New Destinations

NEW DESTINATIONS

MEXICAN IMMIGRATION IN THE UNITED STATES

VÍCTOR ZÚÑIGA AND RUBÉN HERNÁNDEZ-LEÓN
EDITORS

RUSSELL SAGE FOUNDATION, NEW YORK

The Russell Sage Foundation

The Russell Sage Foundation, one of the oldest of America's general purpose foundations, was established in 1907 by Mrs. Margaret Olivia Sage for "the improvement of social and living conditions in the United States." The Foundation seeks to fulfill this mandate by fostering the development and dissemination of knowledge about the country's political, social, and economic problems. While the Foundation endeavors to assure the accuracy and objectivity of each book it publishes, the conclusions and interpretations in Russell Sage Foundation publications are those of the authors and not of the Foundation, its Trustees, or its staff. Publication by Russell Sage, therefore, does not imply Foundation endorsement.

Library of Congress Cataloging-in-Publication Data
New destinations : Mexican immigration in the United States / edited by
    Víctor Zúñiga and Rubén Hernández-León.
        p.   cm.
    Includes bibliographical references and index.
    ISBN 0-87154-988-3
        1. Mexicans—United States.   2. United States—Emigration and immigration—Economic aspects.   3. United States—Emigration and immigration—Social aspects.   4.
    Mexico—Emigration and immigration.   I. Zúñiga, Víctor.   II. Hernández-León, Rubén.
    E184.M5N36   2005
    331.6′272073—dc22   2004058801

Text design by Genna Patacsil.

RUSSELL SAGE FOUNDATION
112 East 64th Street, New York, New York 10021
10 9 8 7 6 5 4 3 2 1

For Constanza, Clara, Nicolás, Aurelio,
Patricia, Paz, and Jesús—V.Z.

For Olín, Paloma, Janna, Emilia, and Aurelio—R.H.L.

CONTENTS

CONTRIBUTORS

RUBÉN HERNÁNDEZ-LEÓN is assistant professor of sociology at the University of California, Los Angeles.

VÍCTOR ZÚÑIGA is dean of the School of Education and Humanities at the Universidad de Monterrey.

ANA MARÍA ARAGONÉS is professor in the Department of Economics at the Universidad Nacional Autónoma de México (UNAM), Acatlán.

CARL L. BANKSTON III is professor and director of Graduate Studies in the Department of Sociology at Tulane University.

CHIARA CAPOFERRO is manager of the Mexican Migration Project of the Office of Population Research at Princeton University.

MIGUEL A. CARRANZA is associate professor of sociology and ethnic studies and director of the Institute for Ethnic Studies at the University of Nebraska at Lincoln.

JASNEY COGUA is a doctoral student of comparative sociology at Florida International University.

KATHARINE M. DONATO is associate professor of sociology at Rice University and associate professor in behavioral sciences at the University of Texas School of Public Health.

TIMOTHY J. DUNN is associate professor in the Sociology Department, Fulton School of Liberal Arts, Salisbury University.

JORGE DURAND is professor and senior research investigator in the Department for the Study of Social Movements at the University of Guadalajara.

LOURDES GOUVEIA is associate professor of sociology and director of Latino/Latin American Studies at the University of Nebraska at Omaha.

MARK A. GREY is professor of anthropology and director of the New Iowans Program at the University of Northern Iowa.

DAVID C. GRIFFITH is senior scientist and professor of anthropology at East Carolina University.

DOUGLAS S. MASSEY is professor of sociology and public affairs at the Woodrow Wilson School of Public and International Affairs of Princeton University.

MARTA MIRANDA is assistant professor of social work at Eastern Kentucky University.

BRIAN L. RICH is associate professor of sociology and Bingham Fellow at Transylvania University.

GEORGE SHIVERS is professor of Spanish and chair of the Department of Foreign Languages at Washington College.

DEBRA LATTANZI SHUTIKA is assistant professor of English at George Mason University.

ROBERT COURTNEY SMITH is associate professor of sociology, immigration studies, and public affairs at Baruch College, City University of New York, and cofounder of the Mexican Educational Foundation of New York.

MELISSA STAINBACK is postdoctoral fellow in the Department of Sociology at Rice University.

ANNE C. WOODRICK is associate professor of anthropology and codirector of the New Iowans Program at the University of Northern Iowa.

INTRODUCTION

VÍCTOR ZÚÑIGA AND RUBÉN HERNÁNDEZ-LEÓN

Mexican immigration to the United States—the oldest and largest un-interrupted migratory flow to this country—is in the midst of a funda-mental transformation. This book is concerned with a central dimension of this change: the rise of new destinations of settled Mexican immigra-tion. During the late 1980s and throughout the 1990s, Mexicans estab-lished new settlements in nontraditional destinations of the Midwest and eastern seaboard regions. Throughout this period, Mexicans began to arrive rapidly and massively in specific localities and counties of states such as Iowa, Nebraska, Minnesota, Idaho, Utah, Arkansas, New York, Georgia, North Carolina, Kentucky, and Tennessee. Although some of these places were acquainted with transient agricultural flows and others were familiar with old and isolated Mexican communities, all of them were taken by surprise with the emerging pattern of rapid and massive settled migration. In addition, with entire families making up a substantial proportion of the new influx, Mexican immigrants moved from the liminality of the farm workers' camps to the main-stream of schools, clinics, shopping centers, and other public spaces. The demographic, social, cultural, and political changes that have en-sued are the subject of this volume.

In the chapters that follow, editors and contributors show that to understand the rise of new destinations it is important to grasp the often overlooked yet central role of geography. As the Mexican immi-grant population in the United States crosses the demographic and symbolic ten million people threshold (Durand 2004), we argue that in addition, scholars need to pay more attention to the spatial distribution of immigrants as well as to the quantity and quality of immigration.

Drawing on micro-level observations, this volume illustrates how, as a factor of social change, the distribution of immigration over space is as significant as its demographic size and composition. Regarding Mexican immigration, social scientists may someday write that at one time this segment of the Latino population lived primarily in the American Southwest. The authors of this volume show how this state of affairs has begun to change in the direction of what Jorge Durand, Douglas S. Massey, and Chiara Capoferro (chapter 1) aptly call "the new geography of Mexican immigration."

THE SIGNIFICANCE OF MEXICAN MIGRATION

The focus of this book is on Mexican migrants, although for all practical purposes their migration is intertwined with others originating in El Salvador, Nicaragua, Guatemala, Costa Rica, and Honduras. The emphasis on Mexican migration reflects not only its demographic significance but also three distinct characteristics of the Mexican and Mexican-origin population in the United States. First, the presence of Mexican-origin communities in the Southwest, their culture, lifestyle and economy predate the arrival of Euro Americans, as the names of streets, rivers, cities, and states attest. Instead of impeding the movement of people, the 1848 annexation of southwestern territories and the Mexican inhabitants there set off migratory flows between Mexico and the United States, which have remained largely uninterrupted.

A second distinguishing characteristic of the Mexican population in this country is its geopolitical and economic importance. Mexico shares a 2,000-mile border with the United States and has become the country's second most important trading partner, with more than $235 billion in commercial exchanges between the two nations in 2003 (U.S. Department of Commerce 2004). The same year, Mexican immigrant remittances reached $13.3 billion (González Amador 2004). It comes as no surprise, then, that migration is a critical issue on the bi-national agenda. Just as this agenda was dominated by oil and drug-trafficking in the 1970s and 1980s, the salient concern of the present is the movement of hundreds of thousands of people from one country to the other. Third, this massive population movement has over time heightened the sociocultural significance of the Mexican immigrant and Mexican-origin people of the United States. Kinship networks, friendship and business ties, intermarriage, and cultural exchanges have expanded and are now part of the social landscape of contemporary American and Mexican societies (Durand 2000).

This landscape underwent a fundamental transformation during the 1990s as Mexican-settled populations began to spring up in nontraditional destinations. Very often communities in formation, these settlements enjoy multiple and multidirectional connections to Mexico and to the political, cultural and demographic capitals of Mexican immigration in the United States—Los Angeles, Chicago, and Houston (Hernández-León and Zúñiga 2003). Due in part to sheer numbers and new destinations, the most recent waves of Mexican immigration are leading to fundamental yet energizing social change in American society.

A NEW GEOGRAPHY

During a century of primarily working-class migrations between Mexico and the United States, cities like Los Angeles, Houston, Chicago, Tucson, San Antonio, and El Paso were the preferred points of entry for Mexican migrants. Many street names, neighborhoods, business districts, schools, and churches across these cities have crystallized distinct histories, aesthetics, and culinary styles—variously referred to as Mexican American, Tex-Mex, Tejano, or simply mejicano. Not surprisingly, radio tunes, newspapers, the aroma of restaurants, the sound of Spanish, the color of houses, and visibly strong family ties give these urban spaces a deep Mexican imprint. All residents, regardless of ethnic origin, appreciate the Mexican presence that has been and is an essential part of the local history and landscape.

This geography of urban places shows that the spatial impact of Mexicans in the United States since 1848 had been strictly regional, limited primarily to California, Texas, Arizona and New Mexico, and Illinois. With the exception of the greater Chicago area, Mexican immigrants had remained near their homeland, forming a sort of territorial strip in the Southwest, where in some instances Mexicans and Mexican Americans made up the majority of the population. Even though some dispersion occurred during the classic migration period of the late nineteenth and early twentieth centuries, when Mexican workers participated in the expansion of railways over most of the United States, and the Bracero period (1942 through 1964), when Mexicans became the preferred source of agricultural labor, the nature of their jobs and the predominantly male composition of the flow made the Mexican presence ephemeral, limited, and frequently almost invisible to residents in various parts of the country. Throughout these two periods, migration between Mexico and the United States was both circular and itinerant, with workers moving from state to state following harvests and rail lines. Still, by the end of the Bracero Program and throughout the 1970s and 1980s, historical Mexican communities swelled with laborers settling out of agricultural streams, former braceros and their families who had become legal permanent residents, and the now predominantly undocumented migrants working in the urban centers of the Southwest and Chicago. Yet despite these growing numbers, the undocumented status that came to characterize Mexican sojourning during the 1964 through1986 period also kept a substantial segment of the Mexican immigrant population temporary and symbolically out of sight (Durand 1998; Durand and Massey 2003).

This volume shows how a new geography is opening a new chapter in the history of the Mexican presence in the United States and seeks to explain its impact on the political, economic, and symbolic dynamics of towns and cities across the country. Data from the 2000 census could not be more eloquent in documenting new settlement patterns. By the mid-1990s, as the proportion of Mexicans concentrated in gateway states like California and Texas was declining, the numbers in nontraditional destinations were rising rapidly, putting states like Idaho, Iowa, Georgia, and New York on the map of Mexican immigration (Massey, Durand, and Malone 2002; Passel and Zimmermann 2001). Between 1990 and 2000 the Mexican immigrant population in non-gateway states had grown dramatically: 645 percent in Utah; more than 800 percent in Georgia; between 500 and 600 percent in Iowa, Indiana, and Nebraska; more than 1,000 percent in Arkansas and Minnesota; between 200 and 400 percent in New York, Pennsylvania, Washington, and Wisconsin; and more than 1,800 percent in North Carolina, Tennessee, and Alabama (U.S. Census Bureau 2004). Although the population base of some of these states was rather small in 1990, a look at the ten most important states concentrating Mexican immigrants in 2000 demonstrates a conspicuous new geography. As table I.1 illustrates, where the top four spots are occupied by traditional states along the border and Illinois, the rest are nontraditional states, such as Georgia, Florida, North Carolina, New York, Nevada, and Colorado (a renewed historical destination). Tellingly, New Mexico is absent.

Thus the pattern of Mexican immigration has shifted from almost exclusive settlement along the southwestern border to other regions of the country. This distinctly patterned presence is evident not only in the labor market but also in school attendance, Spanish-language newspapers and Mexican music radio programming, the spread of Catholicism to regions with other religious traditions, soccer leagues, new businesses, expanded kinship and friendship networks, enriched re-

TABLE I.1   Top Ten State Concentrations of the Mexican
            Immigrant Population in 2000

State	Number of Mexican Immigrants	Percentage of Mexican Immigrant Population
1. California	3,928,701	42.80
2. Texas	1,879,369	20.47
3. Illinois	617,828	6.73
4. Arizona	436,022	4.75
5. Georgia	190,621	2.07
6. Florida	189,119	2.06
7. Colorado	181,508	1.97
8. North Carolina	172,065	1.87
9. New York	161,189	1.75
10. Nevada	153,946	1.67
Total of top ten states	7,910,368	86.14

Source: U.S. Census Bureau (2004).

gional cuisines, new markets for Mexican goods, more ethnically mixed marriages, and closer ties between two neighboring countries that have for centuries remained somewhat aloof.

ORGANIZATION AND CONTRIBUTION

This volume is divided into four parts, an introduction and three thematic sections. Chapter 1 by Durand, Massey, and Capoferro offers a national and historic perspective on the distribution of Mexican immigrant population throughout the twentieth century. The remaining chapters follow a different approach, each studying a particular locality, region, or state. In part I, the chapters focus on processes of immigrant community formation and the economic incorporation of Mexicans into towns and cities and their local industries. The authors describe and analyze localities in Nebraska, North Carolina, and Louisiana. Part II examines the economic, political, and cultural effects of Mexican migration in the new destinations, including the reactions of local residents. These chapters draw on three case studies of Pennsylvania, Iowa, and the Delmarva peninsula, which spans portions of Delaware, Maryland, and Virginia. Finally, the chapters in part III focus primarily on the ethnic and community dynamics between newcomers and residents. They include studies set in Kentucky, New York, and Georgia.

Chapter 1 establishes the geographic, demographic, and historical evolution of the phenomenon. The chapter describes the major periods in the geography of Mexican immigration to the United States using census and current population survey data. The authors present a historical view divided into four main eras: the classic period, from 1880 to 1920; the Bracero era, from 1942 to 1964; the undocumented era, from 1965 through 1986, and the post-IRCA era, from 1987 to the present. Each of these periods produced its own peculiar "geo-demographic pattern." This chapter also shows how in the wake of the 1986 IRCA, many Mexican families living in Texas, Illinois, and California moved to non-traditional states. IRCA's three main components were: amnesty programs for undocumented immigrants, sanctions for employers of unauthorized workers, and reinforcement of border controls. Even though each of these programs had its own set of consequences, it was the amnesty that allowed millions of eligible Mexicans to move freely about the United States, compare labor markets, and settle in new areas. Between 1964 and 1986, the predominantly undocumented and increasingly urban character of Mexican migration inevitably produced its own geography. These destinations were few and multiplied very slowly because each was a "safe haven" guaranteeing a certain degree of invisibility to undocumented migrants. These were found almost entirely in the greater metropolitan areas of major or border cities. There a migrant could find solidarity with other immigrants and co-ethnics, facilitating economic and social incorporation.

The IRCA, which for the most part benefited Mexican migrants, changed these circumstances by inadvertently starting an internal migratory flow within an international one—what we have referred to elsewhere as "new destinations of an old migration" (Zúñiga and Hernández-León 2001, 126). Once permanence and settlement became real possibilities, Mexicans were able to choose the destination best suited to their interests, leaving historic immigrant enclaves and settling out of itinerant migratory streams. Once they became residents in localities in Nevada, Idaho, Iowa, Nebraska, North Carolina, or Georgia, family reunifications gave rise to a second international migratory flow. Amnesty beneficiaries brought their wives and children directly from Mexico, something that had long been impossible or very dangerous. In little more than a decade, an array of new destinations had emerged, attracting fresh undocumented flows from Mexico. The rapid rate of growth explains why the rise of Mexican communities was a surprise and a novelty to both academic observers and inhabitants of the East Coast, the South, and the Midwest alike. This volume seeks to move the discussion beyond describing the new flows to analyze the social and economic dynamics produced by the arrival of Mexicans to nontraditional destinations.

Despite their specific focus, all the essays here narrate social situations, relations, and contexts that remain in a state of flux. The authors document locally specific emergent processes by describing participants' explorations, uncertainties, trials and errors, and multiple attempts to imagine and implement responses to the ongoing changes in each context. The authors are not necessarily in a position, however, to anticipate the definitive direction of these transformations. Instead, they acknowledge the multidimensional and often contradictory nature of social change. The future of the towns and cities described is less than certain as emerging relations will only crystallize into durable forms of interaction after decades have passed. Despite many unknowns, the contributors have taken advantage of the opportunity rarely afforded to scholars to witness social change as it occurs. For this reason, the cases described here are authentic laboratories, in the style of Chicago in the first decades of the twentieth century, in which to rethink findings and to refine and challenge the established conceptual tool kit about immigration and the migratory process.

How can these studies enrich the conceptual tools used to study international migration? We suggest at least four distinct ways. First, by analyzing how new destinations emerge, these studies contribute to the understanding of socioeconomic underpinnings of migration processes. Several chapters (especially those by David C. Griffith [chapter 3], Katharine M. Donato, Melissa Stainback, and Carl L. Bankston III [chapter 4], and Brian L. Rich and Marta Miranda [chapter 8]) complicate perspectives that conceive of migration from Mexico to the United States primarily as the consequence of wage differentials, the economic crises of the 1980s and early 1990s, or the need for undocumented and cheap labor in various sectors of the American economy. As we suggest later, the processes observed in new destinations like North Carolina, Louisiana, and Kentucky are noticeably more complex, with multiple causes operating simultaneously at the local, national, and international levels. In these cases, towns and cities have been affected by profound demographic transformations. Local communities suffer the consequences of technological and market changes that undermine the economic and labor structures that characterized them for decades. At the same time, businesses established in the region have to confront the effects of an increasingly global economy. These processes coincide with networks of experienced Mexican migrants and a migration service industry able to respond to labor demand in a territory as large as the United States. It is the concurrence of multiple factors at the macro-, meso-, and micro-societal levels that allows us to understand the creation of new destinations.

Second, these studies expand the existing conceptual toolkit to study international migration and immigration by examining the dynamics of racialization, categorization, accommodation, and conflict in social interaction not only between newcomers and established residents but also within each of these groups. The studies in parts II and III of this volume pay particular attention to the fact that neither the local receiving population nor the immigrant group are homogenous, and are actually divided along ethnic and class lines, making newcomer-local resident interplay all the more complex. Thus, the often-neglected intragroup negotiations and conflicts emerging in the context of immigration may have a powerful effect on intergroup relations, as the chapters by Debra Lattanzi Shutika (chapter 5), Mark A. Grey, and Anne C. Woodrick (chapter 6), Brian L. Rich and Marta Miranda (chapter 8), and Rubén Hernández-León and Víctor Zúñiga (chapter 10) illustrate. Yet this is at the very least a two-way street: patterns and outcomes of intergroup relations also have the capacity to profoundly affect intragroup dynamics, fostering, for instance, within group conflict.

Third, the authors show that the fluidity of migratory processes results in unintended consequences. At a minimum, changes associated with migration are not uniform or always predictable. The multiple identifications of Mexicans in New York described in Robert Smith's chapter are a case in point. Depending on region of origin at home, age, and migratory experience, Mexicans in this city identify not only with Puerto Ricans but also with academically successful blacks, as one of the strategies to resist stigmatization and integration to the lowest echelons of the urban economy. While older generations of Irish and Greek ethnicities see them as the current incarnation of the long-standing immigrant New York saga, some Mexicans, especially young ones, try to make the most of their Mexican-ness as a novel New York identity. A second instance of an unanticipated outcome of migration processes is the effects of H2B temporary worker visa program controls analyzed by Donato, Stainback, and Bankston: the legality of H2B workers makes them invisible to local residents, due to a high degree of employer control, compared to undocumented workers, who interact with natives in a variety of less restricted social contexts. Similarly unexpected is the positive role of public controversy and conflict within and between groups as a precursor to social integration. Thus, the chapters by Timothy J. Dunn, Ana María Aragonés, and George Shivers (chapter 7), Hernández-León and Zúñiga, and Lattanzi Shutika show how periods of heightened conflict in neighborhoods, workplaces, and schools, have given way to various and at least partial recognition and integration of newcomers through unions, bilingual programs, and public dialogue about the benefits of immigration. Theoretically, the paradoxical and equivocal character of immigration and its effects call for a recovery of what geographers call le flou and le fluide (the blurry and the fluid; Monnet 2001) in contrast to what is unambiguous and institutional. Clearly, immigration produces fear, uncertainty, resistance, controversy, ambivalence, movement, and novelty before it produces institutions and fixed patterns of social interaction.

Finally, several chapters underscore the important role played by dialogue and mediation by actors not aligned with any particular group but willing to act as liaisons, namely, health providers, educators, lawyers, and religious leaders. These actors are not part of the social conflicts in receiving contexts, but catalysts for change responsible for facilitating negotiation, accommodation, and for creating arenas for social consensus. The presence or absence of these liaisons largely explains the stories narrated in each chapter. It is worth noting that the study of these mediators has been conspicuously absent from the community and microsociological study of immigration.

THEMES OF THE VOLUME

The themes of the book represent long-standing concerns in immigration research, which have attracted variable scholarly attention in the past one hundred years. The first theme—the study of immigrants in their communities and workplaces—has been a constant topic of interest since the birth of American sociology in the early twentieth century. In contrast, social scientists have dedicated substantially less energy to the investigation of the impacts and reactions of Americans to immigration, a theme that this volume seeks to illuminate. The third and last theme of the book—the intergroup relations between Mexican immigrants and natives—has been the subject of growing interest in the context of post-1965 immigration, reflecting changes in U.S. society resulting from the civil rights movement.

Community Formation and Incorporation Processes

The chapters of part I focus primarily, though not exclusively, on the process of immigrant community formation and economic incorporation in Nebraska, North Carolina, and Louisiana. All three show evidence of the incorporation of Mexican labor into diverse regional economic sectors: meatpacking, poultry and seafood processing, agriculture (Christmas tree and tobacco plantations), oil extraction and refining, shipbuilding, and operation of ports and canals for the offshore oil industry.

The chapters describe how Mexican workers arrive at their new destinations and become part of these industries, with several combined events explaining the incorporation of Mexican labor. First, the principal detonating factor is the profound local and regional economic transformation. Absent these transformations in the economic structure, the presence of Mexican workers is hard to understand. These changes are in part the result of economic phenomena at the national level and reflect broader effects of globalization. In Nebraska, for instance, since the 1960s the collapse of the sugar beet industry prompted the reorientation of Mexican labor flows to the meatpacking industry, a sector undergoing its own process of restructuring. Second, these changes in economic activity are accompanied by demographic shifts that explain the dearth of local labor. The out-migration of local youth and an aging and low-growth population lead local businesses to acknowledge their enormous dependence on foreign labor, a situation evident in other cases analyzed in this volume as well.

Third, because of these circumstances employers are very active in attracting and ensuring the presence of immigrant workers. They use various recruitment strategies: some take advantage of temporary migration programs (for example, H2B visas), others hire employment agencies, still others offer bonuses to employees who recruit relatives or friends to work at the plants, and others send professional recruiters directly to certain regions of Mexico in search of qualified workers. Finally, the efficient work of migratory networks and the social capital accumulated by generations of Mexican migrants explains their rapid incorporation and "colonization" of industries such as meatpacking in Nebraska, where Mexicans now constitute 75 percent of the workforce.

The chapters in this section also pose questions about the future economic incorporation of migrants. The jobs newcomers hold offer no promising future. Many carry out dirty, unhealthy, unsafe, and poorly paid industrial tasks offering few prospects for mobility. High turnover and work-related accident rates in the poultry processing plants of North Carolina are clear indicators of the limited prospects for the incorporation of Mexican migration into new regions. In the past, the employment prospects experienced by less skilled Mexican workers have been less important because most of these workers did not intend to live permanently in the United States. Many would have returned to their regions of origin in Mexico after a few months. Today many are a permanent part of American society. Their economic incorporation and the occupations of their children thus take on a political and social dimension that they did not have until recently.

The chapters by Donato, Stainback, and Bankston on Louisiana and by Griffith on North Carolina highlight the unanticipated effects of legal status on the process of immigrant incorporation and community formation. The authors observe that undocumented immigration has been more likely than legal immigration to foster social integration, family ties, child bearing, child rearing, and church and school attendance. Donato and her associates use a comparative approach to explain these unintended consequences in southern Louisiana. On the one hand, the H2B program segregates migrant workers socially and spatially by subjecting them to employer control through the provision of housing and transportation services. Due to this segregation, and despite their bona fide legal status, they become invisible and absent as objects of and participants in public debates. If the receiving community perceives that they do not "exist," then no one talks about them. On the other hand, undocumented immigration is not subject to the same kind of employer control, allowing for greater spatial and social contact with local residents. To be sure, visibility may entail confrontation, fear, resistance, and tension. However, in Louisiana, as in other places analyzed here, tension and conflict have given way to consensus, social and symbolic accommodation, and institutional responses. These unanticipated outcomes of legal and undocumented statuses merit further scrutiny.

Local Reactions to Mexican Immigration

The significance of public debate becomes all the more evident in part II. In chapter 5, Lattanzi Shutika analyzes reactions to Mexican settled migration in Pennsylvania. She describes what happens as migrants become socially visible in the small but affluent community of Kennett Square, one of the main mushroom producing regions in the United States. Although Mexican laborers had worked in the industry since the 1960s, they had remained largely hidden from the view of locals. "We knew our place well," some of them affirmed, illustrating their position as outsiders to the local social space. However, as Mexican migrants have become visible in schools, clinics, labor unions (for example, through participation in a 1993 strike), and especially in local neighborhoods, they could no longer be ignored. Their presence has challenged the residents of Kennett Square, a community that has viewed itself as highly educated, liberal, and tolerant and is now reinventing relations between outsiders and insiders. The author describes in detail a series of events and steps local residents have taken to symbolically include newcomers after an initial backlash that produced collective feelings of shame and guilt. Lattanzi Shutika observes that despite the stated goals these efforts may also be marginalizing immigrants from various spaces and institutions.

In the same spirit, Grey and Woodrick examine complex processes of mutual accommodation in Marshalltown, Iowa. In a very short time, the massive presence of Mexican workers transformed the city from a small, predominantly white, and isolated community, into a multiethnic and multicultural city. Such a drastic and visible change immediately produced anti-immigrant attitudes. Local residents associated migrants with crime, drugs, conflict and a corporate plot to weaken unions and lower salaries. Anti-immigrant sentiment found expression in a 1996 INS raid, an event that in turn unleashed anger, sadness, and pain in Mexican workers and their families. Local authorities, churches and community leaders, law enforcement, migrant workers, union representatives, and employers participated in an ensuing public debate on immigration. Organized and facilitated by experts who acted as liaisons between migrants and native residents, this dialogue brought about the acknowledgment that Marshalltown is now part of a binational labor market in which particular sending towns are connected to particular receiving communities. City leaders accepted an invitation to visit one of the Mexican communities that sends most of its people to this region of Iowa. The trip affected the perspective of local actors and produced what the authors identify as processes of mutual accommodation.

The study by Dunn, Aragonés, and Shivers gives an account of Mexican workers' presence in the poultry and seafood processing sectors, the timber industry, and the tourism and health sectors of the Delmarva peninsula. In this region, Mexican immigrants have played a crucial role revitalizing dormant unions in the plants of the poultry industry. The unfolding story of this isolated mid-Atlantic region has a complex plot involving a cast of characters such as migrant workers, African American union representatives, unions like the UFCW, the local and national press, religious leaders, and municipal authorities. The authors describe this complicated web of relations in the context of the debate between citizenship rights theory and human rights perspectives. Undocumented Mexican workers who suffer the consequences of extremely unsafe work find themselves devoid of labor rights. Corporate actors can flagrantly violate the most basic rights with no concern that existing laws will be enforced. In this legal no man's land, unexpected forms of cooperation are emerging, including cooperation between African Americans and Mexicans. At the same time, the liminal status of undocumented workers allows for unrestrained expressions of hostility, such as wildcat strikes. As documented by the authors, public discussion forums have offered a venue for emerging discourses about immigration while public debate continues to run its course.

Conflict and Accommodation in Intergroup Relations

The third and final section of this book includes three case studies that analyze how the arrival of Mexican immigrants affects intergroup and interethnic relations. Each case study documents unfolding processes of racialization, xenophobia, and hostility and the role of immigrants as catalysts for irreversible political, social, and symbolic change in new destinations in Kentucky and Georgia. At the same time, in an immigrant metropolis like New York, the massive arrival of Mexicans has added yet another layer of complexity to the already complicated racial architecture of the city.

In Lexington, Kentucky, the "horse capital of the world," Rich and Miranda identify an ambivalent mixture of community responses toward immigrants, which include paternalistic, benign, and cooperative assistance, as well as negative racialized attitudes. In this city, a profound demographic and ethnic change has started to unfold as Mexicans transition from the invisible work of tobacco plantations and horse ranches to visible urban industrial and service sector jobs (construction, hotels, restaurants, domestic services, and factories). Rich and Miranda note that local authorities and business leaders have been the first to promote a paternalistic response to newcomers. In contrast, working-class whites and blacks are more prone to develop xenophobic and racist responses. In the urban setting, working-class blacks on the lower rungs of the ethnoracial occupational ladder perceive Mexicans as a threat. In contrast, middle-class whites react with a mixture of benign neglect and indifference.

Even though newcomers appear to local residents as a self-reliant group whose members share strong bonds of ethnic solidarity, especially when compared to the perceived fragmentation and disorganization of poorer African Americans, and that local and state authorities acknowledge the economic contribution of immigrants, long time residents still alternate between paternalism and xenophobia. The "Mexican symbolic challenge" that the authors identify is reminiscent of Roger Waldinger's (2003) argument regarding immigrants in general: they are welcomed for their brawn and hard-working attitudes, but rejected as they become more socially visible. Put differently, locals accept single and relatively invisible Mexicans but reject the newcomers the moment they attend schools, go to clinics, shop at supermarkets, organize meetings, or hold public celebrations. In brief, acceptance as a desirable worker does not preclude rejection in other spheres of social life, and even the presumption of greater immigrant integration does not exclude the marginalization of newcomers from all institutional and political representation.

Robert Courtney Smith's chapter on Mexicans in New York focuses more on what immigrants do than on what residents imagine (chapter 9). He asks whether Mexicans in New York will become a marginalized, racialized minority or an incorporated ethnic group. This is an important question because Mexicans do not easily fit into the racial classification systems of either New York or the East Coast in general. Smith compares the outlook and practices of Mexicans according to migration cohort (that is, first, 1.5, and second generations), age (preteens, teens, and adults), social mobility (that is, those who have experienced generational mobility with those who have not), and gender. He is able to document multiple responses suggestive of several trends. Despite the observed diversity, certain cultural bastions of the Mexican community in New York could provide the basis for new categories in the city's racial architecture. In this perennial city of immigrants, some Mexicans see themselves, and are viewed by native New Yorkers, as the newest arrivals looking for a foothold in the city's ethnic ladder. Unlike Puerto Ricans and blacks, who find themselves on the bottom rungs, Mexicans are neither natives nor citizens. To some, Mexican-ness offers a cultural heritage that makes them less vulnerable to the city's vices and dangers. Particularly to young second-generation women employed in the pink-collar economic sector, being Mexican may be cool and hip rather than racializing and stigmatizing. Finally, to second-generation young males, Mexican-ness is a form of racialization. For this reason, they prefer to follow the model of academically successful blacks with whom they interact in high school settings.

Finally, Smith offers a brief comparison of racialization and re-racialization processes in New York and California. He concludes that "processes of ethnicity and race occur differently in different contexts despite the fact that the same national origin group is involved." In New York, Mexicans are seen as hard-working strivers whose children will continue in this vein and will prosper. They do not see themselves as a victimized minority. This is the key to understanding how Mexicans in New York are writing a different story than Mexicans in Los Angeles.

The last chapter narrates how the arrival of Mexican immigrants to Dalton, Georgia—the "carpet capital of the world"—has subverted historical social arrangements in this Appalachian locality. The authors describe different phases of interclass and intraracial social compacts established as a means to solve long-standing labor conflicts between all-white carpet industrialists and blue-collar workers. The absence of black workers from Dalton's industrial workplaces suggests that these settlements were intimately intertwined with the other significant social axis in this town, namely, the black and white divide. Facing this social and historical configuration, the authors analyze intergroup dynamics and agreements from the perspective of social class relations rather than in strictly racial terms. Mexican immigration has disrupted these intraracial and interclass social compacts and as a consequence is destabilizing existing patterns of social interaction in multiple microsociological arenas, such as schools, business districts, churches, government agencies, and workplaces. Clearly, the newly found Mexican presence elicits ambivalent responses that range from nostalgia for an irrecoverable past to the construction of a new future in which, according to various local actors, immigrants will have to be included.

All the studies in this book analyze the consequences of what Lourdes Gouveia, Miguel A. Carranza, and Jasney Cogua call a "tectonic demographic shift" across the United States. Each chapter contributes to a fuller knowledge of incorporation, group dynamics, social responses, and the effects of a migratory flow that for a century hardly crossed strict regional boundaries. This book attests to a turning point and new direction in the history of Mexican migration to the United States. It records the first phases in this shift to new destinations in Oregon, Wisconsin, Utah, Washington, Rhode Island, Oklahoma, Tennessee, Idaho, Massachusetts, New Jersey, and Nevada.

A New Geography and a New Historical Era

This book captures two new and seemingly enduring developments. First, Mexican immigrants are arriving in U.S. communities whose residents have had little or no contact with these newcomers in the past. Second, Mexicans are coming to stay. They are no longer birds of passage but appear to be nesting permanently in their new destinations. The effect of both developments may signal the beginning of a new historical era in Mexican immigration to the United States, spearheaded by a novel geography of diverse receiving contexts to which newcomers are integrating. As several of these essays suggest, each of these contexts has its own racial hierarchy, history of interethnic relations, and ways of incorporating immigrant workers and their families. Just as New York presents very different conditions for Mexicans than Los Angeles and California, new and renewed destinations like Pennsylvania, the historic South, Nebraska, and Iowa also present particularities that will shape the incorporation of Mexican migrants into these areas. The effect of receiving contexts will be especially noticeable in the construction of racial classification systems in each region.

Still other contextual and immigrant specific attributes will also shape the contours of Mexican immigration in this new historical period. A significant feature of new and traditional receiving contexts—one definitely unknown to Mexicans who arrived or lived in Texas or California in earlier decades—is the current normative climate. Recent immigrants are encountering a novel context in which "the right to diversity" is turning into the common ethos (Garcia 2001; Suarez-Orozco 1998). Defined as the right to recapture and develop the fundamental traits that characterize a group as such, the right to ethnocultural diversity is now part of a series of entitlements including political and religious freedom, sexual orientation, and aesthetic taste and lifestyle. But is this new ethos merely a superficial movement characteristic of the most educated and cosmopolitan layers of American society? On the contrary, it appears that the norm of "intolerance for intolerance" is gaining momentum well beyond these strata. In this context, tolerance is something more than "the suspicion that the other fellow might be right" (Wirth 1945/1964, 253). Indeed, it is becoming a moral norm based on the notion that diversity is not only inescapable but also a desirable feature of contemporary social life. At the same time, the multiculturalist ethos is creating its own feelings and behaviors: public shame, indignation, and guilt. These feelings develop as part of the new multicultural morality and the attitudes it rejects and seeks to avoid—hence the shame of being labeled a racist, the horror of being considered a xenophobe, and the guilt of being considered intolerant.

However, nontraditional receiving contexts and a new normative ethos are not enough to explain why the new geography described in this book will likely initiate a new history of Mexican immigration to the United States. Yet another factor is the social capital accumulated by migrants over decades (Portes 1995). Mexican workers arriving at new destinations are not unfamiliar with the institutions and traditions of American society. As we have shown elsewhere, they are experienced immigrants whose social capital allows them to more rapidly and effectively become incorporated into new destinations (Hernández-León and Zúñiga 2003). From a variety of perspectives, several of the essays in this volume support this point. In a very short time, migrants buy homes, create businesses to meet the market demands that they themselves produce, participate in organizations that represent their interests, and build intragroup and intergroup alliances. They are seasoned migrants quite capable of envisioning and negotiating a future for themselves and their children in Nebraska, Louisiana, Pennsylvania, North Carolina, and Georgia.

Finally, the visibility of contemporary Mexican immigration also suggests the beginning of a new historical era. Most new destinations are smaller towns and cities where it is impossible for migrants to go undetected (with the possible exception of those controlled by employers through H2B visas). But it is not just the size of the receiving communities that makes invisibility difficult. Increasingly, Mexican immigration is a family affair. The presence of wives and children, grandparents, and nephews, among other relatives, has an immediate impact on the most important institutions and organizations of receiving towns and cities (churches, schools, clinics, and business districts). Given these conditions, small and medium-sized cities do not face the same stark choices as large metropolitan areas, namely ghettoization or integration. In large U.S. metropolitan areas, immigrants and established residents have generally lived in separate social worlds (Rodriguez 1999). This separation has produced a particular kind of social order, different from small new destination communities where immigrants and residents share multiple social spaces and are building new and distinct notions of community as well as a new repertoire of local identities.

Most likely, the new geography documented in this book will be the source of a fresh stage in the history of Mexican migration to the United States. This new period has been provisionally dubbed the "post-IRCA" and "post-NAFTA era" because its most significant features are still emerging. What we do know now is that in this new era there are factors that more readily make immigrants agents in their own incorporation and integration despite their lowly positions in the labor queue. The visibility of newcomers, a less intolerant normative context, and especially the social capital accumulated by migrants invite them to be agents rather than victims of their fate.

The authors would like to thank David Cook and Veronica Terriquez for their research assistance.

REFERENCES

Durand, Jorge. 1998. *Politica, Modelos y Patron Migratorios: El Trabajo y los Trabajadores Migratorios en Estados Unidos*. San Luis Potosi, Mex.: El Colegio de San Luis.

———. 2000. "Origen es Destino. Redes Sociales, Desarrollo Historico y Escenarios Contemporaneos." In *Migracion Mexico-Estados Unidos, Presente y Futuro*, edited by Rodolfo Tuiran. Mexico: Consejo Nacional de Poblacion.

———. 2004. *La Migración en Cifras*. Unpublished paper. Universidad de Guadalajara, Guadalajara, Mexico.

Durand, Jorge, and Douglas S. Massey. 2003. *Clandestinos, Migracion Mexico-Estados Unidos en los Albores del Siglo XXI*. Mexico: Universidad Autonoma de Zacatecas and Porrua.

Garcia, Eugene E. 2001. *Hispanic Education in the United States*. Lanham and Boulder: Rowman & Littlefield.

González Amador, Roberto 2004. "Las Remesas en EU Mantienen el Consumo Interno en México." *La Jornada* 20(6982): 22. Available at: http://jornada.unam.mx/2004/feb04/040204/020n1eco.php?origen=index.html&fly=1 (accessed February 4, 2004).

Hernández-León, Rubén, and Víctor Zúñiga. 2003. "Mexican Immigrant Communities in the South and Social Capital: The Case of Dalton, Georgia." *Southern Rural Sociology* 19(1): 20–45.

Massey, Douglas S., Jorge Durand, and Nolan Malone. 2002. *Beyond Smoke and Mirrors: Mexican Immigration in an Era of Economic Integration*. New York: Russell Sage Foundation.

Monnet, Jérôme. 2001. "Pour une géographie du fluide et du flou." *La Géographie. Acta Geographica* 1502bis(II): 89–94.

Passel, Jeffrey S., and Wendy Zimmermann. 2001. "Are Immigrants Leaving California? Settlement Patterns of Immigrants in the Late 1990s." Unpublished paper. The Urban Institute, Washington, D.C.

Portes, Alejandro. 1995. "Economic Sociology and the Sociology of Immigration: A Conceptual Overview." In *The Economic Sociology of Immigration*, edited by Alejandro Portes. New York: Russell Sage Foundation.

Rodriguez, Nestor. 1999. "U.S. Immigration and Changing Relations between African Americans and Latinos." In *The Handbook of International Migration: The American Experience*, edited by Charles Hirschman, Philip Kasinitz, and Josh DeWind. New York: Russell Sage Foundation.

Suarez-Orozco, Marcelo M. 1998. "Crossings: Mexican Immigration in Interdisciplinary Perspectives". In *Crossings: Mexican Immigration in Interdisciplinary Perspectives*, edited by Marcelo M. Suarez-Orozco. Cambridge, Mass.: Harvard University Press.

U.S. Census Bureau. 2004. *Census 2000 Summary File 4 (SF 4)—Sample Data.* Washington: U.S. Census Bureau. Available at: http://factfinder.census.gov/ servlet/DatasetTableListServlet?_ds_name=DEC_2000_SF4_U&_lang=en (accessed October 13, 2004).

U.S. Department of Commerce. International Trade Administration. 2004. *U.S. Aggregate Foreign Trade Data.* Washington: U.S. Department of Commerce, International Trade Administration. Available at : http://www.ita.doc.gov/ td/industry/otea/usfth/tabcon.html (accessed October 13, 2004).

Waldinger, Roger. 2003. "The Sociology of Immigration: Second Thoughts and Reconsiderations." In *Host Societies and the Reception of Immigrants*, edited by Jeffrey G. Reitz. La Jolla: CCIS, University of California, San Diego.

Wirth, Louis. 1945/1964. *On Cities and Social Life: Selected Papers.* Chicago and London: University of Chicago Press.

Zúñiga, Víctor, and Rubén Hernández-León. 2001. "A New Destination of an Old Migration: Origins, Trajectories and Labor Market Incorporation of Latinos in Dalton, Georgia." In *Latino Workers in the Contemporary South*, edited by Arthur D. Murphy, Colleen Blanchard, and Jennifer A. Hill. Athens, Ga.: University of Georgia Press.

CHAPTER 1

THE NEW GEOGRAPHY
OF MEXICAN IMMIGRATION

JORGE DURAND, DOUGLAS S. MASSEY, AND CHIARA CAPOFERRO

Mexican immigration has never been spread evenly across the United States. Historically, a few key states, mostly in the southwest, attracted the large majority of immigrants from Mexico. This pattern of regional concentration was partly a matter of geography, of course. The four states that border Mexico—California, Arizona, New Mexico, and Texas—naturally assumed greater importance than others, in part because until 1848 they were part of Mexico. Even among border states, however, geography wasn't everything. Some states consistently outdrew others. One nonborder state, for example, Illinois, has for many years been an important destination. Economic and political factors have also played significant roles.

What we undertake here is a descriptive analysis of the changing geography of Mexican immigration to the United States using representative census and survey data. Beginning early this century and continuing up to the present, we focus on four key periods: the classic era of open immigration before the restrictive policies of the 1920s; the Bracero era of 1942 to 1964, when the United States sponsored a large temporary worker program; the undocumented era, between the end of the Bracero Program and the passage of the Immigration Reform and Control Act of 1986 (IRCA); and the post-IRCA era, from 1987 to the present.

The post-IRCA period has been one of notable change in the forces that promote and sustain Mexico-U.S. migration. First, the border has been selectively militarized (Dunn 1996; Andreas 2000; Nevins 2002). In the fifteen years leading up to 2000, the number of border patrol

1

officers increased by 368 percent and the agency's budget increased by a factor of six. The expansion of the border patrol gathered particular force in the 1990s with the launching of Operation Blockade in El Paso in 1993 and Operation Gatekeeper in Tijuana in 1994. The selective hardening of the border in these two sectors deflected migratory flows away from the most popular destinations and toward crossing points in Arizona and New Mexico (Massey, Durand, and Malone 2002).

At the same time that the militarization of the San Diego–Tijuana border drove up the costs of a California crossing, that state became relatively much less attractive as a potential destination. The post–Cold War recession hit southern California's economy particularly hard, raising rates of unemployment among both immigrants and natives and tarnishing the lure of U.S. jobs. The recession was also accompanied by an anti-immigrant backlash that culminated in the passage of Proposition 187 in 1994. This initiative sought to ban undocumented migrants from receiving public social services and required state and local officials to both verify a client's immigration status and report suspected undocumented migrants to INS officials. The rise in native hostility and the withering of economic opportunity combined to make California much less attractive a destination than it had been.

A third change stemmed from IRCA's legalization programs, which ultimately granted legal permanent residence to some 2.3 million Mexicans between 1988 and 1992, the large majority of whom lived in California (Massey, Durand, and Malone 2002). In other words, just as political and economic conditions for Mexico were deteriorating in California, millions of Mexican migrants received green cards that allowed them freedom of mobility. Kristin Neuman and Marta Tienda (1994) documented a clear pattern of geographic mobility by newly legalized migrants away from areas of Mexican concentration. With documents in hand, they were suddenly free to leave historical Mexican enclaves in search of better opportunities elsewhere (Durand, Massey, and Parrado 1999).

Finally, while the recession was slow to end in California the rest of the country quickly entered a sustained boom, which by the mid-1990s produced tight labor markets, rising wages, and improving work conditions in other regions. In the midwest, northeast, and southeast, *New York Times* correspondent Louis Uchitelle pointed out, regions that had never experienced significant immigration from Mexico, unemployment rates fell to record low levels, generating a sustained demand for unskilled and semi-skilled workers, whose real wages rose for the first time since 1973 (May 23, 1997).

During the latter half of the 1990s, therefore, an unusual constellation of factors came together to push Mexican migrants away from traditional gateways in general and from California in particular: a dramatic increase in the costs and risks of border-crossing in San Diego, a deterioration of the Californian economy, a nasty anti-immigrant political mobilization there, the sudden granting of freedom of mobility to millions of former undocumented migrants, and the emergence of strong labor demand throughout the country. After describing our data and using them to describe historical patterns of Mexico-U.S. migration, we show the effect of these structural changes on the geography of Mexican immigration during the 1990s.

DATA AND METHODS

Our analysis relies on two basic data sources. The first is the Integrated Public Use Microdata Samples (IPUMS), a machine-readable file of public use samples of individual records from the U.S. censuses of 1900 to 1920 and 1940 to 1990, prepared by Steven Ruggles and Matthew Sobek (1997). These data are publicly available online at http://www. ipums.umn.edu. For each census year, we selected records for all persons born in Mexico. The number of such records was too small in 1900 to sustain reliable analysis, so we dropped that year from consideration, yielding an IPUMS-based dataset from 1910 to 1990, excluding the census of 1930 (its manuscripts having not yet been released into the public domain).

Our second source of data is the March supplement of the year 2000 Current Population Survey (CPS), which included a question on place of birth as part of its demographic module. The CPS is a representative household survey of the noninstitutionalized civilian population of the United States. Because we anticipated significant shifts in Mexican immigration as a result of economic and political changes during the 1990s, and given that the census only occurs once per decade, we sought to use the CPS to capture late-breaking developments. As with the IPUMS, we selected all persons born in Mexico to measure the population of Mexican immigrants.

For the period 1910 to 1960, we tabulated foreign-born Mexicans by state of U.S. residence to view the overall geographic distribution of immigration during the classic and Bracero eras. For the period 1970 to 2000 we also present these distributions; but because the geographic distribution of all immigrants in any year is heavily influenced by the behavior of those in the past, we developed an alternative set of tabulations for *recent* immigrants—those who entered the United States during the five years prior to the census or survey. We also consider trends in the distribution of Mexican immigrants by metropolitan area since 1990.

For all geographic distributions, we compute Henri Theil's (1972) entropy index to summarize the diversity of destinations (henceforth the diversity index):

$$E = \frac{-\sum_{i=1}^{n} p_i * \log(p_i)}{\log(n)} \times 100$$

where n is the number of categories (for example, states) and p_i is the proportion of people in category i (for example, state i). The index varies between 0 and 100. Minimum diversity occurs when all people are concentrated in one category and maximum diversity occurs when each category contains exactly the same number of people (see White 1986).

IMMIGRATION IN THE CLASSIC ERA

Table 1.1 presents the distribution of foreign-born Mexicans by state of residence in two historical epochs: the classic era of open immigration (based on the censuses of 1910 and 1920) and the subsequent Bracero era of U.S.-sponsored labor migration (drawing on the censuses of 1940, 1950, and 1960).

The top panel shows the distribution of immigrants among gateway states. As can be seen, during the classic era about half of all Mexican immigrants were in Texas, with the percentage falling slightly between 1910 and 1920 (going from 55 percent to 50 percent). The next closest state is California, which increased from 17 percent to 22 percent over the decade, followed by Arizona, which stayed relatively stable between the two census dates (increasing just two points, from 12 percent to 14 percent). A small but declining number of Mexican immigrants lived in New Mexico, comprising just 3 percent of the total in 1920. Illinois had not yet emerged as a significant destination for Mexican immigration, accounting for less than 1 percent of all Mexican immigrants at both points in time.

During the classic era, therefore, Mexican immigrants flowed primarily to Texas, California, and Arizona. Together, these states absorbed roughly 85 percent of all Mexico-U.S. migrants, with nongateway states getting just 11 percent. The distribution of immigrants among the six categories clearly moved toward greater diversity be-

TABLE 1.1   Distribution of Mexican Immigrants by
State of Residence: 1910 to 1960

	Classic Era		Bracero Era		
State	1910	1920	1940	1950	1960
All immigrants					
Gateway states					
Arizona	11.8%	14.1%	7.2%	6.7%	6.3%
California	16.9	21.6	35.6	34.0	41.9
Illinois	0.3	0.8	2.5	2.6	4.8
New Mexico	4.5	3.2	4.2	2.1	1.8
Texas	55.2	49.9	39.5	44.5	35.9
Other states	11.2	10.5	11.1	10.2	9.4
Diversity index	71.6	74.8	77.8	73.5	75.2
Sample n	947	2,380	4,178	6,818	5,838
Immigrants in nongateway states					
Colorado	9.4%	29.2%	15.8%	11.2%	11.2%
Florida	5.7	0.4	0.4	2.0	2.0
Georgia	0.0	0.0	0.4	0.0	0.2
Idaho	0.0	0.8	1.1	1.2	0.9
Indiana	0.0	0.0	4.5	6.5	8.8
Iowa	1.9	2.0	3.9	4.6	2.0
Kansas	63.2	24.4	18.6	12.0	5.7
Michigan	0.0	0.8	6.3	14.4	10.3
Minnesota	0.0	1.6	3.2	1.9	1.5
Missouri	6.6	2.4	3.0	2.3	3.9
Nevada	0.9	2.4	1.3	1.3	1.8
New Jersey	0.9	0.4	0.9	1.3	1.5
New York	2.8	8.0	9.1	5.8	13.0
North Carolina	0.0	0.0	0.4	0.0	0.4
Oklahoma	4.7	5.6	2.2	1.9	1.7
Oregon	1.9	1.2	1.5	0.7	0.9
Pennsylvania	0.0	1.6	1.7	3.2	2.9
Utah	0.0	5.2	3.2	3.6	2.8
Washington	0.0	2.4	0.4	3.2	11.5
Other	2.0	11.6	22.1	22.9	17.0
Diversity index	47.1	70.9	79.3	82.0	84.9
Sample n	106	250	463	694	546

Source: 1910–1960 Integrated Public Use Microdata Sample.

tween 1910 and 1920, however, as relative numbers in Texas dropped while those in Arizona and California increased, yielding a more even distribution and a slight increase in the diversity index from 72 to 75.

During the late nineteenth and early twentieth century, Mexico experienced a period of political peace and sustained economic expansion under President Porfirio Díaz (1876 to 1910). Under his rule, Mexico acquired a nationwide rail system, a nascent industrial base, growing urban centers, and a new economic structure based on export agriculture and extraction, financed mainly by foreign interests (see Hart 1987; Haber 1989). The Porfirian boom was accompanied by the consolidation of rural landholding, the substitution of cash for staple crops, and the widespread implementation of capital-intensive agriculture. These developments produced massive labor displacements and strong pressure for emigration from rural areas, forces that were exacerbated by the collapse of the Porfirian regime in 1910 and the inauguration of ten years of revolution and civil war (Cardoso 1980; Hart 1987).

In the western United States, meanwhile, the arrival of the railroads connected agricultural and mining areas in the southwest to booming industrial cities in the northeast and midwest, yielding sustained economic growth and rapid growth in labor demand. As the demand for workers grew, traditional sources were progressively closed off, first by the Chinese Exclusion Acts of the 1880s and then by the Gentlemen's Agreement with Japan in 1907 (Keely 1979). In response, U.S. railroads, agricultural growers, and mining companies began recruiting Mexican workers (Durand and Arias 2000).

The integration of the Mexican and U.S. rail systems (financed by the same American interests) provided the link to connect labor supply with demand, and recruiters followed the tracks into Mexico to initiate the first waves of migration to the United States (Cardoso 1980). By the 1920s, the flows became a "floodtide" as first World War I, then the creation of the Soviet Union, and finally the imposition of restrictive quotas cut industrialists off from traditional European labor sources (Massey 1996).

The effects of these macro-level forces are evident in the shifting distribution of Mexican immigrants between 1910 and 1920. Texas was the state most closely tied to Porfirian economic development (Hart 1987); but by 1920 California had emerged as the new economic power in the west, and Los Angeles, rather than San Antonio, had become the principal center of Mexican settlement north of the border. Thus, we observe an increasing percentage of immigrants located in California accompanied by a decreasing percentage in Texas between 1910 and 1920.

Although small sample sizes in nongateway states caution against drawing strong conclusions, we see that other salient destinations early in the century were Colorado and Kansas, both containing important rail junctions and industrial centers (Kansas City and Denver), reflecting the growing importance of Mexicans as rail and factory workers (Cardoso 1980).

THE GEOGRAPHY OF BRACERO MIGRATION

The last three columns of table 1.1 show the geographic distribution of Mexicans at points before, during, and just after the peak of the Bracero Program in the 1950s. Following the surge of Mexican immigration during the 1920s, the onset of the Great Depression triggered a wave of mass deportations and the population of foreign-born Mexicans fell during the 1930s (Hoffman 1974). By 1942, however, tight wartime labor markets had replaced the joblessness of the late depression and the United States once again turned to Mexico for workers, negotiating an agreement known as the Bracero Accords to arrange the annual importation of Mexican farmworkers under supervision of the U.S. government (Craig 1971). Although enacted as a "temporary" wartime measure, it was successively renewed and expanded for twenty-two years before finally being terminated in 1964 (Calavita 1992).

The Bracero years coincided with an unprecedented boom in California that dramatically increased labor demand in all economic sectors. Within Mexico, meanwhile, post-revolutionary governments distributed millions of hectares of land to peasants but failed to provide sufficient capital to allow them to begin producing, generating intense needs for cash among rural dwellers (Massey et al. 1987). The Mexican policy of import substitution industrialization yielded high rates of industrial growth in urban areas but failed to provide enough jobs for the rising tide of rural in-migrants (Hansen 1971). With pressures for out-migration building and a program in place to connect the burgeoning supply with rising demand, Mexicans quickly came to dominate farm labor within California and made significant inroads into manufacturing and service industries as well.

The geographic distribution of Mexican immigrants in 1940 illustrates the effect of forces in play ten years earlier, at the onset of the Great Depression. Given the emigration of Mexicans during the 1930s and the absence of new arrivals in the interim, the geographic distribution prevailing in the late 1920s was essentially frozen in time. Although California represented a major locus of settlement on the eve of the Bracero Program, containing just over a third of all Mexican immigrants in 1940, it was still second to Texas, which contained 40 percent. But during the 1920s and 1930s, Illinois had also emerged as a gateway state, although still containing only a small share of all Mexican immigrants (2.5 percent). Compared with 1920, Arizona declined substantially in importance (to 7 percent) while New Mexico and the "other" category stayed roughly the same. Given the increase in the share of Mexicans in California and the decrease in Texas, the diversity index rose to nearly 78.

The geographic profile of Mexican immigration changed little between 1940 and 1950. Texas briefly reasserted its dominance as an immigrant destination, increasing its share from 40 percent to 45 percent and lowering the diversity index to 74. California remained roughly constant at 34 percent, and the share attributable to Arizona, Illinois, and other states stabilized. The real change is observed between 1950 and 1960, dates that bracket the largest expansion of the Bracero Program. As late as 1950, only sixty-seven thousand Braceros were imported into the United States; but during the late 1950s the number never fell below four hundred thousand (Calavita 1992). A disproportionate share of these migrants were sent to growers in California, and by 1960 that state had surpassed Texas as home to the largest concentration of Mexican immigrants. From 1950 to 1960, while the percentage of Mexicans in Texas fell sharply from 45 percent to 36 percent, the relative number in California rose from 34 percent to 42 percent. At the same time, the percentage located in Arizona, New Mexico, and other states declined. The era of Californian dominance had begun.

Besides California, only Illinois grew as a destination for Mexican immigrants during the 1950s. By 1960 roughly 5 percent of all Mexican immigrants were located in that state. Nearly all of these migrants went to Chicago, but figures for Illinois alone understate this urban area's importance as an immigrant destination. As the bottom panel of table 1.1 shows, over the period 1940 to 1960 Indiana also increased its salience among nongateway states. The vast majority of these immigrants settled in Chicago suburbs such as East Chicago, Hammond, and Gary, where they worked in the steel mills and factories (see Taylor 1932). When Mexican immigrants to Indiana are added to those in Illinois, the total reaches about 6 percent in 1960.

From 1940 to 1960, the states of Colorado and Kansas, which had been of some importance for Mexican immigrants in the classic era, faded into obscurity as points of destination. At the same time, Mexican immigration to industrialized states such as Michigan and New York rose, as did the relative importance of Washington, where Mexicans constituted the backbone of its fruit-picking workforce. Among non-gateway states, the long-term trend since 1910 has been one of increasing diversity, with the index rising from 47 in 1910 to 85 in 1960. Against this backdrop of diversification among secondary destinations, however, the lasting legacy of the Bracero era was a growing concentration of Mexican immigrants in California.

IMMIGRATION DURING THE UNDOCUMENTED ERA

The first two columns of table 1.2 show the geographic distribution of Mexican immigrants in the years immediately following the Bracero Program, a period characterized by rapid expansion in Mexican immigration through both legal and illegal channels (Massey, Durand, and Malone 2002) but especially illegal (illegal migrants are, of course, undercounted in the census figures we use). Although the U.S. economy faltered during the 1970s, the demand for unskilled labor continued unabated, and Mexicans expanded their presence in economic niches where they had already established themselves during the Bracero era. In Mexico, the discovery of vast oil reserves set off an economic boom that intensified the desire for income, capital, and security available through U.S. migration.

From 1970 to 1980, California continued to grow in importance as a destination for Mexican immigration. By 1970, a clear majority (53 percent) of foreign-born Mexicans were located in this state, and by 1980 the total reached 57 percent. With the exception of Illinois, which rose from 6 percent to 8 percent, the percentage of Mexican immigrants in all other states fell, with Texas leading the way. As a result of California's growing dominance, the index of diversity among gateway states fell from 75 in 1960 to 71 in 1970 and reached 67 in 1980. At the same time, the percentage of Mexican immigrants in nongateway states fell, although the variety of destinations grew, with the diversity index climbing from 76 in 1970 to 84 in 1980.

GEOGRAPHIC CHANGES IN THE WAKE OF IRCA

During the era of undocumented migration that prevailed before the passage of the Immigration Reform and Control Act (IRCA) of 1986,

TABLE 1.2   Distribution of Mexican Immigrants by
State of Residence: 1970 to 2000

State	Undocumented Era		Post-IRCA Era	
	1970	1980	1990	2000
All immigrants				
Gateway states				
Arizona	4.5%	3.3%	3.4%	5.3%
California	52.7	57.0	57.8	47.8
Illinois	6.2	7.7	5.2	5.8
New Mexico	0.8	0.8	1.9	1.0
Texas	26.5	22.6	22.1	19.0
Other states	9.4	8.5	10.3	21.1
Diversity index	70.5	67.8	68.6	76.1
Sample n	33,757	22,492	43,116	5,543
Immigrants in nongateway states				
Colorado	6.1%	7.9%	8.5%	10.7%
Florida	3.8	7.6	14.7	11.5
Georgia	0.6	0.4	4.4	3.3
Idaho	1.1	4.0	3.2	2.5
Indiana	6.9	6.0	1.3	1.1
Iowa	1.2	0.9	0.5	2.5
Kansas	4.1	3.0	3.0	2.3
Michigan	10.5	4.9	2.7	1.6
Minnesota	1.2	1.0	0.6	2.9
Missouri	2.4	0.9	1.0	0.6
Nevada	2.0	5.1	8.3	9.7
New Jersey	1.6	1.3	2.3	1.7
New York	7.3	6.3	8.1	8.7
North Carolina	0.5	0.6	1.7	6.8
Oklahoma	1.6	3.7	3.3	1.0
Oregon	2.2	5.5	7.6	6.4
Pennsylvania	2.1	1.6	1.0	0.1
Utah	2.4	2.4	2.8	3.7
Washington	3.0	8.9	11.0	6.6
Other	39.4	28.0	14.0	16.2
Diversity index	76.0	84.2	88.8	88.1
Sample n	3,156	1,916	4,425	1,055

Source: 1970–1990 Integrated Public Use Microdata Samples; 2000 Current Population Survey.

the clear trend in Mexican immigration was one of growing concentration in California, accompanied by a progressive diversification of immigrant destinations among all other states. Although the IRCA passed in late 1986, its various programs and provisions were gradually implemented in the period 1987 through 1989, so trends through the 1980s primarily reflect the pre-IRCA pattern of growing concentration in California and increasing diversification everywhere else. The percentage of foreign-born Mexicans in California peaked at 58 percent in 1990, while the share in Texas bottomed out at 22 percent; the share in other states rose very slightly (see the third column of table 1.2). Among nongateway states, the diversity index reached a high of 89 in 1990.

The full effects of the new regime of immigration were not felt until after 1990, when the IRCA's legalization program was completed and its employer sanctions fully implemented (Massey, Durand, and Malone 2002). As a result of the IRCA's general amnesty and a special legalization program enacted for farmworkers, some 2.3 million Mexicans acquired legal documents between 1987 and 1990 (U.S. Immigration and Naturalization Service 1991). Roughly 55 percent of those legalized lived in California, and 40 percent were in the southern portion of the state (in Los Angeles, Orange, Riverside, San Bernardino, or San Diego counties).

This massive legalization had two immediate consequences for Mexican immigrants in California: first, it flooded local labor markets (particularly those around Los Angeles) with newly legalized immigrants; and, second, it gave the latter new freedom to move. Where illegal migrants generally seek to find a steady job and hold it, avoiding mobility to minimize the risk of detection, newly legalized immigrants suddenly had full U.S. labor rights and lost their fear of arrest. Not only did they have the freedom to move, other changes provided them with strong incentives to do so, for the legalizations occurred against a backdrop of new employer sanctions, deteriorating economic conditions, and growing hostility toward immigrants in California.

The IRCA for the first time made it illegal for employers to hire undocumented workers, imposing both civil and criminal penalties against those who did. In response, employers shifted to labor subcontractors to satisfy their needs (Martin and Taylor 1991). Subcontractors are typically citizens or legal immigrants who sign a contract with an employer to provide a specific number of workers, for a specified period, to engage in a particular task, at a set fee per worker. By working through a subcontractor, employers avoid the risk of prosecution under IRCA and escape the law's burdensome paperwork requirements. In return for absorbing these risks and burdens, the subcontractors keep a share of the migrants' earnings, thus lowering the wages of the immigrants themselves (Phillips and Massey 1999). Because enforcement was targeted to sectors known to employ undocumented migrants, the effects of restructuring were naturally greatest in California.

IRCA also increased the budget of the U.S. Border Patrol, and in response it launched a series of repressive crackdowns at the nation's two busiest sectors—San Diego and El Paso (Dunn 1996; Andreas 2000). As a result, flows of undocumented migrants arriving at the Mexico-U.S. border were diverted away from California and Texas toward less intensively patrolled regions in Arizona and New Mexico (Massey, Durand, and Malone 2002).

Just as employer sanctions were putting downward pressure on wages in California's labor markets, moreover, that state experienced a severe economic recession as a result of cutbacks in defense industries stemming from the end of the Cold War. As unemployment rose and wages stagnated, public sentiment turned sharply against immigrants. The anti-immigrant movement culminated in 1994 with the passage of Proposition 187. Passed with massive support from alienated natives, the referendum sought to bar undocumented migrants from receiving publicly provided health, education, and welfare services.

Thus the early 1990s witnessed an unusual coincidence of conditions in California: an IRCA-induced restructuring of immigrant employment toward subcontracting, declining net wages for immigrants, a severe recession and high unemployment, growing native hostility, and greater wage competition triggered by a flood of newly legalized immigrants entering local labor markets. All of these changes occurred precisely at a point in time when vast numbers of former undocumented migrants had acquired new geographic mobility thanks to the IRCA-authorized legalization.

On the heels of these changed circumstances north of the border, Mexico entered a profound economic crisis in December 1994, when a bungled peso devaluation led to a recession that not only created a need for greater income among poor families in traditional immigrant-sending states, but fostered new needs for capital, credit, and security among middle-class households in states that heretofore had not sent many migrants to the United States. As new migrants entered the binational labor market, they naturally sought to avoid the difficult and radically changed circumstances in California.

The end result was a rapid shift of Mexican immigrants away from California toward nontraditional destinations. The changed geography is clearly observed between 1990 and 2000. In just a decade, the percentage of Mexican immigrants located in California dropped 10 points—from 58 percent to 48 percent. At the same time, in Texas it continued to fall, reaching an all-time low of 19 percent in 2000. In contrast, the relative number of Mexicans rose in most of the other gateway states. The percentage of Mexicans in Arizona went from 3 percent to 5 percent and in Illinois from 5 percent to 6 percent.

More important, the share located in nongateway states more than doubled during the 1990s, reaching the highest percentage in the history of Mexico-U.S. migration: 21 percent. After three decades of declining diversity, the variety of destinations increased dramatically in the early 1990s, with the diversity index going from 69 to 76 in just ten years. Looking at long term increases among nongateway states since 1970, it is clear that new centers of attraction are emerging in Florida, Idaho, Nevada, New York–New Jersey, North Carolina, and elsewhere.

Because the geographic distribution of immigrants at any point in time is heavily conditioned by where earlier cohorts of immigrants decided to settle, table 1.3 replicates the geographic analysis of table 1.2 selecting only Mexican immigrants who arrived in the United States over the prior five years. This table accentuates all of the trends observed earlier and underscores the recency of the geographic transformation. Whereas the large majority (63 percent) of Mexicans who arrived between 1985 and 1990 went to California, among those who arrived between 1995 and 2000 the percentage dropped dramatically to just 35 percent. As a consequence, the diversity index increased from 64 to 79.

At the same time, the percentage going to nongateway states rose from 13 percent to 35 percent, a radical shift unprecedented in the history of Mexico-U.S. migration. By the late 1990s, more than a third of all Mexicans were settling somewhere other than gateway states. Trends since 1970 once again document the emergence of Florida, Idaho, Nevada, New York–New Jersey, and North Carolina as destinations, but also hint at the emergence of Georgia, Iowa, Oregon, and Minnesota as poles of attraction, in addition to the re-emergence of Colorado as a significant receptor. As a result, immigrant destinations are now more diverse than ever.

Table 1.4 further documents this fact by showing the metropolitan area of residence for Mexican immigrants who arrived in the last half of the 1980s and the last half of the 1990s. The numbers going to Los Angeles and San Diego fell between the two periods, but rose for almost

TABLE 1.3   Distribution of Recent Mexican Immigrants (Those Arriving in Previous Five Years) Among Nongateway States: 1970 to 2000

	Undocumented Era		Post-IRCA Era	
State	1970	1980	1990	2000
All recent immigrants				
Gateway states				
Arizona	4.4%	2.6%	3.7%	6.2%
California	59.0	58.7	62.9	35.4
Illinois	8.2	8.7	4.9	6.1
New Mexico	0.5	0.6	0.9	0.8
Texas	20.7	20.6	14.9	16.4
Other states	7.4	8.7	12.8	35.3
Diversity index	66.9	66.3	64.2	78.8
Sample n	4,042	7,173	12,795	1,055
Recent immigrants in nongateway states				
Colorado	4.0%	9.3%	6.5%	12.1%
Florida	8.4	8.8	15.7	13.0
Georgia	0.3	0.0	7.0	3.0
Idaho	0.3	5.9	3.3	1.3
Indiana	8.4	3.4	0.6	0.2
Iowa	0.3	0.3	0.1	4.3
Kansas	0.3	3.5	1.9	1.0
Michigan	5.7	2.9	1.3	1.5
Minnesota	0.3	1.9	0.8	1.3
Missouri	0.3	0.5	1.0	0.0
Nevada	3.0	6.5	6.6	7.1
New Jersey	3.7	1.3	3.8	0.0
New York	8.4	7.5	10.9	7.5
North Carolina	0.7	0.5	2.4	11.2
Oklahoma	0.3	3.8	3.0	0.0
Oregon	1.4	5.1	9.0	6.9
Pennsylvania	2.4	2.4	1.2	0.0
Utah	1.4	2.1	2.7	4.0
Washington	1.7	10.5	10.7	5.6
Other	48.7	23.8	11.5	19.9
Diversity index	64.6	84.6	87.3	80.9
Sample n	297	627	1,643	462

Source: 1970–1990 Integrated Public Use Microdata Samples; 2000 Current Population Survey.

TABLE 1.4   Distribution of Recent Mexican Immigrants
             (Those Arriving in Previous Five Years)

Metropolitan Area	Recent Mexican Migrants	
	1990	2000
Los Angeles–Riverside–Orange County	32.9%	17.0%
Chicago-Gary-Kenosha	4.3	5.9
New York–Northern New Jersey	4.9	2.5
Houston-Galveston	3.2	2.7
Phoenix	2.0	4.6
Dallas–Fort Worth	1.6	6.7
Las Vegas	0.5	2.3
Denver-Boulder-Golden	0.5	3.6
McAllen-Edinburgh	1.3	1.0
Salinas-Seaside-Monterrey	0.8	1.4
Fresno	1.4	1.6
Albuquerque	0.2	0.1
San Diego	4.4	2.3
San Francisco–Oakland–San Jose	3.0	5.9
Brownsville-Harlingen	1.0	0.3
Bakersfield	0.9	1.1
El Paso	1.8	0.9
Minneapolis	0.1	0.5
Visalia-Tulare	1.1	1.2
Other metro area	23.2	30.0
Diversity index	63.8	79.3
Nonmetro area	10.9	8.5

Source: 1990 Integrated Public Use Microdata Samples; 2000 Current Population Survey.

all other destinations. Thus the percentage going to Los Angeles fell from 33 percent to 17 percent, but to Chicago rose from 4 percent to 6 percent, to San Francisco from 3 percent to 6 percent, and to Phoenix from 2 percent to 5 percent. Although Los Angeles continues to dominate as a pole of attraction for Mexican immigrants, its importance appears to be slipping and newer metropolitan areas are coming to the fore. Although space limitations preclude us from presenting the data, tabulations suggest that this shift away from traditional destinations was not led by a random cross-section of Mexican immigrants, but by a particular subset of migrants composed predominantly of working-age men working disproportionately in agriculture, who by 2000 were already shifting rapidly into urban jobs where they were joined by growing numbers of women and children (see table 1.5).

CONCLUSIONS

Our analysis of the changing geography of Mexican immigration from 1910 to 2000 suggests several long-run trends linked to developments in the binational political economy. Early in the century, Mexican immigration was strongly oriented towards Texas, which had stronger financial and material interests in Porfirian Mexico than other U.S. states. As late as 1920, half of all Mexicans living in the United States were in Texas. The unraveling of the Porfirian regime after 1910 coincided with a heightened demand for Mexican workers elsewhere in the United States, and as Mexican immigration surged, destinations shifted, with California and, to a lesser extent, Chicago, emerging as alternative poles of attraction. This epoch came to an abrupt end in 1929 with the onset of the Great Depression.

The creation of the Bracero Program in 1942 and its massive expansion during the 1950s dramatically altered the geographic profile of immigration to the United States. As Texas faded in relative importance, California became the preeminent destination. By 1960, 42 percent of all Mexican immigrants lived in California, 36 percent in Texas, and 6 percent in Illinois or northwest Indiana. The termination of the Bracero Program in 1964 ushered in an era of extensive undocumented migration, during which California increasingly came to dominate among U.S. destinations. By 1990, California alone housed 57 percent of all Mexican immigrants, whereas Texas was home to only 22 percent and Illinois around 5 percent (6 percent including migrants in Indiana, who were mostly located in Gary). At the end of the 1980s, therefore, the diversity of Mexican immigrants' destinations reached an all-time low.

The Immigration Reform and Control Act broke with the past to establish a new regime of binational migration. The implementation of the act's tough new enforcement provisions coincided with a severe recession in California. The result was an unprecedented deflection of Mexican immigration away from that state toward new destinations that heretofore had received few Mexicans. Among those arriving over the five years prior to 1990 and 2000, the percentage going to California fell from 63 percent to 35 percent.

The new destinations include Florida, Georgia, Iowa, Minnesota, Ne-

TABLE 1.5   Characteristics of Recent (Those Arriving in Previous Five Years) Mexican Immigrants to the United States, 1990 and 2000

	1990			2000		
	Gateway		Non-gateway	Gateway		Non-gateway
Characteristic	California	Other	gateway	California	Other	gateway
Geographic[a]						
Central city	44.8%	40.5%	21.1%	59.7%	56.7%	28.0%
Suburbs	43.0	12.1	22.9	40.3	34.9	51.1
Nonmetropolitan	12.2	47.4	44.0	0.0	8.4	20.8
Demographic						
Age						
Under eighteen	29.8%	35.9%	29.4%	25.8%	25.1%	22.9%
Eighteen to						
sixty-four	69.4	62.6	70.1	71.4	74.2	76.2
Sixty-five or older	0.8	1.5	0.5	2.8	0.8	0.9
Average age	21.9	22.1	22.3	23.4	25.0	25.1
Family status						
Male	58.2%	53.3%	63.1%	52.8%	53.9%	61.0%
Married	32.9	35.8	36.6	34.5	30.3	26.5
Socioeconomic						
Years of schooling						
Less than twelve	75.7%	77.7%	74.9%	80.1%	78.0%	75.8%
Twelve	16.1	12.6	15.4	13.8	14.4	16.3
Thirteen or more	8.2	9.7	9.6	6.1	7.7	7.9
Labor force[b]						
Employed	82.9%	77.7%	82.0%	55.3%	65.1%	69.6%
Unemployed	7.7	8.3	7.2	11.7	3.9	6.1
Out of labor force	9.4	14.0	10.8	33.0	31.0	24.2
Occupation						
Managerial-						
technical-						
professional	12.8%	15.4%	13.1%	2.3%	2.8%	2.7%
Service workers	23.8	29.9	23.8	34.2	37.1	30.4
Skilled manual	37.2	32.2	27.1	24.8	29.3	32.3
Unskilled manual	15.7	15.1	12.2	15.1	22.0	15.3
Farm workers	10.5	7.4	23.7	23.6	8.8	19.4
Sample n	8,042	3,110	1,643	288	305	462

Sources: 1990 Integrated Public Use Microdata Samples; 2000 Current Population Survey.
[a]In about 13 percent of the samples the Central city metropolitan statistical area status code is "not identified." These distributions are based on the other 87 percent of the sample.
[b]In the sample, 20.0 percent of the migrants are not in the universe (age fourteen or younger). The distribution of the labor force is based on migrants fifteen years or older.

vada, New York, New Jersey, North Carolina, and Oregon. The movement of Mexicans away from California and Texas was led by young single men of labor force age who worked in agriculture. By the mid-1990s, however, they had already begun moving to cities, where they were joined by growing numbers of women. While the number of Mexican immigrants going to large metropolitan areas in California (Los Angeles, San Diego, and San Francisco) fell during the early 1990s, the number going to New York, Houston, Phoenix, Dallas, Las Vegas, and Minneapolis rose. The diversity of immigrant destinations reached new highs. In a few short years Mexican immigration has been transformed from a narrowly focused process affecting just three states into a nationwide movement.

This transformation has transfigured the political landscape of both countries. As they have put down roots in the United States, Mexican immigrants have come to value political participation as never before. They have begun to participate in its public debates, political organizations, and electoral contests, and ultimately to become important social and political actors on both sides of the border.

The interplay between politics in Mexico and the United States worries officials in both countries, but it is nonetheless a harbinger. Post-IRCA policies in the United States, when combined with political and economic developments occurring under the North American Free Trade Agreement, have had unexpected social, economic, and political consequences. Both Mexican and American authorities now face a mobilized population of Mexican immigrants simultaneously working to defend their rights in the United States while helping to bring about political change in Mexico, and ultimately contributing to greater integration—social, economic, and political—within North America.

REFERENCES

Andreas, Peter. 2000. *Border Games: Policing the U.S.-Mexico Divide.* Ithaca: Cornell University Press.

Calavita, Kitty. 1992. *Inside the State: The Bracero Program, Immigration, and the I.N.S.* New York: Routledge.

Cardoso, Lawrence. 1980. *Mexican Emigration to the United States: 1897–1931.* Tucson: University of Arizona Press.

Craig, Richard B. 1971. *The Bracero Program: Interest Groups and Foreign Policy.* Austin: University of Texas Press.

Dunn, Timothy J. 1996. *The Militarization of the U.S.-Mexico Border, 1978–1992: Low-Intensity Conflict Doctrine Comes Home.* Austin: Center for Mexican American Studies, University of Texas at Austin.

Durand, Jorge, and Patricia Arias. 2000. *La Experiencia Migrante: Iconografía de la Migración México-Estados Unidos.* Guadalajara: Altexto.

Durand, Jorge, Douglas S. Massey, and Emilio A. Parrado. 1999. "The New Era of Mexican Migration to the United States." *Journal of American History* 86(2): 518–36.

Haber, Stephen H. 1989. *Industry and Underdevelopment: The Industrialization of Mexico 1890–1940.* Stanford: Stanford University Press.

Hansen, Roger D. 1971. *The Politics of Mexican Development.* Baltimore: Johns Hopkins University Press.

Hart, John M. 1987. *Revolutionary Mexico: The Coming and Process of the Mexican Revolution.* Berkeley and Los Angeles: University of California Press.

Hoffman, Abraham. 1974. *Unwanted Mexican Americans in the Great Depression: Repatriation Pressures 1929–1939.* Tucson: University of Arizona Press.

Keely, Charles B. 1979. *U.S. Immigration: A Policy Analysis.* New York: The Population Council.

Martin, Philip L., and J. Edward Taylor. 1991. "Immigration Reform and Farm Labor Contracting in California." In *The Paper Curtain: Employer Sanctions' Implementation, Impact, and Reform,* edited by Michael Fix. Washington, D.C.: The Urban Institute.

Massey, Douglas S. 1996. "The New Immigration and the Meaning of Ethnicity in the United States." *Population and Development Review* 21(3): 631–52.

Massey, Douglas S., Rafael Alarcon, Jorge Durand, and Humberto Gonzales. 1987. *Return to Aztlan: The Social Process of International Migration from Western Mexico.* Berkeley: University of California Press.

Massey, Douglas S., Jorge Durand, and Nolan J. Malone. 2002. *Beyond Smoke and Mirrors: Immigration Policy in an Era of Free Trade.* New York: Russell Sage Foundation.

Neuman, Kristin E., and Marta Tienda. 1994. "The Settlement and Secondary Migration Patterns of Legalized Immigrants: Insights from Administrative Records." In *Immigration and Ethnicity: The Integration of America's Newest Immigrants,* edited by Barry Edmonston and Jeffrey Passel. Lanham, Md.: Urban Institute.

Nevins, Joseph. 2002. *Operation Gatekeeper: The Rise of the "Illegal Alien" and the Making of the U.S.-Mexico Boundary.* New York: Routledge.

Phillips, Julie A., and Douglas S. Massey. 1999. "The New Labor Market: Immigrants and Wages After IRCA." *Demography* 36(2): 233–46.

Ruggles, Steven, and Matthew Sobek. 1997. *Integrated Public Use Microdata Series: Version 2.0.* Minneapolis: Historical Census Projects, University of Minnesota.

Taylor, Paul. 1932. "Mexican Labor in the United States: Chicago and the Calumet Region." In *University of California Publications in Economics,* vol. 7, no. 2, edited by Carl C. Plehn, Ira B. Cross, and Melvin M. Knight. Berkeley: University of California Press.

Theil, Henri. 1972. *Statistical Decomposition Analysis.* Amsterdam: North Holland.

U.S. Immigration and Naturalization Service. 1991. *1990 Statistical Yearbook of the Immigration and Naturalization Service.* Washington: U.S. Government Printing Office.

White, Michael J. 1986. "Segregation and Diversity: Measures in Population Distribution." *Population Index* 52(2): 198–221.

PART I

PROCESSES OF IMMIGRANT COMMUNITY FORMATION AND ECONOMIC INCORPORATION

CHAPTER 2

⋈

THE GREAT PLAINS MIGRATION:
MEXICANOS AND LATINOS IN NEBRASKA

LOURDES GOUVEIA, MIGUEL A. CARRANZA, AND JASNEY COGUA

At first glance, Nebraska meets the definition of a new destination for Mexican migration. A combination of forces converging toward the end of the 1980s culminated in an unprecedented growth of the state's Latino population. However, as we take stock of what is "new," it is important not to lose sight of what is old. Mexicans began arriving in Nebraska at the beginning of the twentieth century, although relatively few settled permanently in the state when compared to this latest wave. Given this historical precedent, Nebraska may be best characterized as a re-emerging destination for Mexican immigrants and a new destination for immigrants from Central and South America. Today, the latter group makes up about 23 percent of the total Latino population in the state and their numbers are increasing apace.

Despite pronounced ebbs and flows in Mexican migration to Nebraska, some key historical and structural connections tie the fates of these older and newer settlement communities and shape newcomers' chances for successful incorporation. One thread is woven by the uneven, yet largely uninterrupted, demand for low-wage Mexican labor, primarily in the agro-food sector. The second is defined by the formation of well-defined Mexican communities and social networks of co-ethnics that tend to accompany the clustering of populations around a small set of labor markets. These pre-existing communities are both revitalized by and reconstituted into important springboards for the settlement and incorporation of new arrivals.

It is the question of immigrant settlement and incorporation that concerns us in this chapter. As in the rest of the nation, the people of this state are slowly awakening to the tectonic demographic shift fueled by new immigration. Rather predictably, many welcome the badly needed injection of a young labor force to a state faced with an aging population and persistent brain drain. Yet many others express concern about the new immigrants' capacity to "assimilate." Our main objective is to identify the main factors that facilitate or impede successful incorporation for Mexican and other Latino populations moving into this particular region of the country, and the extent to which they may differ from those found in other immigrant destinations.

The analysis includes an overview of old and new communities' sociodemographic profiles and histories of incorporation and a succinct summary of the labor markets and industrial sectors into which Mexican migration streams have tended to concentrate. Our primary data collection focused on an examination of governmental and nongovernmental institutions and the extent to which they seem to be adapting to better serve the needs of new arrivals. It is too early in the process for conclusive statements, and data presented here are insufficient to make predictions about the direction such incorporation will take. It is possible, however, to outline the various paths of incorporation confronting newcomers in Nebraska and, one hopes, help move policy and institutional changes toward the most productive of such paths.

Much of the data for this chapter were compiled during a recently completed project sponsored by the State of Nebraska Mexican American Commission.[1]

THEORETICAL AND ANALYTICAL FRAMEWORK

Ours is a largely descriptive account of the barriers to incorporation that Mexican and other Latino groups arriving in the state confronted during the last decade and a half. Nonetheless, data collection and analyses were guided by the rich theoretical and empirical scholarship on immigrant incorporation that both revisits and problematizes the old assimilation canon. Contrary to the old theories of "assimilation" informed by the somewhat mythologized experience of European immigrants, successful integration does not presuppose a necessary and progressive shedding of one's cultural and ethnic heritage. For many immigrants, it is the resources provided by their ethnic communities, composed of older and newer arrivals, that account for their successful integration (Rumbaut and Portes 2001). Most immigration scholars today also agree that the integration process is uneven, largely contingent on contextual factors, and often segmented. Children born to the most economically vulnerable immigrant groups are more likely to experience downward assimilation accompanied by a distancing from their parents' ethnic identity. Conversely, those occupying more favorable positions in the labor market, as well as in other racial and class hierarchies, tend to experience integration paths closest to the idealized views of assimilation in which eventually ethnicity becomes a matter of choice (Portes and Rumbaut 2001). As Gary Gerstle and John Mollenkopf (2001, 10) argue, the "received wisdom" inherited from earlier views of assimilation as a straight-line process hardly applies to the current wave of immigrants and it probably never did to earlier waves either.

The central thesis emerging from this new integration literature and informing our work is that successful incorporation is largely a function of the opportunities and barriers immigrants encounter in the host society, as opposed to simply the level of skills (human capital) or cultural attitudes they allegedly bring with them. In addition to contextual factors, which include the strength of existing and emerging ethnic networks and labor market conditions, the literature on incorporation stresses how general or targeted programs, institutional cultures, and national as well as local policies can have a considerable impact on immigrant integration (Fix and Zimmerman 2000; Crul and Vermeulen 2003;Waldinger 2001). It is this second dimension we tried to capture with our institutional survey and focus groups. Census data and previous research addressed the first. We focus mainly on various measures of socioeconomic progress, or the more structural, as opposed to the cultural dimensions of integration. Structural integration includes measures of educational attainment, income, and labor force participation. The sociocultural dimension, addressed more tangentially here, is often captured by the degree to which groups speak English, have become naturalized, participate in various mainstream civic and political institutions, or intermarry.

PIONEER MEXICANS AND LATINOS IN NEBRASKA: DEMOGRAPHIC COMPOSITION AND HISTORIES OF INCORPORATION AS SOCIAL CONTEXT FOR NEW ARRIVALS

The large wave of Mexicans arriving in Nebraska by the late 1980s and early 1990s encountered relatively small pockets of earlier settlements in both urban and rural communities across the state. According to the 1920 census, there were 2,452 foreign-born Mexicans living in Nebraska by 1919. With the passage of national-origin quota laws in the 1920s, and opportunities for older European arrivals to move out of the wage labor, the supply of German-Russians who had worked in the sugar beet fields dried up. As a result, more than two thousand Mexican-origin laborers were contracted annually to work in the fields. The majority resided in the rural part of the state, around communities such as Grand Island, Lexington, North Platt, and, significantly, Scottsbluff where the sugar industry was particularly strong. By 1929, a growing number of Mexicans were found in urban communities as well, particularly in Omaha, where many had been recruited to work in the railroad industry (Lopez 2000). The Mexican population declined by 50 percent during the Great Depression and rebounded only slightly during the years of the Bracero program, which lasted from 1942 to 1964 (Grajeda 1976). By the 1970s, ironically, just as the industry was experiencing a historic decline in Omaha, Mexicans were estimated to have made up about one-third of the meatpacking industry labor force. Most of these workers were second generation, sons (and some daughters) of immigrants, but new arrivals were also evident (Lopez 2000).

The 1980 census counted 28,000 individuals of Hispanic origin, 10 percent of whom were foreign-born. Community agencies estimated, however, as Eileen Wirth and Sibyl Myers noted in an article on Omaha, that the real number was closer to 44,000 ("Estimate: City Total 13,000; 2,000 May Be Illegal Aliens," *Sunday World Herald*, September 9, 1979, p. 15B). By the end of the decade, the percentage of foreign-born in the state had doubled. A chance for more permanent employment as old European and even Mexican immigrants exited this labor market, together with the collapse of the sugar beet industry in the mid-1960s, the end of the Bracero program in 1964, and the 1965 immigration legislation undoubtedly contributed to this visible population increase and more concentrated presence in meatpacking (C. David Kotok, "Crackdowns on Working Aliens Anger State Mexican-Americans," *Lincoln Sunday Journal & Star*, September 3, 1978, p. 1B, 2; Gouveia and Juska 2002).

From this information, it becomes clear that this wave of Mexican migration to the state was primarily labor migration. This type of migration is commonly associated in the literature with restricted opportunities for upward mobility. In fact, despite high rates of labor force participation, Mexican oldtimers in Nebraska have tended to concentrate in "blue-collar" jobs, have higher poverty rates, lower rates of home ownership, and lower median incomes than non-Latino whites (Lopez 2000). The outcomes of this incorporation are partly captured in earlier censuses. In 1990, mimicking national trends, only 9 percent of Hispanic adults in Nebraska had completed college degrees when compared to 19 percent for non-Hispanic whites. Poverty rates of individuals of Hispanic origin in places like Omaha or Grand Island were twice and three times as high, respectively, as those for non-Hispanic whites (U.S. Census Bureau 1990). Possibilities for self-employment had been rather limited for this group, especially during the first half of the twentieth century. Although precise numbers are not available, journalistic and historical accounts about the presence of Latino businesses in the state, around the 1960s and 1970s, suggest these amounted to no more than one to two Mexican restaurants in every town and a handful of other small service and manufacturing businesses. The small population size, as well as intense interethnic competition, both in labor markets and for investment capital with European-origin groups did not generate a particularly favorable climate for Mexican business creation. Although residentially segregated and clustered in a small set of labor markets, the Mexican community did not exactly fit the definition of an ethnic enclave, whereby high levels of human capital and entrepreneurial assistance appeared to be readily accessible to newer arrivals.

On the other hand, there has been a progressive increase in the number of second- and third-generation Latinos who have completed at least some college (about an equal number of Latinos and non-Latino whites had completed two-year associate degrees in 1990). Like their European counterparts, earlier Mexican generations left the meatpacking industry when conditions deteriorated and many chose to go back to school when faced with few other options. The number of Nebraska Latinos with a college degree was also slightly above the national average for Latinos (Bureau of Business Research 1997).

Additionally, it is said that when communities lack human capital resources to facilitate upward mobility, social capital can become an important substitute. Historical accounts also depict another side of this ethnic identity that underscores a strong preservation of Spanish in many households, commitment to family, and sense of collective responsibility toward their co-ethnics has remained strong across generations as evidenced in dense networks of voluntary work. However small the institutional infrastructure ready to facilitate incorporation of newcomers, the proportion of businesses and nonprofit organizations to service and advocate for the Latino community grew with the years. Some have been there for more than thirty years, as is the case of the Chicano Awareness Center and a community clinic in Omaha (Lopez 2000; Grajeda 1976). It is clear that these institutions and stronger co-ethnic networks have played an important role in the incorporation of new arrivals, certainly in Omaha and Lexington. In communities where human and social capital are weakest, and the context of reception has been historically hostile, as is the case of Grand Island, institutional changes necessary to facilitate incorporation have lagged behind.

POPULATION GROWTH AND NEW ARRIVALS

The most dramatic Latino population increase occurred between 1990 and 2000. According to census figures, the Hispanic and Latino population in Nebraska more than doubled (155 percent), going from 36,969 to 94,425 during this decade (U.S. Census Bureau 2001b). In looking at table 2.1, the comparison of percentage change from 1990 to 2000 between the total population and the Hispanic and Latino population in cities is even more dramatic.

Rural communities were the main beneficiaries of Latino population growth. Nearly half of the total Hispanic and Latino population enumerated by the 2000 census lived in cities of less than twenty-five thousand; this helped reverse the severe population decline during the 1980s

TABLE 2.1   Growth and Percentage Changes in Populations for
Selected Nebraska Cities

Cities	1990		2000		Percentage Change	
	Total	Hispanic and Latino	Total	Hispanic and Latino	Total	Hispanic and Latino
Omaha	335,719	10,288	390,007	29,397	16.2	185.7
Lincoln	191,972	3,764	225,581	8,154	17.5	116.6
Grand Island[a]	39,386	1,887	42,940	6,845	9.0	262.7
Lexington	6,601	329	10,011	5,121	51.6	1456.5
Scottsbluff[a]	13,711	2,720	14,732	3,476	7.4	27.8
S. Sioux City	9,677	545	11,925	2,958	23.2	442.8
Bellevue	30,928	1,213	44,382	2,609	43.5	115.1
Schuyler[a]	4,052	164	5,371	2,423	32.6	1377.4
Norfolk[a]	21,476	299	23,516	1,790	9.5	498.7
North Platte[a]	22,605	1,355	23,878	1,596	5.6	17.8

Source: U.S. Census Bureau (2001a).
[a]Cities located in nonmetropolitan counties.

in rural Nebraska counties that Joe Brennan noted in an article on the subject ("More Nebraska Counties Than Ever Lost Population Between 1980, '90," *Omaha World Herald*, August 23, 1990, pp. 1, 5). For example, between 1990 and 2000 Dawson County lost 10 percent of its population and an even larger share of its working-age population, yet its Latino population grew 22 percent in the same period. Lexington, the city where most Latinos in Dawson County live, experienced a 1,456 percent increase in Latino population, the largest increase in the state. Even Omaha, the largest city in the state, would have likely experienced net out-migration had it not been for international migration. Yet, Omaha experienced a 16.2 percent gain in overall population while its Latino population alone grew by 185.7 percent.

While immigration contributed the most to the recent Latino population growth (42 percent of the total Hispanic population is foreign-born, an increase of 539 percent between 1990 and 2000, compared to a 63 percent growth among native-born Hispanics), age and fertility have been important contributors to the emergence of a whole new second generation in the past ten years alone. The Latino population in Nebraska is very young and fertility rates are more than twice the state averages—31 percent versus 14.4 percent (Nebraska Department of Health and Human Services 2001).

The new Latino immigrant population is also more diverse than it was in 1980 or even 1990. The "Other Hispanic or Latino" category comprises almost 24 percent of the state's Hispanic and Latino population. Central Americans, especially Guatemalans and Salvadorans, make up the second-largest foreign-born group. However, this is still an overwhelmingly Mexican population. Slightly more than 75 percent of Latinos living in Nebraska claim Mexican ancestry.

AGRO-FOOD RESTRUCTURING AND THE LABOR MARKET RE-CLUSTERING OF IMMIGRANTS

Earlier settlements of Latinos in Nebraska arose largely from labor migration streams journeying toward sugar beet fields, railroad jobs, and meatpacking plants. Today, Latino immigrants have again responded to new and persistently high demands for their labor in a handful of agro-industrial sectors in the Midwest (Gouveia and Saenz 2000). Table 2.2 offers a comparison of demographic transformations in Nebraska and other Great Plains states. A common denominator has been the reorganization and revitalization of the meat processing industry as well as other sectors that now depend on immigrants.

TABLE 2.2   Growth and Percentage Changes in Populations for Selected Northern Plains States

State	1990 Total	1990 Hispanic and Latino	2000 Total	2000 Hispanic and Latino	Percentage Change Total	Percentage Change Hispanic and Latino
Iowa	2,776,755	32,647	2,926,324	82,473	5.4	152.6
Kansas	2,477,574	93,670	2,688,418	188,252	8.5	101.0
Missouri	5,117,073	61,702	5,595,211	118,592	9.3	92.2
Nebraska	1,578,385	36,969	1,711,263	94,425	8.4	155.4
North Dakota	638,800	4,472	642,200	7,786	.5	74.1
South Dakota	696,004	5,568	754,844	10,903	8.5	95.8

Source: U.S. Census Bureau (2001a).

The meatpacking industry's search for immigrant labor pools was at the core of new strategies to increase profits and revitalize the industry that began in earnest by the end of the 1980s and beginning of the 1990s. As old-line and decreasingly competitive packers such as Swift, Armour, and Morrell were succeeded by the new "Big Three" (IBP, Cargill/Excel, and ConAgra/Monfort), so were their largely European immigrant labor pools followed by Mexican and Central American immigrants. This latest wave of meatpacking industry restructuring had resulted in weakened unions, relocation to nonmetropolitan counties in the Great Plains, lower wage structures, further de-skilling of labor force, more limited career paths, and production line speeds that tripled in the last two decades. High injury rates, as a result, became a hallmark of this industry (Hackenberg et al. 1993; Schlosser 2001). Large pools of Latinos heeded recruiters' calls for their labor just as older Mexicanos in cities such as Omaha left the industry, along with their Anglo counterparts, in search of better jobs and educational opportunities (Gouveia 1994; Grey 1995). Mexican and other Latino workers sought new opportunity in the Midwest such as more permanent jobs, and a better quality of life (Gouveia and Saenz 2000).

As network recruitment created an abundant and constantly replenished labor supply, plants expanded or opened into new large-scale operations in a growing number of communities and states (Gouveia and Stull 1996; Fink 1998). In Nebraska, communities such as Lexington, Grand Island, and Schuyler became emblematic examples of meatpacking restructuring and rural transformation in the 1980s and 1990s. Grand Island and Lexington had been part of the sugar beet growing and processing region of the early part of the twentieth century (Gouveia 2000). A small Latino middle class, made up of a half dozen families, flourished among second-generation Mexicans in places like Lexington, a county seat. Grand Island did not seem to provide similar opportunities for human capital creation that could later, as in Lexington, be mobilized into proactive Latino organizations.

Sugar beets were not a mainstay of Schuyler's old economy and a Mexican-origin population was virtually absent from the area until the late 1980s. However, Schuyler had built a meatpacking plant in the heyday of industrial restructuring but also fell victim to the profit-squeeze of the 1970s, and by 1981 the plant closed. It re-opened eighteen months later, after a significant rollback of wages and benefits (Gouveia and Sanchez 2000).

Between the late 1980s and beginning of the 1990s, each of these communities was sporting a new or refurbished meatpacking plant owned by one of the "Big Three." Excel bought Schuyler's plant in 1987; Lexington became home to IBP's newest plant in 1990, built on the site of a defunct agricultural machinery factory; and Monfort (soon to become a subsidiary of ConAgra) purchased Grand Island's Swift plant in 1987. The consolidation of a Great Plains–directed immigrant network also revived Omaha's old meatpacking district, commonly referred to as "South Omaha."

It has almost become a truism that Mexicans, and low-skill immigrants as a whole, do the dirty jobs European Americans no longer wish to do. This is as true in Nebraska as it is anywhere. Meatpacking jobs, along with all the menial services no longer performed by European Americans, and even African Americans, have become identifiable Mexican and Latino immigrant niches in the state. Their work ethic is celebrated by employers and townsfolk but such celebrations may unwittingly or conveniently stigmatize and racialize Mexicans as the group that is best fitted to do the dirty work and to occupy the lower rungs of our social institutions. Framed in this manner, institutions of all kinds, from universities to state agencies, tend to accommodate this vision rather than invest in strategies aimed at socioeconomic upward mobility.

The clustering of Latinos in a small set of low-wage labor markets and dead-end occupations continues to be one of the major threads that links older and newer arrivals. In 2000, about 64 percent of all Latino male workers in Nebraska were found in just two occupational categories (production and construction). Another 20 percent are concentrated in the low-end of the service industry (U.S. Census Bureau 2000). Among those Latinos found in manufacturing, 23 percent were working in meatpacking, and the overwhelming majority of them were foreign-born. Conversely, 34 percent of non-Latino whites were found in the higher ranked-management and professional occupations. Only 12.5 percent of Latinos fit under this category and the majority are native born (U.S. Census Bureau 2003).

As numerous studies have also made clear, it is the second generation that will shape the character of these communities. The children of immigrants will, at least in part, reflect the current socioeconomic successes and immigrant experiences of their parents as well as their surrounding co-ethnic network. Local labor market structures do not appear to offer significant upward mobility for immigrants. It remains to be seen whether other factors, such as institutional adaptation and host-community attitudes can make up for these failings or are more likely to reinforce segmented incorporation.

METHODOLOGY

To understand the direction of Mexican and Latino incorporation into new destinations such as Nebraska, we conducted a survey and held a series of focus groups among local and state agencies as well as immigrant workers and older community members.[2] We selected both settled Mexicano communities and those that experienced significant growth between 1990 and 2000.

The survey was sent to more than 1,100 agencies or organizations in fifty-four communities. The response rate was acceptable for a mail questionnaire (approximately 25 percent) but lower than we had hoped. A total of 72 percent of the responses came from agencies or organizations in communities with populations of less than twenty-five thousand, where the majority of Mexicans and Latinos are concentrated. We grouped agencies and organizations into eight categories: schools and education, city and state government, justice and law enforcement, economic and business, churches and civic organizations, human and social services, media, and "other." Schools had by far the highest response rate. The overwhelming majority of the surveys returned were completed by organizations in which Latinos make up fewer than 10 percent of the workforce. Given our knowledge of these communities, the finding was not entirely surprising but guided our decision to conduct focus groups with greater Latino representation.

Focus group discussions proved particularly useful for uncovering the operation of more hidden and mutually reinforcing barriers to integration. They also helped unpack community attitudes and expectations toward newcomers which in surveys show up as much more dichotomous and unidimensional than they really are. We conducted four focus groups in a metropolitan city, three in a small community, and one in a medium-size city. All host meatpacking plants and have been important immigrant communities. Some had experienced earlier Mexican migration, though others, such as Schuyler, had not.

The selection was also guided by our familiarity with these communities, where we had conducted research that might complement our findings. We did not try to achieve equal representation by type of participants, but instead used our knowledge of and interest in exploring "hot-button" issues or challenges (for example, INS presence and lack of good housing) unique to each community. Our local focus group coordinators assembled groups of participants who would be knowledgeable about such challenges. We highlight similarities and differences among communities we found particularly significant and offer comparisons across types of organizations we believed particularly informative.

Focus group representatives were from governmental and nongovernmental Latino and non-Latino community service agencies in all three communities. We wanted to explore their views about and their roles in addressing barriers to Latino socioeconomic incorporation. One was composed of primarily Latino service providers. The rest were largely non-Latino whites. In the metropolitan, as well as in one of the nonmetropolitan communities, we assembled a "grassroots" focus group with Latino and Latina workers and family members. The size of the focus groups ranged from as few as six to as many as thirty-five individuals.

ATTITUDES AND INSTITUTIONAL RESPONSES OF HOST COMMUNITIES AND GOVERNMENTS

To ascertain some measure of community views concerning the nature and source of barriers to integration confronted by the new immigrant population, we asked respondents to identify the three greatest assets and the three greatest challenges Latinos bring to their community that facilitate or impede incorporation. In both instances respondents were asked to rank order the assets and challenges.

Assets and Challenges to Incorporation: Group Traits or Institutional Barriers?

Regarding Latino immigrant assets, answers were classified three ways: Latinos provide a much-needed labor supply and exhibit a strong work ethic; they are a source of cultural enrichment to the host community; and they hold strong family and religious values. In answer to the question of challenges posed by immigrants, regardless of rankings, all agencies surveyed included responses that were largely, but not entirely, associated with group traits. We clustered these into three main categories: language, cultural conflicts or racism, and lack of assimilation and understanding of the law. A smaller set of responses interpreted "challenges" as "structural barriers" to integration. Those respondents mentioned the quality of jobs held by new immigrants, insufficient educational and skill acquisition opportunities, and barriers associated with national immigration policy and inadequate access to services.

Organizations closer to the plight of newcomers tended to view this population as workers and families trying to improve their lives against enormous odds. As such, they were more likely to focus on institutional rather than individual barriers to successful immigrant integration (for example, more than 12 percent of educational institutions, versus fewer than 9 percent of religious institutions and only 2.5 percent of law enforcement agencies saw low wages and lack of educational opportunities as main barriers to integration). Local police departments considered lack of assimilation and understanding of local community norms and laws as the most important challenge that Latino newcomers posed.

With overwhelming concurrence, organizations recognized the negative impact of factors such as intolerant, racist, and prejudicial attitudes held by old-timers and prevalent in local institutions. In fact, survey responses demonstrated the presence of these attitudes in somewhat unexpected settings. For example, church members were just as likely as law enforcement respondents to view newcomers as norm violators and individuals who had "disregard for the laws and community norms." Such well-entrenched views were confirmed by other church representatives holding opposite views. As one of them aptly put it: "many/most of the members with power in the church don't want 'them' in our congregation." On the other hand, it is often said that the most segregated hour in America is at 11:00 o'clock on Sunday morning. This is certainly true in most Nebraska churches today. In South Omaha alone, Latinos can choose from at least four Catholic churches to attend Mass, mostly in Spanish but also in English, with an entirely Latino congregation.

Focus groups added to our understanding of these complex community attitudes and the inflexibility of institutions confronted with ethnic transformation. They also revealed how these change as the process of settlement deepens. A newly appointed Latino minister of a Protestant denomination also spoke of his church's ambivalence toward Hispanics at the time of his arrival.

> They wanted me to come and start a Hispanic ministry, but were not willing to let me change anything that could make that happen. I had to ask if I could bring the children to church, and they would tell me no, that they would destroy everything, that they are very dirty; and we were not supposed to go there either [to their homes or community events], as that was dangerous for us ministers." Eventually, he said, "I ended up losing only two non-Hispanic families from the congregation, unhappy with the arrival of Hispanics to our church.

While it is true that nonmetropolitan communities tend to suffer from an even more serious lack of institutions and programs responding proactively to new immigration, we found that attitudes that could hinder or facilitate incorporation did not always line up neatly along this urban-rural divide. In some rural communities, institutional response to the new realities of massive and sociolinguistically diverse immigration lagged behind others in significant ways. The attitude toward Mexicans as outsiders and transient laborers was particularly prominent in one community where Mexicans fared quite poorly in earlier years. As one participant put it: "I must say that we are behind the curve here in (community's name). It has taken us a long time to realize that immigrants are here to stay and that they are a very important part of our survival as a community." She went on to remark how local agencies lacked translators or culturally competent personnel in almost every area of social services, including an absolute absence of bilingual mental health providers in the entire state.

Focus group participants ultimately converged toward a characterization of Latinos that differentiated between two qualitatively different segments of the population. The first was characterized as the "core" and largest segment, and was associated with positive attributes, similar to those highlighted in the survey, such as a strong work ethic and family values. The second was characterized as a much smaller, transient, and peripheral group, and was associated with negative traits such as drug distribution and other illegal activities, which, respondents argued, have contributed to an unfair stigmatization of the entire population. These distinctions were just as likely to be drawn in nonmetropolitan as in metropolitan communities.

SPECIFIC BARRIERS TO INTEGRATION EXAMINED

Respondents' perceptions of barriers to incorporation are clearly bound by the institutional spaces they occupy. The answers also are often just as revealing, if not more revealing, of the lack of human capital resources in agencies addressing newcomers' issues and the typical absence of a structural perspective of the root issues determining those clients' placement in the lower rungs of the socioeconomic hierarchy.

Language

Language, as Wayne Cornelius (2002) pointed out, has become the "lightning rod" for anti-immigrant sentiments and lack of English language proficiency is a major irritant to many monolingual Americans. Spanish dominance and bilingualism are often taken as evidence of cultural fragmentation and a looming threat to the imagined cohesiveness of "American" culture. Anxieties over language are as salient in Nebraska as in other parts of the country. However, the reality is that, in 2000, 30 percent of Latinos in Nebraska spoke only English and 62 percent spoke it well or very well (U.S. Census Bureau 2004). That still leaves 38 percent of Hispanic and Latinos who do not speak English well or at all, which indeed constitutes a serious barrier to successful integration. Thirty-three percent of educational organizations, 24 percent of religious organizations, and 28 percent of social service agencies ranked language as the number one barrier to incorporation. Only law enforcement agencies ranked it second to "lack of assimilation/understanding of the law." Each of these organizations ranked cultural conflicts or racism as the second major challenge to integrating Mexican and Latino newcomers.

While many focus group participants conceptualized the language barrier as a Latino cultural deficiency, others constructed it as the outcome of intolerant attitudes and lack of institutional support necessary for immigrants to acquire this important human capital resource. "We should all learn Spanish," was as common a response as was "why should we learn Spanish?"

Participants often offered analyses of how disadvantages, such as lack of transportation and childcare, as well as excessive work hours and double shifts, accrue over time and are barriers to integration. They noted that their female clients, who already suffer from the effects of traditional gender roles, are particularly disadvantaged by these structural barriers.

A lack of institutional flexibility and energetic response to this need is evident in the state's English as a Second Language (ESL) system. Community representatives concur that more often than not ESL classes lack standardization, consistent curriculum, qualified staff, sufficient funding and are not equipped to provide students with English language skills beyond elementary levels.[3] Despite such obstacles, ESL classes are filled to capacity and waiting lists for them are long. However, teachers participating in focus groups also noted how newcomers tend to get discouraged after realizing these classes are time consuming and yield few tangible results. "They just stop coming; time is extremely costly and valuable to them." Latino workers in the focus groups offered their own interpretation of these barriers:

> Let's accept the fact that there may be people who don't want to learn English; but there are many more who do because they want to improve their lives; because after all that's why we came, to improve our lives. . . . English is not an easy language; experts say it takes about ten years to learn English. Precisely because we don't speak English we have to take the hardest jobs, then many times it becomes physically impossible to study after such hard work all day; that is one of the most difficult things.

Labor Markets and Quality of Jobs

As in the rest of the country, Latinos in Nebraska show labor force participation rates that equal or exceed those of non-Latinos. In 2000, such rates ranged between 63 percent and 70 percent for native- and foreign-born Latinos of different origins, compared to 69.9 percent for non-Latinos. As shown earlier, despite such high rates of labor force participation, Latino newcomers in Nebraska end up in the lowermost jobs with few opportunities for advancement. Due to the unstable nature of many of the jobs they fill, unemployment rates for Mexicans and Central Americans are almost three times as high as those of non-Hispanic and non-Latinos in the state. For example, 9 percent of Central Americans in 2000 were unemployed, though only 3.4 percent of non-Hispanics were. A lack of serious recognition of the significance of this barrier and parallel public and institutional resolve to address it does not augur well. In fact, institutional agents responding to our survey did not rank labor market barriers among the top three barriers to immigrant incorporation. It was only after much discussion and probing during focus groups that some participants chose to speak at length about the associations between poor jobs, poverty, and few opportunities for advancement that affect immigrants.[4] Here, the ethnic divide across responses was salient. Latino respondents were much more likely to elaborate, often quite eloquently, about how cumulative barriers to integration are erected upon a foundation of precarious employment to which one must add lack of institutional support for immigrants during the early stages of settlement.

> This [immigrant community] is a very unstable community. The main reason is their economic situation. Maybe their jobs are new and they cannot pay the deposit, or the husband lost his job. They don't have a safety net that can help them get back on their feet. Or they are stuck in a low-wage job because they are not able to adjust their legal status or don't speak English. The families are young and are having children, the husband gets injured in a job and they have no health insurance, usually because they don't think they can afford it or are even eligible for it.... They often don't qualify for benefits from the county or state help or this is simply not sufficient.... Their health issues we see everyday are related to poverty.... I think they just need an opportunity to start, get a job, have some money, and they will prosper from there.

In a focus group with thirty Latino workers, working conditions and the quality of jobs were similarly identified as the primary obstacles to economic stability and adaptation to their new communities. Complaints about the lack of job ladders, poor benefits, line speeds, injuries, and maltreatment by supervisors in meatpacking plants echoed those Gouveia collected more than twelve years ago. Immigrants remain unimpressed about a newly implemented Meatpacking Workers' Bill of Rights declared by Nebraska Governor Johanns. The bill's objective is to remind employees as well as employers of exiting constitutional and legislative sanctions against violation of labor laws. The comment echoed by most was: "What happens is that what it says out there [on the bill posted outside the working area] is not followed inside."

Finally, neither survey results nor focus groups revealed a particularly heightened awareness of the gendered character of immigrant labor markets and the unique disadvantages Latina immigrants face in Nebraska host communities. Female employment in meatpacking plants is limited and seldom exceeds 30 percent. Given the small size of rural economies and their over-reliance on a single manufacturing industry, alternative employment opportunities for women are also limited. A rural-to-urban migration of Latino newcomers is already evident and often spurred on by these employment needs. Census figures do not adequately capture the true dimensions of female unemployment as many immigrant women are discouraged from entering the paid labor market from the start. For Mexicans, the unemployment rates for men and women are similar, though for Central America they are not (10.8 percent for women compared to 8.1 percent for men).

Education, Legal Status, and Immigration Policies

Access to education will be the most critical factor determining upward mobility among the children of these newer Mexican and Central American arrivals. Educational attainment for Latino foreign-born lags far behind the already disadvantaged Latino native-born population in Nebraska. Parental education is, in turn, one of the factors that correlates highly with their children's educational achievement levels. In 2000, almost 75 percent of Latino foreign-born, 25 years old or older, residing in Nebraska did not have a high school diploma, and college rates for males were half of those found among the Latino native-born. Institutional intervention will be critical if factors associated with first-generation educational levels and other disadvantageous contextual factors are to be overcome.

Survey and focus group participants from mainstream institutions did not seem to register the level of concern that would seem to correspond more closely with the seriousness of the situation. To be sure, all participants considered education a barrier, but ranked it far lower than cultural and linguistic issues. As expected, educational institutions were the most aware and concerned. Focus groups with Latino parents, confirming findings from various national research projects, demonstrated a high level of concern for their children's education and focused primarily on legal status as a main barrier standing between aspiration and reality. One mother, an undocumented Mexican herself, echoed a common concern being heard in communities and the media around the nation today:

> My children are eight and six years old. The oldest has no papers and the youngest was born in the United States. We are very

thankful about the fact that our children have access to free public education until the twelfth grade. But at the same time that one pushes our kids to get an education and aspire to a professional career, we know that at the end of the road everything stops because they have no papers and no social security. We work from sun up to sun down hoping that our children will have a better life. But we have no way to get legal papers so they can do so. Today I got the reports from my eight-year-old. He got the honors band and he was so excited about having earned the honor to have lunch with the principal. It breaks my heart when I think that some day soon I will have to tell him, no more education. We contribute a lot to the economy of this state. This is not fair.

Community agency representatives also expressed concerns about adult newcomers' limited access to language classes, vocational training, and opportunities to pursue or complete their higher education. Participants pointed to the lack of flexibility in existing educational institutions and their failure to accommodate to the particular working schedules and other constraints faced by newcomers.

Aside from laws denying undocumented children a college education, respondents expressed a degree of concern with how the absence of a legal status denied immigrant families access to health insurance, credit, bank accounts, public benefits, and state driver's licenses. The lack of legal protection is thought to be having even more dire consequences for immigrant families in some cases. One focus group of health and human service providers in Grand Island discussed new cases in which parental rights are being terminated when mothers are deported after minor child abuse and neglect infractions, and then find it hard to return to claim their children. Emboldened by a heightened presence of immigration law enforcement officers in these interior communities, local police officers feel the need to arrest parents suspected of being undocumented for offenses they were seldom or ever arrested for in the past. Once in custody, the police have the right to call upon these officers if undocumented status is suspected and it quickly spirals downward from there.

As children come into our care, you know, they are placed with a foster family. It's just hard because once they come into our care you have all these professionals (allegedly advocating for the child). You have the county attorney, a judge, the attorney ad litum; we don't have people who are bilingual and we all come from different backgrounds, we are not educated in their culture. If anything can stop the train [to try to re-unite the children with the parents] is when INS gets involved. Maybe the parent has been deported and we have the issue of, you know, part of it is to show that they can provide for their children. And if they are undocumented [the parent left behind or returning after being deported] they cannot work legally. Well, that's the reason right there for termination of parental rights. Because how are you going to prove that you can, you know, maintaining your household, and that these children will be safe, and well taken care of? . . . you can't prove that.

These fears, participants agreed, are having a serious negative impact on the use of social services, even among legal immigrants, and particularly in rural communities where advocacy organizations are less visible. As in the rest of the country, post–September 11 immigration enforcement actions have increased a sense of vulnerability and fear among newcomers, the effect of which will not be known for some time.

THE FUTURE: ASSIMILATION OR SEGMENTED INCORPORATION?

As figures 2.1 and 2.2 illustrate, most survey respondents believed their agencies are being increasingly successful at creating a positive environment for assimilation and felt quite optimistic about the future.

One focus group participant expressed a sentiment commonly heard in all focus groups and replicated in the survey responses: "I personally feel very, um, very positive that new immigrants are going to be assimilated, ah, very well and expeditiously." It is hard to interpret such findings. Polls consistently show that non-Latino whites tend to hold much more positive views about interethnic and inter-racial relations as well as optimistic views about opportunities for mobility and equality for all than do populations of color. In fact, Latina agency representatives, as well as non-Latinos with long histories of immigrant advocacy, tended to qualify their optimism in ways that are more consonant with views of assimilation as a highly segmented and contingent process:

I think that we will have two layers, one are the kids that become successful, that get their high school and college degrees and become medium-size business owners. And the other will be those kids who get into the system [become assimilated] but are not able to make it because of social and economic situations.

FIGURE 2.1   Community Success at Latino Integration

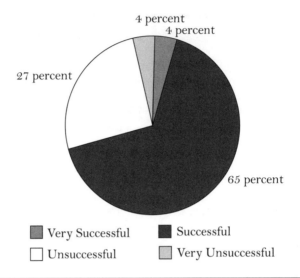

4 percent
4 percent

27 percent

65 percent

▩ Very Successful   ■ Successful
□ Unsuccessful   ▨ Very Unsuccessful

Source: Authors' compilation.

FIGURE 2.2   Optimism for Agency Contribution to
              Latino Community Integration

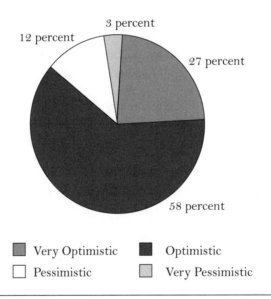

3 percent
12 percent

27 percent

58 percent

▩ Very Optimistic   ■ Optimistic
□ Pessimistic   ▨ Very Pessimistic

Source: Authors' compilation.

A second agency director picks up on this latter point:

> However, those who get into the system are losing their cultural connection, their cultural values. Their parents want them to become Americanized, to speak English without an accent . . . so these kids become "American" but that does not necessarily make them successful. They end up assimilating into all these material values and want new and expensive shoes and other things their parents cannot afford. They become frustrated and have no system in place or their own cultural values they have now rejected to protect them.

The loss of cultural values and native language was often cited, as it is in the research literature, as leading to the loss of parental authority and family cohesion which can in turn direct children toward the formation of an identity that rejects parental and more positive mainstream values such as education (Portes and Rumbaut 2001).

Conclusions

The recent arrival of large numbers of new Mexican and other Latino immigrants in new destinations such as Schuyler, Nebraska, is transforming local demographics and sociocultural landscapes in profound and not totally understood ways. The question most often raised by these changes, and addressed in this chapter, has to do with the pace and degree of success with which newcomers will integrate into these "coastless" communities. Do these heartland communities provide better contexts of immigrant incorporation than their larger urban counterparts? It is too early to provide more definitive answers. A large part of the answer will depend on local and national institutional responses and the mobilization of political resources that can tilt the incorporation process, inherently sensitive to social contexts, up or down. We can, however, summarize our findings and present additional insights that both increase our awareness of the barriers to immigrant upward mobility and, conversely, reveal the resources waiting to be mobilized to productively hasten incorporation along its path.

As in the rest of the country, Mexicans and other Latino groups are concentrated in a small set of occupations and industries characterized by low wages and poor opportunities. On the other hand, the scarcity of labor in Nebraska offers local Latinos unexpected opportunities to combine household incomes not found in areas, such as California, where intra-immigrant labor market competition is severe and the cost of living is significantly higher. Meatpacking plants today have to compete with a growing number of local labor markets that are taking advantage of this new labor supply windfall. Benefits associated with an abundance of jobs are tempered by the low wage structure that characterizes them. Despite high rates of labor force participation, the rate of Latinos' poverty remains unacceptably high.

On the other hand, there is evidence that income-pulling strategies may be paying off. Median household income for Nebraska Hispanics, most of who are of Mexican origin, increased 19 percent between 1990 and 2000. With regard to Latino foreign-born, their median household income is only about $3,500 below that of Latino native-born, $35,000 and $31,500 respectively (U.S. Census Bureau 2003). In Lexington, the median income gap between Latinos and non-Latino whites is reduced to a mere $200 (U.S. Census Bureau 2000). In addition, despite low levels of human capital and uneven levels of social capital found among earlier and recent arrivals, self-employment rates among Latinos have increased significantly in recent years. Latino businesses grew at double the rate of other minority businesses and their total numbers was just below that of African Americans (U.S. Census Bureau 1997). Latino-owned establishments occupy many, if not the bulk, of downtown business districts in most of the new, or resurgent, destination communities highlighted here. Many of these locales were boarded up during the 1970s and 1980s after the exodus of European Americans to the suburbs of urban communities such as Omaha, or more serious economic decline in rural communities such as Lexington. Unlike earlier Mexican arrivals, Latino newcomers do not compete in the same business sectors or labor markets with white immigrants where they had inexorably occupied the next-to-the-last step in the ethnic cue. Such businesses cater to an ethnic population base that has also expanded significantly and prefers to do business in familiar surroundings. Besides these great efforts to overcome barriers to economic mobility, newer Mexican arrivals mirror national trends related to high levels of house ownership as well as naturalization rates that have more than tripled each year between 1999 and 2002 (U.S. Department of Homeland Security 2003).

There is a visible explosion of nonprofit community and advocacy organizations dedicated to facilitating immigrant incorporation, though these are still inadequate to the need. Old-timers and non-Latinos dominate these organizations, but more recent arrivals are increasingly visible in both boards and staff. In fact, while Nebraska also mirrors the schizophrenic nature of public attitudes toward immigrants at the national level, it lacks the virulence of anti-immigrant sentiments and historical baggage of intense interethnic and interracial conflicts found in older destinations. This has created an unexpected and fertile environment for experimenting with legislative and other initiatives promoting integration that may have provoked much more heated opposition than one encounters here (see Gouveia and Juska 2002 for one prominent example).[5]

All this notwithstanding, the barriers to mobility that immigrants and native-born Latinos confront in Nebraska are serious. Institutional responses on the part of the state to remove the barriers are woefully inadequate. Despite Herculean efforts by nonprofit organizations, the challenges facing Latino immigrants and their host communities are as evident here as in other urban destinations. They suffer from the highest uninsured rates, unprotected day laborers are a growing phenomena, safety nets are inaccessible (as are adequate documentation and transportation), and educational opportunities are patently limited given this combination of barriers documented in our survey and focus groups.

Data also hints at the slow if not neglectful pace at which institutions and political leaders are adopting policies and creating programs to meet the needs of a population that has become the lifeline of the state. Local school districts share an uneven burden when it comes to educating immigrant children and their special needs. School funding formulas do not take into account such disparate resource needs. Recently, four school districts across the state joined forces and are suing the state of Nebraska for precisely this reason. The governor's initiative to introduce a Meatpacking Workers' Bill of Rights was heralded as a historic move by a Republican governor. However, conditions in these plants have barely changed and complaints filed by workers under this new law have never been analyzed for the purpose of effecting more systemic changes in immigrant-dependent industries. If anything, we have all come to accept, it would seem, the employers' mantra that "meatpacking is just hard work." The state's commitment to expand opportunities for learning English, training programs for adults, or educational support programs for the second generation to close the educational achievement gap and reduce drop-out rates is questionable at best.

New research on immigrant integration at the national and international level, as well as initiatives such as the Immigration Taskforce of the Chicago Council on Foreign Relations, document similar challenges, and propose innovative and visionary solutions that require more than just political will. Some of these suggestions were informed by the unique character of new destinations in midwestern states. It behooves us to learn from all of them.[6]

This largely Mexican-origin population also carries with it a heavy sociopsychological burden gathered along its unique migration history and laced with exclusion and racialization. A hint of such history is registered in our surveys and focus groups. A barrage of recent studies paints a rather pessimistic outlook for this future generation of Mexicans. Yet we must move carefully along the fault lines that identify the unique challenges facing this population group on one side and paint an unduly fatalistic outlook on the other.

The authors wish to thank the State of Nebraska Mexican American Commission and the Nebraska Legislature's Task Force on the Productive Integration of the Immigrant Workforce Population. Funding for this project was also provided by a grant from the U.S. Department of Education. We want to recognize the support of our universities and programs as well as all those community agencies and members who donated much of their generous time to us during the research process. We also thank our research assistants, Jasney Cogua, Katrina Ondracek-Sayers, and Esperanza Camargo. Jerry Deichert, from the Center for Public Affairs Research at the University of Nebraska at Omaha, assisted us with a major portion of the census data reflected in our tables and text. Finally, we wish to acknowledge the work of the Nebraska Appleseed Center for Law in the Public Interest whose dedication to defending the rights of immigrants and the poor helped inspire the legislation and call for proposals that culminated in our report and this chapter.

NOTES

1. As a result of Legislative Bill 1363, the Nebraska legislature created the *Task Force on the Productive Integration of the Immigrant Workforce Population* (Legislature of Nebraska 2000). Besides holding public hearings, the *Task Force* commissioned a study on this topic. The first two authors were principal investigators in the study while the third served as a research assistant. The report, "The Integration of the Hispanic/Latino Immigrant Workforce: Final Project Report," can be located on the websites for the University of Nebraska at Omaha, Office of Latino/Latin American Studies as well as that of Nebraska Appleseed Center for Law in the Public Interest.

2. The data was collected as part of a project sponsored by the Nebraska State Legislature and the Mexican American Commission (see Carranza and Gouveia 2002).

3. The seriousness of this problem is underscored by the recent organization of an ad hoc coalition of representatives from various Omaha agencies and individuals concerned with this issue. They have recently mailed a questionnaire to governmental and non-governmental agencies teaching ESL as a first step to find more adequate solutions.

4. This was likely an effect of the instruments used rather than particularly meaningful differences between survey and focus group participants, albeit the proportionately larger presence of Latinos in the focus groups may indeed account for the differential attention paid to economic barriers in the two sets of responses.

5. Among some of the advocacy organizations, the Nebraska Appleseed Center for the Public Interest and the Iowa-Nebraska Immigrant Rights Network have done some of the most nationally and locally prominent work. Community organizations now include a Latina Resource Center as well as an array of old organizations that have retooled to serve the newcomer population.

6. See for example the various references for the work on the second generation by Alejandro Portes, Rubén Rumbaut, and the special issue of the International Migration Review edited by Maurice Crul and Hans Verneulen (Portes and Rumbaut 2001; Rumbaut and Portes 2001; Crul and Vermeulen 2003). See also the Chicago Council on Foreign Relations (2004) for a midwestern perspective on these issues and their solutions.

REFERENCES

Bureau of Business Research. 1997. *The Educational Status of Hispanics/Latinos in Nebraska: A Statistical Profile.* Vol. 2. Lincoln: University of Nebraska-Lincoln.

Carranza, Miguel A., and Lourdes Gouveia. 2002. "The Integration of the Hispanic/Latino Immigrant Workforce: Final Project Report." Submitted to the State of Nebraska Mexican American Commission and Task Force on the Productive Integration of the Immigrant Workforce Population. Lincoln, Neb. (May 31, 2002).

The Chicago Council on Foreign Relations. 2004. *Keeping the Promise: Immigration Proposals from the Heartland. Report of an Independent Taskforce.* Chicago: Chicago Council on Foreign Relations.

Cornelius, Wayne. 2002. "Ambivalent Reception: Mass Public Responses to the "New" Latino Immigration to the United States." In *Latinos Remaking America*, edited by Marcelo M. Suarez Orozco and Mariela M. Paez. Berkeley: University of California Press; Boston: David Rockefeller Center for Latin American Studies, Harvard University.

Crul, Maurice, and Hans Vermeulen. 2003. "The Second Generation in Europe." *International Migration Review* 37(4): 965–87.

Fink, Deborah. 1998. *Cutting into the Meatpacking Line: Workers and Change in the Rural Midwest.* Chapel Hill: University of North Carolina Press.

Fix, Michael, and Wendy Zimmerman. 2000. "The Integration of Immigrant Families." Washington, D.C.: The Urban Institute.

Gerstle, Gary, and John Mollenkopf. 2001. "The Political Incorporation of Immigrants, Then and Now." In *E Pluribus Unum? Contemporary and Historical Perspectives on Immigrant Political Incorporation,* edited by Gary Gerstle and John Mollenkopf. New York: Russell Sage Foundation.

Gouveia, Lourdes. 1994. "Global Strategies and Local Linkages: The Case of the U.S. Meatpacking Industry." In *From Columbus to ConAgra. The Globalization of Agriculture and Food,* edited by Alessandro Bonanno, Lawrence Busch, William H. Friedland, Lourdes Gouveia and Enzo Mingione. Lawrence: University Press of Kansas.

———. 2000. "From the Beet Fields to the Kill Floors: Latinos in Nebraska's Meatpacking Communities." Unpublished paper. University of Nebraska at Omaha.

Gouveia, Lourdes, and Arunas Juska. 2002. "Taming Nature, Taming Workers: Efforts to Separate and Re-Link Meat Consumption and Meat Production." Unpublished paper. University of Nebraska at Omaha.

Gouveia, Lourdes, and Rogelio Saenz. 2000. "Global Forces and Latino Population Growth in the Midwest: A Regional and Subregional Analysis." *Great Plains Research* 10(2): 305–28.

Gouveia, Lourdes, and Thomas Sanchez. 2000. "Incorporation of Latinos/Immigrants in Rural Nebraska Communities: Grand Island and Schuyler." Report to Texas A&M Research Foundation, July 21, 2000. College Station: Texas A&M University.

Gouveia, Lourdes, and Donald D. Stull. 1996. "Latino Immigrants, Meatpacking and Rural Communities: A Case Study of Lexington, Nebraska." *JSRI Research Report* No. 26. East Lansing: Michigan State University.

Grajeda, Ralph. 1976. "Chicanos: The Mestizo Heritage." In *Broken Hoops and Plains People,* edited by Nebraska Curriculum Development Center. Lincoln: University of Nebraska-Lincoln.

Grey, Mark. 1995. "Turning the Pork Industry Upside Down: Storm Lake's Hygrade Work Force and the Impact of the 1981 Plant Closure." *The Annals of Iowa* 54(3): 244–59.

Hackenberg, Robert A., David Griffith, Donald Stull, and Lourdes Gouveia. 1993. "Creating a Disposable Labor Force." *The Aspen Institute Quarterly* 5(2): 78–101.

Legislature of Nebraska. 2000. "Legislative Bill 1363." Ninety-Seventh Legislature, Second Session. Lincoln.

Lopez, David A.. 2000. "Latinos in Omaha: A Socio-Economic Comparison of Non-Latino Whites and Latinos in the City of Omaha." *JSRI Statistical Brief.*

No. 12. East Lansing: Julian Samora Research Institute, Michigan State University.

Nebraska Department of Health and Human Services. 2001. *2000 Births by Sex, Race and Hispanic Origin by Place of Residence.* Available at: http://www.hhs.state.ne.us/cedtabl5.htm. (accessed May 30, 2002).

Portes, Alejandro, and Rubén Rumbaut. 2001. *Legacies: The Story of the Immigrant Second Generation.* Berkeley: University of California Press.

Rumbaut, Rubén G., and Alejandro Portes. 2001. "Introduction—Ethnogenesis: Coming of Age in Immigrant America." In *Ethnicities: Children of Immigrants in America,* edited by Rubén Rumbaut and Alejandro Portes. Berkeley: University of California Press.

Schlosser, Eric. 2001. *Fast Food Nation: The Dark Side of the All-American Meal.* Boston: Houghton Mifflin.

U.S. Census Bureau. 1990. Summary File 3. Washington: U.S. Census Bureau.

———. 1997. *Minority- and Women-Owned Businesses.* 1997 Economic Census. Washington: U.S. Government Printing Office.

———. 2000. U.S. Bureau of the Census 2000 Summary File 4 (SF 4)—Sample Data, Table QT-P27. Occupation by Sex. Washington: U.S. Census Bureau.

———. 2001a. Census 2000 Redistricting Data (Public Law 94-171) Summary File, Matrices PL1 and PL2. Washington: U.S. Census Bureau.

———. 2001b. Census 2000, Summary File 1 and Unpublished Data. Internet Release Date: October 22, 2001. Washington: U.S. Census Bureau.

———. 2003. Census 2000 Public Use Microdata Sample (PUMS), various tables.

———. 2004. Census 2000, Summary File 4 (SF4) PCT38.

U.S. Department of Homeland Security. 2003. *2002 Yearbook of Immigration Statistics.* Washington, D.C.: Office of Immigration Statistics.

Waldinger, Roger. 2001. "Up From Poverty? 'Race,' Immigration and the Fate of Low-Skilled Workers." In *Strangers at the Gate: New Immigrants in Urban America,* edited by Roger Waldinger. Los Angeles: University of California Press.

CHAPTER 3

⋉⋊

RURAL INDUSTRY AND MEXICAN IMMIGRATION AND SETTLEMENT IN NORTH CAROLINA

DAVID C. GRIFFITH

Sometime during the early 1990s, while I was conducting studies of workers and work in the Midwest and mid-Atlantic states, a labor contractor who moved work crews among southern states for agricultural harvests told me that he refused to take crews north of the North Carolina–Virginia line. When I asked him why, he said, quite frankly, that when you crossed that state line you entered a region with more stringent labor law enforcement. He was talking mainly about the enforcement of the Migrant and Seasonal Agricultural Workers Protection Act (MSAWPA), a federal law that should protect farmworkers in North Carolina as fully as in Virginia, yet he was correct in his view that enforcement differed from one side of the border to the other. Virginia lies in a different U.S. Department of Labor region than North Carolina, and historically the two regional offices have approached labor law enforcement with varying degrees of enthusiasm. Perhaps because of its southern heritage, the Atlanta Regional Office of the Department of Labor had been less strict than the Philadelphia office. In so far as this translates into farm labor contractors refusing to take crews north of the North Carolina–Virginia line, it means that, for many Mexican farm workers, even deep inside the United States a border remains a significant force in their lives.

Certainly not all Mexicans settling in North Carolina realize that labor law enforcement varies between North Carolina and Virginia, yet most, even those living and working legally in the state, may perceive that not only is labor law loosely enforced but immigration law as well. The Immigration and Naturalization Service (INS) steps so lightly in the state that when the Raleigh *News & Observer* ran a front page story about a new undocumented Mexican immigrant and his family, the immigrant felt confident enough about his residence in the state to give the reporters his name and place of employment and let them photograph him and his home for publication. While the INS, after this story, couldn't not apprehend and deport this man, it was widely rumored that, after his deportation, he returned to the state with the assistance of the newspaper reporter, his employer, and several concerned citizens (Gigi Anders, "Heart Without a Home," *News & Observer*, March 8, 1998, pp. A1, A16).

Openness about their status among undocumented Mexicans in North Carolina is not uncommon, raising interesting issues regarding the terms of Mexican immigration into the state and, by extension, throughout those parts of the South and the rest of the United States that did not experience high levels of immigration until the 1990s. As recently as the summer of 2000, a research associate and I were traveling through the state studying the employment of children in agriculture, focusing primarily on Mexican farmworkers. Stopping at a Mexican-owned and -operated restaurant early on a Friday evening, being the only customers, we struck up a conversation with one of the Mexican cooks, a woman neither of us had ever met. We asked her where she was from and how long she had been in the area. She said that she had come from Zacatecas five years earlier. When we asked about her family back home, she said that she had two children whom she missed dearly, along with her parents and the rest of her family, but that, despite her sadness, she had no plans to return any time soon. "No tengo papeles," she said. She had, that is, no papers.

The following afternoon, we visited a Mexican man and a woman who worked, legally, for a crabmeat factory, carrying H-2 (temporary employment) visas. I had known and worked with this couple for three years, visiting them several times in Mexico and the United States. Despite what I thought to be a trusting, open relationship, they hesitated before answering several questions about the terms of their employment, the treatment they received from their bosses and their hopes for the future. Although they did eventually answer our questions, their hesitation and wariness stemmed from their fear that, somehow, being too frank about the H-2 program would jeopardize their jobs.

What strikes me about these two incidents happening over the same weekend was that the people who were living and working in North Carolina legally seemed far more reticent about revealing much about themselves and their employment experiences than those who were living and working in the state illegally. Why should the woman at the restaurant, whom we had only just met, have been more forthcoming about her conditions of residence in North Carolina than two individuals whom I had known for years and who lived and worked in the country completely legally? How does this reflect on state practices and federal policies toward immigrants and immigration? Finally, what might this tell us about the ways that Mexican and other immigrants enter and take up residence in North Carolina?

Here I explore the possibility that the differences we observed that weekend at the turn of the century illustrate one of the central paradoxes of Mexican immigration into North Carolina. On the one hand, the state has been at the forefront of legal immigration, using the H-2 program as heavily as any state in the South and more heavily than most, and the home state of the principal organization responsible for the recent growth of the program all along the east coast. On the other, the state's undocumented immigration has been equally robust yet has been more apt than the H-2 program to generate family ties to towns, neighborhoods, schools, and other social resources of North Carolina. While legal immigration encourages young, single men and women living in dormitories, separated from most of their families, migrating cyclically instead of settling—a kind of military model of immigration— illegal immigration into the state seems to be encouraging the family formation, child bearing and child rearing, church and school attendance, and other attributes we normally associate with the development of community. Indeed, this seems common in other parts of the United States, and in particular in those nontraditional destinations where new immigrants have been arriving in large numbers only since the late 1980s and early 1990s.

Studies of U.S. immigration agree that the recent growth in immigration from Mexico and Central America began following the immigration reforms of the late 1980s, primarily the 1986 Immigration Reform and Control Act (Grey 2000; Haines and Rosenblum 1999; Stull, Broadway, and Griffith 1995; Portes and Rumbaut 2001). Rural communities in many parts of the United States—particularly California, Florida, Illinois, New York and New Jersey, and Texas—have received Mexican, African, Southeast Asian, Southern and Eastern European, and other so-called "new" immigrants at least since the 1950s and in some cases much earlier, though in many cases on a seasonal basis and confined primarily to the agricultural labor market.

What is different about the new waves of immigration into the United States is their diffusion across economic landscapes and geographical areas: more and more, new immigrants are moving out of those states and areas of employment that have been considered traditional destinations for immigrants, such as California agriculture, and into other areas where employment is less seasonal and more secure, such as food processing, construction, light manufacturing, and fast food. From this movement across landscapes and industrial sectors, many areas of the United States—and particularly its rural areas— seem to be in flux, with people moving in and out of communities across the nation, internationally, and among small towns within regions.

This demands a revision of the idea of community, of course, as less of a physical place than a social unit connected by various threads— such as the raitero networks, switchboard labor markets, and anchor households described in previous works (Griffith et al. 1995; Kissam et al. 2000)—to several physical places that go by names like Hendersonville and Belhaven, North Carolina, Immokalee, Florida, Dalton, Georgia, and Chandler Heights, Arizona. Just as networks connect families throughout regions like the South or the Midwest, more distant ties link families with similar migration and ethnic backgrounds across the United States, containing the potential for apparently disparate communities and neighborhoods to become parts of a much larger social ecology in which we understand behaviors in Kennett Square, Pennsylvania, or Newton Grove, North Carolina, in terms of the political and economic landscapes of Marshall, Minnesota, or Villachuato, Michoacan.

These individual and group movements across the country, combined with growing settled immigrant populations, create their own internal markets for informal economic activity (Zlolinski 1994; Kearney 1996). These include, for example, traditional food preparation and/or vending (including the establishment and staffing of restaurants), childcare services, and various services oriented toward negotiating a noncitizen status. Securing identification, translating, and locating and providing transportation to various agencies and businesses that address immigrant needs for education, health care, and employment are all part of the immigrant and refugee experience in the United States today.

These developments, driven by economic need, have spawned several social and cultural developments. First, many of the "traditional" regions and occupations continue to attract immigrants, in the United States and elsewhere, but immigrants from different socioeconomic and ethnic backgrounds or with different immigration statuses. Sherri Grasmuck (1982) found Haitians filling jobs in the Dominican Republic that Dominicans either wouldn't or couldn't fill, Jorge Duany (1990) found Dominicans filling jobs in Puerto Rico that Puerto Ricans either wouldn't or couldn't fill, and David Griffith and Manuel Valdés Pizzini (2002) found Puerto Ricans filling jobs in New York that New Yorkers either wouldn't or couldn't fill.

Similar class and ethnic successions are taking place inside Mexico and Central America and in traditional immigrant receiving occupations and regions in the United States. In the highly industrialized agricultural production sites along the Pan-American Highway, near the marketing center of Los Mochis, women, children, and indigenous workers have moved in to fill positions vacated by women and men working in North Carolina as H-2 workers or undocumented immigrants. In Oaxaca, Jeff Cohen's (2001) recent examination of people who don't have the means to migrate found some who had moved into jobs vacated by emigrants. With the expansion of the H-2 program and the growth of Mexican immigration to the United States since 1990, new sending areas have emerged in Mexico and new social and cultural features have been turning up throughout the United States. The rural United States has been particularly transformed by these changes. As numbers of H-2 workers increased in agriculture, for example, they composed work groups of almost exclusively young, single males. New sending areas and new indigenous groups in Mexico and Central America have emerged to staff industries once staffed by Mestizo Mexicans from traditional sending regions like Michoacan and Hidalgo. Thus one of the largest nurseries on the East Coast hires, along with low country African Americans from Gullah backgrounds (descendants from isolated southern coastal slave plantations who speak a distinct language and recognize themselves as ethnically distinct), predominantly young, single Mixtec women from Oaxaca who speak little or no Spanish and even less English. Similarly, one of the largest poultry producers in Maryland uses predominantly Mayans—such as X'anjobal, Chuj, and Jacaltec—to work its disassembly lines beside prisoners on work release programs and local whites and African Americans.

At the same time as many of these traditional labor markets are attracting single male and indigenous workers, immigrant settlement has begun creating a second generation of Mexicans and other immigrant groups (Portes and Rumbaut 2001). Increased employment opportunities and labor demand associated with growing immigrant populations have underwritten immigrant settlement, the elaboration of kinship networks within immigrant populations and between immigrant and native populations, and more children of Mexican immigrants being born in the United States. The tensions that attend the concentration of immigrants in farm work, meatpacking, and similar low-wage, hazardous occupations—specifically those where employers use immigrants to undermine labor organizing, foster indentured servitude or debt peonage, and engage in excessive labor control—may become less pervasive as immigrants develop their own opportunities within immigrant networks, develop skills through increased interactions with community opportunities for learning English and developing human capital, and access a wider variety of economic opportunities (wage labor, salaried, and business) in their communities.

Like the midwestern meatpacking regions, the South, with the glaring exception of Florida, has been one of those regions with a relatively shallow history of Mexican immigration as compared to areas like California, the Southwest, and the Northeast. This is particularly true in the lowland plantation belt where the majority of the country's African American descendants of slaves continue to live, and the Appalachians, with its legacy of small farming mixed with subsistence hunting, fishing, and gathering and often hazardous work in mining, forestry, and light manufacturing. With its lowland, heavily African American coastal plain and its Appalachian region, an examination of Mexican immigration into North Carolina is thus a small window into Mexican immigration into the South.

HISTORY OF MEXICAN IMMIGRATION INTO NORTH CAROLINA

Although Mexican immigration to North Carolina is perceived as new among a number of observers, Mexican immigrants have been working in North Carolina agriculture—from coastal fruit and vegetable production to mountain apple and Christmas tree production—at least since the early 1980s. As a consequence, Mexicans have been settling out in the state since the middle 1980s, originally in rural industry such as poultry processing and meatpacking and later in rural and urban manufacturing (primarily of furniture), construction, landscaping and nurseries, and the restaurant and hospitality trades. As in other parts of the United States, Mexican immigration into North Carolina increased markedly following the immigration reforms of the late 1980s and early 1990s, particularly since the amnesty provisions of the Immigration Reform and Control Act (IRCA) of 1986.

With the legalization of large numbers of Special Agricultural Workers (SAWs), many Mexicans familiar with North Carolina's labor markets, now free to move between the United States and Mexico, began facilitating travel and employment among new immigrants from their home communities. Interviewing H-2 workers in Mexico in 2000, village residents in Hidalgo and other Mexican states told us that large-scale emigration began in 1987; H-2 flows only enhanced the larger emigration (Griffith, Heppel, and Torres 2001). Several factors came together during the late 1980s and early 1990s to make Mexican-North Carolina migration feasible among many rural Mexicans: North Carolina's expanding economic base, and particularly its food processing, construction, and furniture manufacturing industries; greater numbers of legal immigrants with knowledge of North Carolina returning to Mexico for brief visits and recruiting friends and family to North Carolina jobs; an expansion of links between labor contractors, raiteros (those who provide rides from the Mexican border to the Eastern United States); and greater overlap between agricultural and rural industrial labor markets. SAWs were instrumental in these developments, a fact that will become clearer in the section on poultry processing.

Between 1988, when I first studied poultry industry hiring practices in the state, and the early 1990s, more poultry firms in the state had begun hiring Mexican immigrants and those that hired Mexicans in 1988 hired more in 1990 (Griffith 1993). These trends have continued through the 1990s in poultry, accompanying growing numbers and percentages of Mexicans across the state (Striffler 2001). The 2000 census revealed over fourfold increases in the numbers of Mexicans across the state, from 76,726, or 1.16 percent of the population in 1990, to 328,963, or 4.7 percent of the population in 2000 (http://factfinder.census.gov). During this same period, the total state population grew by around 21 percent, or from 6.6 to 8 million. Mexicans counted in the census made up 21 percent of this growth.

Specific county-level data are somewhat more telling than the state-wide figures, in part because the 2000 figures separate Mexicans and other Mexicans from Puerto Ricans and Cubans, a distinction that is important because the latter two groups are less likely to be illegal and have greater ranges of opportunities in the state. The figures in table 3.1 feature counties where agriculture and food processing are common occupations attracting Mexican immigrants, along with the urbanized counties near these areas.

Clearly, in most of these counties, the Mexican population, usually less than 1 percent of the total in 1990, grew by three to four times during the 1990s. These figures are undercounts, of course, not including many undocumented, or the H-2 workers, of which there are somewhere between fifteen and twenty thousand in the state. The H-2 workers in Pamlico County would swell the total number of Mexicans from

TABLE 3.1   Mexican and Latino Population Estimates for Selected North Carolina Counties

County	1990 Total	Number Latinos	Percentage Latino	2000 Total	Number Latinos	Percentage Latino	Mexican	Other Latino
Beaufort[a]	42,283	197	.46	44,958	1,455	3.2	1,219	173
Bladen	28,663	150	.52	32,278	1,198	3.7	919	222
Brunswick	50,985	376	.73	73,143	1,960	2.6	1,381	365
Duplin[b]	39,995	1,015	2.5	49,063	7,426	15.1	4,698	2,552
Henderson[c]	69,285	846	1.2	89,173	4,880	5.5	4,043	643
Martin[b]	25,078	99	.39	25,593	528	2.1	370	119
Pamlico[a]	11,372	61	.54	12,934	171	1.3	117	35
Pender	28,855	273	.95	41,082	1,496	3.6	1,077	308
Pitt	107,924	977	.90	133,798	4,216	3.1	2,992	802
Sampson					6,477	10.8	4,907	1,342
Wilkes[b]	59,393	362	.61	65,632	2,262	3.4	1,625	555

Source: U.S. Census Bureau (various years).
[a]Seafood processing county.
[b]Poultry processing county.
[c]Apple or Christmas tree county.

171 to between two hundred and fifty and three hundred and fifty, and in Beaufort from 1,455 to between seventeen hundred and eighteen hundred. In Martin County, where Mexicans made up only around 2 percent of the population in 2000, the increase accounted for over 80 percent of the total number of individuals added to the county's population.

Two somewhat contradictory processes have accompanied these developments. First, the growth in settled populations of Mexicans has led to more elaborate families living in North Carolina, including increasing numbers of children born in North Carolina to immigrant Mexicans. The settlement of Mexican families, in turn, has created a demand for several services specifically oriented toward Mexican consumers, including transportation and communication services (including wire money transfers), Spanish-speaking media, translation services, churches, bilingual education, native entertainment and cuisine, and childcare.

Second, as we have noted, the growth in H-2 programs throughout the state has created a Mexican work force of primarily single males in agriculture and single females in blue crab processing. Although the use of singles in H-2 programs may seem to contradict the growing reliance on families in other industries in the state, the two forms of Mexican immigration are in fact complementary.

The ways they complement one another are quite varied, ranging from the simple interactions at local grocery stores, bars, and flea markets to the exchange of labor market information to co-residence and intermarriage. H-2 workers from Pamlico County, for example, clean houses of local residents as well as work in the mid-summer blueberry harvests in Craven County during slow weeks in crab. H-2 workers in Beaufort County have dropped out of the program to stay through the year, caring for the children of other H-2 workers as they return to Mexico to renew their visas. During the summer of 1999, after two H-2 workers in the crab industry were fired for disputing their pay, the owners of the crab plant escorted the two women to the bus station in New Bern, refusing to hand them their passports (which they kept while they worked in their crab plant) until they had physically stepped onto the bus. Once on the bus, the two women waited for the owners to leave the station, then got off the bus and, within twenty-four hours, secured work as chambermaids at a local motel and temporary housing with two other Mexican chambermaids.

This last incident reveals a few attributes of Mexican tenure in North Carolina. While employers attempt to manipulate legal status for their own ends, such as enforcing work place discipline or increasing labor control—whether by invoking H-2 visa provisions, controlling passports or other means of identification, or taking advantage of the inherent vulnerability of undocumented immigrants—Mexicans in North Carolina are sometimes capable of exchanging enough information and at least temporary support to reduce the effectiveness of tactics that might undermine their ability to protest working conditions or pay. Without overemphasizing the power that Mexicans may garner from the increase in Spanish-speaking neighbors, business owners, workers, and employers, this increase has meant that more and more services for health care, finances, education, legal advice, and employment are becoming available in Spanish.

One important feature of this increasingly Spanish-speaking landscape has been the Mexican grocery store. Nearly all towns of more than 15,000 in North Carolina, and many with far lower populations, now have a store owned by a Mexican family or catering to a primarily Mexican clientele. Commonly this begins as a grocery store, selling spices, tortillas, fruit drinks, and sodas with brand names well known in Mexico, but rarely are these merely corner grocery stores. Additional goods and services these stores provide usually include money wire transfers, phone card machines, information on bus transportation to Mexico, Spanish-speaking video rentals, and sales of cooked food. Equally important, they usually have bulletin boards or places where people place flyers and other advertisements about dances with Mexican bands (many of which have cover charges of twenty dollars), ESL classes, employment opportunities, child care services, and other items of interest to immigrants and Mexicans. The more elaborate establishments, in addition to canned goods and dried spices, sell clothes, boots, shoes, hats, votive candles, baptism blankets, and other goods, stock fresh produce and skilled butchering departments, and have entertainment in the form of pool tables and video games, liquor sales, and full-service restaurants.

As important as the layouts and inventories of stores are their locations: typically they take over abandoned commercial space or old buildings in parts of downtown that have been deteriorating or on lonesome highways in rural areas where there few other services exist. Often they are within walking distance of neighborhoods where Mexicans have settled in moderate numbers, usually beside African American and poor Anglo families. In this way, while growth along the outskirts of towns associated with the uniform shopping and eating habits of most Americans have abandoned inner cities and rural wastelands (Schlosser 2001),

Mexican stores provide shopping and other services similar to those of colmados and rum shops throughout Latin America and the Caribbean.

One final note about these stores and ancillary businesses is that they are often managed, staffed, and owned by women. In Greenville, the town where I live, one of its three Mexican stores was founded by two sisters. Migrating to California from Mexico in 1985, they worked for six years in San Diego in factories, before moving to North Carolina in 1992 to work in crab-picking, first in Belhaven (about fifty miles east of Greenville) and then in Washington (about twenty miles east of Greenville). It took six years of working in seafood before they gathered enough information and capital to open the store in Greenville. These sisters cite the lack of Spanish-speaking people in much of the state as one factor in their success. That is, shortly after arriving in the state, they were forced to learn English because, they said, "no one would speak a word of Spanish to us." Their English ability was critical to their success, because their most informative sources about opening a business in Eastern North Carolina were primarily English-speaking natives. Other stores I have visited were operated principally by women and owned by either women or couples, and in some cases elder female relatives, abuelos, have been brought to the state to assist in preparing Mexican snacks or meals.

AGRICULTURE AND RURAL INDUSTRY'S ROLE IN ENCOURAGING MEXICAN IMMIGRATION

I noted earlier that Mexican immigrants have been coming to North Carolina since the 1980s, and in some cases even earlier, primarily to work in agriculture. In addition to agriculture, two other sectors of the North Carolina's rural economy were instrumental in drawing Mexican immigrants into the state: poultry processing and the blue crab industry. Features inherent to all three of these industries have encouraged the expansion of Mexican immigrants into other sectors of the economy.

Agriculture: Seasonal Labor and Rural Settlement

Work in the apple orchards and on the Douglas fir farms of western North Carolina has attracted Mexican farmworkers at least since the early 1980s. By 1988, the apple and Christmas tree farms of the mountain region and the vegetable and tobacco harvests along the coastal plain had converted, nearly completely, from predominantly Anglo and

African American to predominantly Mexican labor. Explanations for this shift vary, with most employers and other observers citing superior work habits among migrant Mexicans, but one of the most telling came from Allen Hews (pseudonym), a tobacco and pickle cucumber grower in the eastern part of the state.

In his mid-forties, Hews grew up farming in eastern North Carolina, working closely with African American farmworkers and tenants who sharecropped for his family farm from his youth until the mid-1980s. He claimed that his family was unique for not using what he called "the white man's pencil" (or deducting for so many inputs from sharecropper earnings that they ended up in debt at the end of the season); as a result, his family had closer, more trusting relations with African Americans than most, adding, "the black woman who carried me home from the hospital and helped raise me lives rent free on our farm, and is welcome to stay until she dies."

Despite these close relations, he said that in the 1960s, African Americans his own age refused to take orders directly from a white man. Instead, there were elder African American men who served as liaisons between white farmers and African American farmworkers, tenants, and sharecroppers. After these elders retired or died, dealing with younger African American labor became problematic. As with most of his neighbors, he switched to Mexican workers, first relying on contracted crews based in Florida and later, after IRCA, on the Seasonal Agricultural Worker (SAW) program and finally on the H-2 program, which he continues to use today.

The transition from African American to predominantly Mexican labor has been common throughout rural North Carolina, although many farmers have not made the transition to H-2 workers from the contracted crews. Most farmers, however, do have Mexican individuals or families (often former SAWs) who act as liaisons between them and the more temporary harvest crews, and in many cases these families have settled in North Carolina as permanent hired hands. One statistical residue of the transition from contracted crews to H-2s, however, is seen in table 3.2, which is based on a survey of 734 H-2 workers in the United States (primarily the mid-Atlantic and southern states) and rural Mexico. Around one quarter of workers interviewed admitted to being former illegal immigrants, and over two-thirds of the work force saying that they would either consider or would work in the country without legal documentation.

The numbers in table 3.2 may reflect the close contact that, more and more often, we find between migrant agricultural workers and settled

TABLE 3.2   H-2 Workers Willing to Work Illegally in the
United States

Have worked without papers	25.8%
Say they would work without papers	25.5
Would consider working without papers if their contracts were not renewed	32.9

Source: Griffith, Heppel, and Torres (2001).
Note: n = 734

populations. Slightly over one-half (51 percent) of the H-2 workers interviewed reported that they worked in areas where other Mexicans were living year-round, and most reported that there were places where they went, usually weekly, where other Mexicans gathered. Of those who live in such areas, over three-quarters (76 percent) report that they interact with these individuals on a regular basis, visiting the same stores, bars, churches, soccer fields, and other locations. Around two-thirds, or 68 percent, have only known these individuals for six months, so most other Mexicans are not from their home villages.

Acquaintances such as these serve as the basis for a wealth of labor market, shopping, and other information useful to H-2 workers in the event that they regularize their work status or slip into the undocumented labor force. For most, if the opportunity to interact with Mexicans who were not other H-2 workers presented itself, they took advantage of it, and thus were able to move around in a Spanish-speaking world on and off the job, and contributing to what has been called, by several observers, the Latinization of rural America (Heppel and Amendola 1991; Griffith et al. 1995). Along with agriculture, poultry processing, meatpacking, and other food processing have contributed to the changing faces of rural America.

Poultry Processing and Meatpacking

In North Carolina, as throughout the entire South and many parts of the Midwest, poultry processing and meatpacking have been primary rural industries to attract and hire immigrants. They are multifaceted industries, with ties to agriculture on farms where livestock are grown, consisting of grow-out facilities, feed mills, and hatcheries (in poultry) or other operations where young animals are prepared for feeding out on farms. Most poultry producers are either owned by large food conglomerates (for example, ConAgra), with related firms scattered across the United States and other parts of the world, or have several plants across the South and other parts of the United States, allowing for a vast exchange of labor market information across states and regions. Plant personnel managers often move from one region to another or from one firm to another, facilitating further information exchange about methods of accessing different labor supplies. Attributes of these occupations encourage a steady stream of immigrant workers not only onto their factory floors, however, but also across them. Poultry processing and meatpacking are both hazardous, high-turnover occupations, generally with cores of long-time workers supplemented by several groups of workers more or less attached to the work. Within these plants, some positions are higher turnover than others, and newer workers—new immigrants among them—tend to be placed into the least desirable jobs.

Most jobs in meatpacking and poultry processing plants are disassembly-line positions, although all plants have sections of the plant for receiving live animals or birds and other areas for storage and shipping. In poultry, the "live-hang" or receiving area is the most high turnover, because the jobs there consist of pulling live birds directly from plastic crates and hanging them upside down on hooks for their lethal journey through the plant. Workers wear gas masks and work in rooms lit only by dim blue bulbs because the dark supposedly calms the birds. Following several mechanized killing and plucking machines, the birds are eviscerated and routed to different sections of the plant based on their conditions. The most flawless birds are packaged as whole birds, while those with bruises and other marks travel through several cutting and deboning stations; some plants process the flesh further by seasoning and cooking for the specialty sandwiches of fast food chains (Griffith 1993; Schlosser 2001; Striffler 2001).

Hazards greet workers throughout these plants, beginning with respiratory problems from the dust and feathers of live-hang. Carpal tunnel syndrome or repetitive motion sickness is the most pervasive form of occupational injury, but workers also walk over floors slippery with fat and risk cutting themselves with scissors or knives. The industry has developed several methods of underreporting or hiding occupational illness, and plant nurses routinely deny that workers' complaints are truly physiological, often blaming factors such as menopause or vitamin deficiencies and treating workers with little more than Advil and vitamin B-12.

North Carolina is one of the top five poultry producers in the United

States, first in turkey production and fifth in broiler production (USDA 2002), with processing plants scattered across the state. Turkey production is more concentrated than broiler production. Among the largest counties for turkey production are in the southeast part of the state, most in the Cape Fear River watershed. Sampson, Pender, Bladen, Lenoir, and Onslow counties all either border or are near Duplin County, home to Carolina Turkey, the largest turkey producer in the world and among the earliest in the state to recruit and house Mexican workers. At least three other large processing plants are located in this region, which annually produces around twenty-two million turkeys.

Broiler production is much more geographically dispersed than turkey production. With the exception of the far western, mountainous and forested region of the state and the horseshoe-shaped urban strip along Interstate 85 between Charlotte and the Raleigh–Durham–Chapel Hill triangle, nearly all North Carolina counties produce broilers. Combined, the top ten North Carolina counties employ more than eight thousand workers to process more than four hundred and twenty million birds annually. Because the industry rule of thumb is to place processing plants within twenty-five miles of chicken production areas, these plants are located across the coastal plain, in the Appalachian foothills, and across the central piedmont. Many plants are inside small and medium-sized towns such as Siler City, Robersonville, and Willkesboro, while others are near the large metropolitan areas of Raleigh and Charlotte, giving poultry workers access to urban occupations and factory work in other industries that have been, historically, important to North Carolina, primarily furniture and textiles.

Recruitment into the poultry industry has been through networks since the first poultry processing plants replaced butchers in supermarkets, when African American and women workers dominated the industry's work force (Griffith 1993). The arrival of Mexicans did not change this practice, and network recruitment has been instrumental in the ability of SAWs and other Mexican workers to encourage travel to and employment in North Carolina generally. Many plants give bonuses for network recruitment, offering checks of between $25.00 and $100.00 for those who recruit new workers as long as the new workers last ninety days. While only around one-third of North Carolina plant managers were using a bonus system during the early 1990s, fully 100 percent of managers indicated that network recruitment was their most common method of recruitment (Griffith 1993, 159–60). Some plants enhance their recruiting efforts among new immigrant Mexicans by providing housing or aiding new workers in seeking low-cost housing in the community. The largest turkey processor in the state maintains company housing of trailers that they commonly use as a tool of labor control. I cite the following example of this in my book on low-wage labor. Speaking of this turkey company housing, I wrote:

> Rents are deducted from workers' paychecks and couples may occupy trailers together only on the condition that both work at the plant. The plant reserves the right, moreover, to assign new workers to already occupied trailers. In one case, the company assigned two workers to a trailer that was occupied by a couple. The woman worked the day shift and the man worked the night shift; the two new workers were also assigned one day shift and one night shift. The man complained to company officials that he couldn't leave his wife alone with a strange man at night, but the company refused to modify the arrangement, forcing the couple to quit. (Griffith 1993, 181)

One interesting postscript to this predicament: when the Mexican man who complained related this story, he said that the personnel director was puzzled by his objection to the arrangement and even said, "I don't understand. Aren't you all Mexicans?" Foolishness of this type was common during the early years of Mexican immigration into the state.

Because turnover is a constant problem at the plants, particularly in some of the more onerous jobs, and opportunities to recruit workers are constant, Mexicans returning home can promise individuals there work with near certainty. By the same token, Mexicans can leave plants for extended visits to Mexico or to test the waters of alternative labor markets, knowing that returning to the plants will be relatively easy. Indeed, some plant personnel managers have loosened leave policies around Christmas, allowing Mexicans to return home for extended visits without losing any benefits they have accumulated.

As Mark Grey (2000) found in Iowa, workers in poultry, Mexican or otherwise, often treat processing employment as seasonal work, coming and going as new opportunities arise and as they suffer injuries or other problems at work. I found this to be the case among African American poultry workers in North Carolina and other parts of the South prior to Mexican immigration (Griffith 1993). Typically, African American workers would move in and out of the poultry industry for many of the same reasons Grey documented for Mexicans in Iowa: to attend to household or community responsibilities, to recover from repetitive motion disease, and simply to take a break from the rigors and hazards of factory life. During the late 1980s, however, Mexicans began moving into the job vacancies that African Americans created, making it more difficult for African Americans to enter and leave the plants at will. With each opening in the plant once filled by an African American, it became easy for personnel mangers to fill these positions with Mexican workers. As in agriculture, it has been primarily African American jobs that Mexicans initially filled in North Carolina, although more in the coastal and central portions of the state than in the Appalachians. This process has been driven from both the labor demand and supply sides of the labor process. On the one hand, Mexican workers are usually familiar with many individuals—family members, friends, and even casual acquaintances—who are willing to take these jobs at a moment's notice. On the other hand, plant personnel managers readily admit to a preference for Mexican over African American workers. During a plant tour in northern Georgia, a plant manager asked me to compare for myself the different working habits of African American and Mexican workers, specifically directing my attention to workers returning from the bathroom. He commented that Mexican workers nearly ran back to their positions on the line, while African Americans took their time, stopping along the way to talk to other workers.

Mexican displacement or replacement of African American workers is not confined to the plants. Many of the trailer parks, neighborhoods, and parts of communities that house new immigrant Mexicans are those that have traditionally housed other low-wage workers, including African Americans. Mexican turkey and meatpacking workers around Newton Grove, interviewed on Palm Sunday 2002, said that of all North Carolina natives, African Americans were the most unfriendly toward them and the most likely to treat them with disrespect. Thus any discussion of Mexican immigration into North Carolina and the South generally cannot ignore relations between African Americans and Mexicans in neighborhoods and jobs.

Seafood Processing and Fisheries

Like poultry processing, seafood processing in North Carolina was fueled by African American labor until the late 1980s. Seafood processing is distinct from poultry processing in that most seafood plants are small and seated firmly in a fishing economy characterized by large numbers (six thousand or more) of family- and household-based fishing operations. The most labor-absorbing of seafood processing is the blue-crab industry, which is also the state's largest fishery. It was this sector of the industry that sponsored Mexican immigration into coastal counties.

Three separate and pioneering employers laid the groundwork for H-2 workers in the mid-Atlantic blue crab processing industry: three employers, from different mid-Atlantic communities, all suffering from labor supply problems, accessed H-2 workers by different paths. One used the Virginia Employment Service, one learned of the program through a crab processor in Mexico, and the third worked with Del Al Associates, the largest contractor of H-2 workers in Mexico. The second two were based in North Carolina, and it took little time for North Carolina with its Mexican labor to eclipse Maryland and Virginia in processing blue crab.

These three efforts led to a new phase of crab processing, one accompanied by capital concentration, increased pressures to supply blue crabs to North Carolina from other regions, and the development of small crabbing fleets using Mexican labor. The use of Mexican labor on crabbing vessels was particularly disruptive in the local fishing economy of Pamlico and Beaufort counties, coming at a time of increased regulation of fisheries, fleet development using Vietnamese fishers in other areas of the Albemarle-Pamlico Estuarine System (North Carolina's productive fishing grounds), and coastal development that threatened water quality (Griffith 1999). To understand how the transition from African American to Mexican labor took place in the crab houses, and its influence over other aspects of the fishing economy, it is instructive to consider, first, developments within the African American labor force that led to processors seeking alternative labor supplies.

Briefly, the transition was a highly uneven process, with some African Americans feeling they had been pushed out of work by imported Mexican labor and others using the influx of Mexicans as an opportunity to work toward alternative job opportunities. Based on ninety-four interviews with current and former African American crab pickers, all agreed that declines in work available for them in the plants coincided with the arrival of Mexican workers. This is because each plant, daily, receives a finite amount of crabs to pick. Once that amount is picked, the work is finished for the day. Prior to the arrival of the Mexican women, with sporadic absenteeism accompanying a gradual decline of African American women in the plants (the reasons for which I describe later), crab pickers had plenty of crabs to pick every day. Pay rates were based on the number of pounds of crab picked. Thus crab-picking income and amounts of work of each worker depended on the number of crabs at the plant each morning relative to the number of workers.

With Mexicans coming into the plants in the late 1980s, there was less crab to pick per individual worker, resulting in losses to African American workers of both income and amounts of work.

African Americans responded to reduced work in the crab industry in different ways. Some used the reduced workloads to seek training and gain other employment, others looked for other jobs, while still others relied more heavily on social support systems to make up for the loss in income. Reactions to the Mexican women were similarly mixed, though aimed more at plant owners than the Mexican women themselves. Everyone agreed that work in the plants fell off for the African Americans, but there was disagreement over the question of whether or not Mexican labor was necessary, along with differing emotional responses. Some African American women saw importing Mexicans as sending a strong negative message, as the following quote indicates:

> Malcolm [crab plant owner] didn't need them [the Mexican workers]. They were full of workers, excellent workers who picked fifty pounds a day, even with bad crabs. They made their living, built their houses off this money . . . It's like they said, "You black people, we are through with you."

Yet others believed that, in fact, younger women in the industry had become less reliable workers and that importing Mexican labor was justified. In the words of another displaced worker: "*Now* there was a time when the young blacks wouldn't work, so they brought in the Mexicans. So it was the young blacks that hurt the faithful workers."

In any case, both emotional and occupational responses were uneven, very likely due to alternative opportunities that had been developing in seafood processing and fishing counties through the 1980s and 1990s. At this time, three areas of opportunity expanded: educational opportunities for young African American women at community colleges, in part related to local economic developments; a growth in tourism; and a growth in health care services directed toward the local aging and retiring population. The latter economic development corresponded with increased training for nurses' aides at community colleges, and developments in tourism took place during a general growth in fast food restaurants, other restaurants, and similar services.

As noted earlier, fisheries and seafood processing were suffering during this period. A groundfishing crisis in New England and a net ban in Florida brought more fishing families into the state at a time that processors, now faced with regular surpluses of Mexican *and* African

American labor, were building up fleets or sponsoring fishing excursions to keep that labor gainfully employed. The waters of North Carolina became crowded, and territorial disputes ensued. Political actions directed against newcomers to the fishery (particularly a moratorium on issuing new commercial fishing licenses) were, in some counties, directed toward new Mexican or Vietnamese fishers, whom crab processors had set up with vessels and gear. Ill feelings coursed through the entire blue crabbing community (Griffith 1999).

By the end of the twentieth century, the crisis had abated. Capital concentration occurred in the processing industry, shaking out many of the less productive plants and leaving those with their own fleets or who deal with only with blue crab dealers (instead of directly with fishers), buying crabs from neighboring and distant states as well as from local supplies. The waters remain crowded, and occasionally tempers flare over the Mexicans and Vietnamese on the water, but Hurricane Floyd and its accompanying flood, in 1999, damaged water quality to the extent that many crabbers left fishing or moved into other fisheries. In the plants, the few African American women who remain, fewer than 10 percent of the total, are primarily elder women for whom the processors attempt to find as much work as possible. Others believe they could return to crab processing, and some do on occasion, but in general those African Americans who left, have left for good.

Despite their temporary worker status, H-2 workers have moved toward settlement in small, significant ways. As earlier passages indicate, many H-2 workers have learned how to access other jobs in the community during times that work in the plants is slow, others have intermarried with locals or with settled Mexicans, and still others have entered the ranks of the undocumented. Some find other jobs and stay in the United States beyond the terms of their contracts, working most of the year in North Carolina and returning for only a month or two instead of for the entire winter. The program has also forged linkages between North Carolina and Mexican communities that have begun to approximate the "social remittances" that Peggy Levitt (2001) has found in Dominican communities, stimulating substantial knowledge about coastal North Carolina to facilitate immigration outside of the H-2 program.

In what is perhaps the strongest inducement to settle, a few H-2 workers have arrived in North Carolina pregnant and had children on U.S. soil. Though processors frown on this, and have even penalized workers who have done this by not renewing their H-2 contracts, there have been several cases of this. Women I knew explained it as less of an attempt to settle than the recognition that they were of childbearing and child rearing age, and that having and rearing children in the confines of the H-2 program was simply far easier if the child was born on U.S. soil. Nevertheless, having children in North Carolina and bringing them with them year after year facilitates establishing more and more links with North Carolina. Daycare, preschool and schooling, church, playing at public parks, attending one of the state's many, many festivals, and interactions with other settled families in these and other contexts—all provide Mexican H-2 workers with the social tools for permanent settlement.

CONCLUSION

As we begin the twenty-first century, the two predominant forms of Mexican immigration into North Carolina—H-2 program expansion and increasing undocumented immigration—show signs of converging. Legal distinctions between Mexican immigrants may be ultimately far less important than the general growth of the Mexican population, its implications for heterogeneity, and Mexican claims on permanent residence and the goods and services that permanent residence entails. Low levels of immigration enforcement, aggressive recruiting of undocumented immigrants by North Carolina employers, increasing reliance on the H-2 program, and Mexican network recruiting all spell even greater population growth in the state over the coming decade. Another fourfold increase in the Mexican population would result in at least 1.3 million Mexicans in the state; with similar growth in the state's general population, Mexicans would increase to between 10 and 15 percent of the population. These projections are similar to those for other nontraditional destinations, such as Iowa and Minnesota (Bushway 2001; Grey 2001; Iowa State Public Policy Group 2001).

Yet North Carolina differs from many nontraditional Mexican destinations like Iowa and Minnesota in two important respects: first, the state's population has not been stagnant or declining in recent decades and, second, it has, like other southern states, a large pool of African American workers with low levels of training and education, many of whose jobs have been either undermined by or abandoned to Mexicans. During periods of economic expansion, as in coastal counties during the growth of tourism and health care, opportunities have developed for African Americans to move into alternative jobs or take advantage of educational opportunities. In addition, low-income North Carolinians, black and white, have always combined multiple livelihoods to make ends meet, relying not only on wage work but also on subsistence hunting, fishing, and gathering, social support networks, and social services (Griffith 1993).

Despite the opportunities such livelihoods entail, the state has not been through a prolonged period of economic contraction since the Mexican population began to grow in the late 1980s and early 1990s. Indeed, North Carolina weathered the mild recession of the first Bush administration relatively well, going so far as to erect billboards that read: "We heard there was a recession. We decided not to participate." Whether this good fortune can continue may in fact depend very much on continued infusions of low-wage, immigrant labor, yet the growth of Mexican communities in the state, and the opportunities they present new immigrants, is certain to undermine the abilities of employers to continue the highly exploitative labor relations of the 1990s.

Several factors are likely to contribute to the increasing power of Mexicans, including the tendency for H-2 programs to become institutionalized in labor markets and, perhaps more important, the increasing tendency toward family and community formation among Mexicans in the state. Earlier we have seen that, in a few important ways, the H-2 program is imperfect as a true "guestworker" system in that workers have been able either to leave the program altogether or alter its terms to suit changing circumstances. The presence of large numbers of migrant and settled Mexicans in the state is clearly the most important element in H-2 workers' abilities to manipulate the program, as seen in cases of workers leaving abusive employers only to remain in the state and find alternative employment through connections with other Mexicans. Equally important, the opportunities that come from connections with settled and other Mexicans clearly temper the extreme forms of labor control that have attended H-2 labor relations in the past (particularly in the sugar program—see U.S. Congress 1991).

Settled Mexicans are important to these processes, particularly in those parts of the state where large food-processing industries have relied on Mexican immigration for the past decade and a half. The southeast part of the state, or the region where turkey and chicken processing, pork packing, agriculture, and seafood processing all overlap, is one such region. Two of its counties—Sampson and Duplin, which border one another—revealed the highest proportions of Mexicans in the state and the small Sampson County community of Newton Grove has emerged as a principal locus of health care, social services, and religious services for Mexicans. Originally oriented toward a migrant population, these services have since evolved to reach the growing settled population in the region, while maintaining links to migrants and to natives.

As is common among service providers in areas of growing immigrant populations, the Tri-County Health Services, an Episcopal Church, and a Catholic Church have all recruited bilingual Mexicans from the settled population to serve on their staffs. The priest at the Catholic Church reported that he now serves at least six hundred to seven hundred Mexican families in the area, and has begun performing religious rites at quinceañera festivities and blessing new trucks. Most of these families are young, settled couples with small children; my casual observations at Palm Sunday church services at the Episcopal and Catholic churches revealed fewer than ten people over the age of forty, out of more than eight hundred at the two services. Most teenaged youth can switch easily and comfortably between Spanish and English.

In addition to founding businesses directed toward a Mexican and other clientele, settled Mexicans have also begun branching out into other industries and other occupations. While it is too soon to determine the rate at which Mexicans are moving into industries other than the traditional fields of food processing, landscaping, agriculture, and construction, it is now common to order and receive food from Mexicans in fast food restaurants (particularly in the Raleigh–Durham–Chapel Hill area), to see Mexicans emptying trash and cleaning restrooms in North Carolina airports, motels, and hotels, and to see Mexicans working in offices in hospital, schools, and local agencies. Despite the evident expansion of opportunity these observations suggest, most Mexicans remain confined to low-wage and lesser skilled occupations. Thus while processes of community formation are underway, it remains unclear how much these processes will foster large social and economic gains among Mexicans.

At the same time, we do not fully understand what divisions within the Mexican population—whether based on ethnicity, class, or other factors—will develop over the coming decades or how they will play into economic development initiatives, party politics, disputes over public and private waters and lands, ethnic relations, or other problematic social areas within North Carolina's social and cultural landscapes. Recent data suggest that more indigenous communities of Mexico and Central America have been contributing immigrants to southern neighborhoods and labor markets. Fieldwork conducted in 1998 and 2000 found Mixteco Alta, Mixteco Baja, Otomi, Mam, Zapotec, Trique, and Tzotzil speakers working in southern agriculture, landscaping, construction, and similar fields (Kissam et al. 2000; Kissam, Garcia, and Alarcón 1999). Earlier research documented similar labor market behaviors among Jacaltec, Q'anjobal, and Chuj speakers (Burns 1993; Griffith et al. 2001; Wellmeier 1994). Chiapas, Oaxaca, and northwest Guatemala have become major suppliers of labor to the U.S. South (Cohen 2001). At the same time, traditional sending regions, such as Michoacan and Hidalgo, remain important labor-supply regions, yet, as indicated by Otomi speakers in Florida, the compositions of migrating units from these locations may have changed, including more indigenous groups, women, children, and elderly (Heppel and Torres 2000).

Historically, the changes that take place in southern agricultural labor precede by only a few years those taking place in low-wage labor markets and neighborhoods throughout the rural South. These, in turn, precede similar changes in urban areas. With current high levels of Mexican immigration, however, the pace of these changes may accelerate as more and more individuals with English and cultural brokerage skills emerge within the Mexican population. Along with more rapid change, we will likely see a faster pace of ethnic, linguistic, class, and other forms of social differentiation within the Mexican population of North Carolina and other nontraditional immigrant destinations.

REFERENCES

Burns, Allan. 1993. *Maya in Exile*. Philadelphia: Temple University Press.

Bushway, Deborah. 2001. *The Vitality of Latino Communities in Rural Minnesota*. Mankato: Mankato Center for Rural Policy and Development, Minnesota State University.

Cohen, Jeffrey. 2001. "Transnational Migration in Rural Oaxaca, Mexico." *American Anthropologist* 103(4): 954–67.

Duany, Jorge. 1990. *Los Dominicanos en Puerto Rico: Migración en la semiperiferia*. Río Piedras, Puerto Rico: Ediciones Huracán.

Grasmuck, Sherri. 1982. "Migration Within the Periphery: Haitian Labor in the Dominican Sugar and Coffee Industries." *International Migration Review* 16(2): 365–77.

Grey, Mark. 2000. "Marshalltown, Iowa and the Struggle for Community in a Global Age." In *Communities and Capital: Local Struggles against Corporate Power and Privatization*, edited by Thomas W. Collins and John D. Wingard. Athens, Ga.: University of Georgia Press.

———. 2001. *Welcoming New Iowans, a Guide for Citizens and Communities: Building Respect and Tolerance for Immigrant and Refugee Newcomers*. Cedar Falls: University of Northern Iowa Institute for Decision Making.

Griffith, David. 1993. *Jones's Minimal: Low-Wage Labor in the United States*. Albany: State University of New York Press.

———. 1999. *The Estuary's Gift: An Atlantic Coast Cultural Biography*. University Park: Penn State University Press.

Griffith, David, and Manuel Valdés Pizzini. 2002. *Fishers at Work, Workers at*

Sea: A Puerto Rican Journey Through Labor and Refuge. Philadelphia: Temple University Press.

Griffith, David, Monica Heppel, and Luis Torres. 2001. *Guests of Rural America: Profiles of Temporary Worker Programs from U.S. and Mexican Perspectives.* Report to the Ford Foundation, New York.

Griffith, David, and Ed Kissam, with Jeronimo Camposeco, Anna Garcia, Max Pfeffer, David Runsten, and Manuel Valdés Pizzini. 1995. *Working Poor: Farmworkers in the United States.* Philadelphia: Temple University Press.

Griffith, David, Alex Stepick, Karen Richman, Guillermo Grenier, Ed Kissam, Allan Burns, and Jeronimo Camposeco. 2001. "Another Day in the Diaspora: Changing Ethnic Landscapes in South Florida." In *Latino Workers in the Contemporary South,* edited by Arthur Murphy, Colleen Blanchard, and Jennifer Hill. Athens, Ga.: University of Georgia Press.

Haines, David, and Karen Rosenblum, eds. 1999. *Illegal Immigration in America: A Reference Handbook.* Westport, Conn: Greenwood Press.

Heppel, Monica L., and Sandra Amendola. 1991. *Immigration Reform and Perishable Crop Agriculture: Compliance or Circumvention?* Vol. 2. Washington, D.C.: Center for Immigration Studies.

Heppel, Monica, and Luis Torres. 2000. "Field Research Report: Hidalgo, Mexico." Report prepared for a project entitled, *The Conditions Facing Children in Agriculture.* Washington: U.S. Department of Labor and Aguirre International, 1999–2000.

Iowa State Public Policy Group. 2001. *Snapshot in Time Close-up: A Detailed Look at the Value, Importance, and Impacts of the Latino Population in Central Iowa.* Des Moines: Iowa State Public Policy Group.

Kearney, Michael. 1996. *Reconceptualizing the Peasantry.* Boulder, Colo.: Westview Press.

Kissam, Ed, Anna Garcia, and Rafael Alarcón. 1999. *Work-Related Injuries, Illnesses, and Health Risks Faced by Teenage Farmworkers in Immokalee, Florida.* Final Report to the California Institute for Rural Studies, University of California at Davis.

Kissam, Ed, David Griffith, Anna Garcia, Monica Heppel, Luis Torres, and Nancy Mullenax. 2000. *Children No More: Conditions of Children Working in Agriculture.* Final Report to the U.S. Department of Labor, Office of the Assistant Secretary of Policy, Washington, D.C.

Levitt, Peggy. 2001. *The Transnational Villagers.* Berkeley: University of California Press.

Portes, Alejandro, and Rubén Rumbaut. 2001. *Legacies: The Story of the Immigrant Second Generation.* Berkeley: University of California Press.

Schlosser, Eric. 2001. *Fast Food Nation: The Dark Side of the All-American Meal.* New York: Houghton Mifflin.

Striffler, Steve. 2001. "Poultry Workers and Latin American Immigration in the New Southern Economy." *Global View: The University Center for Inter-*

national Studies, The University of North Carolina at Chapel Hill (spring): 1, 6–7.

Stull, Donald, Michael Broadway, and David Griffith, eds. 1995. *Any Way They Cut It: Meat Packing and Small Town America.* Lawrence: University Press of Kansas.

U.S. Census Bureau. Various years. *American Factfinder.* Washington: U.S. Census Bureau. Available at http://factfinder.census.gov/ (accessed October 18, 2004).

U.S. Congress. 1991. "Report on the Use of Temporary Foreign Workers in the Florida Sugar Cane Industry." Serial no. 102-J. Washington: U.S. Government Printing Office.

U.S. Department of Agriculture (USDA). 2002. "Broiler Production by States." *National Agriculture Statistical Service.* Washington: U.S. Government Printing Office.

Wellmeier, Nancy. 1994. "Rituals of Resettlement: Identity and Resistance Among Maya Refugees." In *Selected Papers on Refugee Issues, III*, edited by Jeffrey MacDonald and Amy Zaharlick. Arlington, Va.: American Anthropological Association.

Zlolinski, Christian. 1994. "The Informal Economy in an Advanced Industrialized Society: Mexican Immigrant Labor in Silicon Valley." *The Yale Law Journal* 103(8): 2305–2335.

CHAPTER 4

⋉

THE ECONOMIC INCORPORATION
OF MEXICAN IMMIGRANTS IN SOUTHERN
LOUISIANA: A TALE OF TWO CITIES

KATHARINE M. DONATO, MELISSA STAINBACK,
AND CARL L. BANKSTON III

By the end of the twentieth century, the United States had witnessed dramatic demographic changes. Among these were shifts in immigration. Since 1965, more than twenty million migrants have entered the United States, more than the largest wave entering between 1880 and 1914 (U.S. Department of Justice 1997). Not only have they arrived in greater numbers (Borjas 1999), immigrants began to work and settle in communities not traditionally associated with migration in the past. These include the nonmetropolitan towns of Dalton, northwest Georgia, an area well known for its carpet production (Hernández-León and Zúñiga 2000) and Garden City, Kansas, where meatpacking employers have sought low-wage workers (Stull, Broadway, and Erickson 1992). Other examples represent urban areas that did not attract specific national origin groups in the recent past, such as Mexicans in New York City and in Atlanta (Sassen and Smith 1992; Smith 1996; Durand, Massey, and Charvet 2000). One consequence is that approximately 24 percent of all U.S. counties gained at least one thousand Hispanics or Asians between 1990 and 1996 (Frey 1998). Certainly a gain of that magnitude, especially in small nonmetropolitan counties, is likely to have profound social and economic consequences. Both the immigrants themselves and the places that receive them face new kinds of opportunities and challenges.

As immigrant destinations have diversified, so too has the early migrant experience in the United States. Understanding the experience, the social forces that influence it, and how it unfolds over time, are the objectives of this chapter. By comparing the initial migrant experience in two new destinations, our analysis highlights the complicated, contradictory, and at times, paradoxical, paths that immigrant incorporation takes. In one locality, for example, early controversy and resistance from native-born residents spurred the formation of a stable Mexican migrant community that has clear signs of permanence. In another, the very absence of controversy worked together with a high degree of emyployer control to impede the emergence of a strong Mexican community. Here government policies that facilitated the legal immigration of workers, such as the H-2B visa program, helped intensify employer control over migrants and undercut the formation of a stable migrant community.

To illustrate these processes, we examine the early social and economic incorporation of immigrants attracted to two small cities in southern Louisiana in the 1990s. Drawing from a larger project that examines the community impact of new immigrant populations in this area (Donato 1998), we analyze data collected from employers, community leaders, foreign-born workers, and other residents in the late 1990s to describe how new immigrants first incorporate in these communities. Our analysis examines variations in the economic incorporation of immigrants by community of residence, and portrays these differences as the different faces that incorporation takes early on in a receiving community's history of migration. By doing so, we argue that emerging foreign-born populations in nontraditional U.S. destinations offer us a new venue in which to observe the assimilation process, beginning at its earliest point.

We begin by describing the two communities in which we conducted our research. In many ways, the two were similar in the late 1990s. The oil industry represented the key economic activity in both communities, and as a result, both shared a similar profile with respect to labor supply and demand. The two communities also shared similar demographic profiles. Despite the similarities, however, immigrant incorporation differs dramatically across the two local economies. Therefore, after discussing the settings, data and methods used, we then continue by describing the factors that motivate international migration decisions, in general, and the particular conditions that led to immigrant workers moving to nontraditional destinations in southern Louisiana. Drawing from prior studies on the segmented assimilation of U.S. immigrants, we offer a framework for understanding how immigrants incorporate in these two communities and use it to guide our discussion of the early stages of economic incorporation of immigrants in the two communities. Our key findings suggest that Mexican immigrants initially incorporate in different ways and at different rates into local economies, and that these differences are a consequence of social forces specific to the destination community. Together, the findings illustrate considerable segmentation in the early process of the economic incorporation of Mexican immigrants.

PROFILES OF TWO COMMUNITIES IN SOUTHERN LOUISIANA

Describing the communities is a first step toward understanding differences in the process of economic incorporation of Mexican immigrants in southern Louisiana. Although Louisiana has not been a common destination area for U.S. immigrants, field reports suggested that many Latino migrants were working in shipbuilding and fabrication yards in the southern coastal areas of the state in the late 1990s. We focus our discussion on two areas: Morgan City and its surrounding area in St. Mary's Parish, and Houma and its surrounding area in Terrebonne Parish (see figure 4.1). Both locales have been unusually tied to oil production and refining during the twentieth century. They house many fabrication and shipbuilding companies, and operate ports and canals to service offshore oil industry.

The two communities share many characteristics. For example, both witnessed dramatic growth in the oil and gas industry during the first half of the twentieth century. Given that wetlands cover much of the geographic area, growth in the development of support construction services in these two communities was spurred on by the development of submersible drilling barges in shallow water in the 1930s (Grambling 1996). As a result, many migrated to the area, lured by economic opportunities and new federal investments in highways. They settled on land next to the natural levees found in the marshlands, also known as "string town" settlements (Kniffen 1968).

More able-bodied workers led to the development of new canal networks. Critical to Houma was the Houma Navigational Canal, completed in 1961 as a thirty-mile connection between Terrebonne Bay and the Gulf of Mexico. In Morgan City, the port has operated since the mid-1950s to service a wide variety of vessels in the Gulf of Mexico.

In addition to the development of canal networks, new technology permitted drilling for oil offshore. In 1947, Morgan City became nationally known when its waters housed the first offshore oil well. This set in motion debates about land ownership, which once settled, led to the

FIGURE 4.1   Houma and Morgan City, Louisiana Map

1. Houma
2. Morgan City

Gulf of Mexico

Source: Authors' compilation.

implementation of newly refined offshore technology that permitted drilling and processing in up to thousands of feet of water and in places located hundreds of miles offshore (Grambling 1996). The new technology included seismic imaging, deepwater production and processing, and remotely operated vehicles. These and other developments fueled growth in offshore oil production and onshore support services through much of the century, including the 1990s.

One consequence is that these two communities rely heavily on the oil industry for employment. For example, of the major private industry employers in each of these two areas in 1998, more than 80 percent were in oil and related services (http://leap.ulm.edu). Moreover, among all employees in the major private companies, more than 80 percent were employed in oil and related industries.

Despite these similarities, however, the demographic profiles of these two communities are quite different (see http://leap.ulm.edu or http://www.census.gov). Data from the 2000 decennial census show that the population of St. Mary's Parish was about half that of Terrebonne (58,000 versus 97,000, respectively). Moreover, where the figures represent a population decline of 7.9 percent for St. Mary's Parish, for Terrebonne they represent an increase of approximately the same rate.

Census data also suggest considerable shifts in the Hispanic composition of the two parishes in the 1990s. St. Mary's increased its overall Hispanic population by just 2.1 percent, but the Hispanic population in Terrebonne increased at a rate of 18.5 percent. Differences in the growth of the Hispanic population during the decade are more dramatic when we make city comparisons. For example, Houma (in Terrebonne) experienced a 32.5 percent increase during the 1990s, but Morgan City (in St. Mary's) saw a 9.9 percent decline. These gains and losses compare to a 15.8 percent increase in Hispanic population for Louisiana as a whole.

Therefore, although the oil industry represented the key economic activity in both areas in the 1990s, their demographic profiles are remarkably different. One question that arises is whether and how these differences signal differences in the economic assimilation of Mexican immigrants.

DATA AND METHODS

Our data collection effort was twofold. First, we gathered information from guided conversations with community stakeholders (leaders such as the mayor, school board president, medical expert, and director of social services), employers, and immigrants, to provide the basis for assessing the impacts of immigration (Lofland and Lofland 1995). Second, we gathered interview data with information from a telephone survey of two hundred randomly selected households in Morgan City and Houma.

The guided conservation methodology used in this project is articulated in an interview guide (available on request). Table 4.1 summarizes the numbers and types of our guided conversations completed as part of this project. Of the total ninety-four guided conversations, we spoke with twenty-one community officials involved in civic organizations and local government, forty-three employers, and thirty immigrant workers,

TABLE 4.1   Number of Guided Conversations by Type and
            Community

Community	Employer	Community Leader	Immigrant Worker	Total
Morgan City	17	14	19	50
Houma	26	7	11	44
Total	43	21	30	94

Source: Louisiana Migration Project (2001).

of whom all were directly involved in oil and gas development activities (Grambling 1996). With permission from respondents, we recorded these conversations on tape to avoid normal interruptions that occur from taking notes (either on a computer or by hand). Our interviewers conducted most worker interviews in Spanish, which we had translated into English.

WHY MIGRATE TO LOUISIANA?

Three types of conditions influence people to migrate: supply side factors that push individuals to move to another country; demand side factors that pull individuals into a new receiving nation; and network factors that represent a system of support bridging the two places (Escobar Latapí et al. 1998). These forces often operate simultaneously and may be mutually dependent. For example, with a system of network support that promotes migration as a cultural rite of passage in many Mexican communities (Massey et al. 1987), many migrate in search of reasonable employment to the United States. Armed with the information and social support they need to cross the border, potential migrants eventually make a first U.S. trip.

Although many scholars agree that Mexico–U.S. migration flows developed from the demands of U.S. employers for workers, they also agree that shifts in conditions in Mexico have disengaged many Mexicans from their land and origin communities (Escobar Latapí et al. 1998; Massey 1988). Changes in agricultural production, including declining government crop subsidies and volatility in the Mexican economy, have led to earnings declines, peso devaluations, and high unemployment. Coupled with these shifts was an important demographic change. As a result of high fertility rates in mid-century, there were many more people of working age in Mexico's population. One consequence was that Mexico had many more people than jobs—even when the economy was strong—and many were pushed off their land to search for reasonable employment elsewhere.

Whether emphasizing demand or supply side factors, however, Mexico-U.S. migration has persisted in recent decades because of the strength of migrant networks. They provide the crucial bridge between supply and demand conditions by offering migrants social support that reduces risks, and increases benefits, related to making a U.S. trip (Massey and Espinosa 1997). Social ties to friends and relatives in the United States, once established, spur potential migrants to make a first trip and encourage recurrent migration.

Although Louisiana has not been a common destination for the foreign-born during most of the twentieth century, it has become a destination for immigrants from Mexico since 1990. Propelled into movement by shifting supply conditions in Mexico, migrants primarily went to coastal communities in southern Louisiana searching for work. Here jobs in the oil industry were plentiful and offered reasonable wages because employers faced a serious shortage of skilled labor. Mexican workers were recruited to the area in formal and informal ways. Employers formally recruited workers by traveling to Mexico and arranging their transportation, housing, and legal documents while they lived and worked in the United States. After the first Mexican immigrants arrived, however, employers also offered these workers cash to recruit their friends and family members. New workers then arrived because they heard about high-paying, skilled, and semi-skilled jobs in the fabrication centers and shipbuilding companies that supply and service offshore drilling platforms. Therefore, consistent with prior studies, employer demand for labor provided jobs that were subsequently filled by a supply of immigrants employers actively recruited.

The oil industry in southern Louisiana houses employers with specific types of traits (Donato, Bankston, and Robinson 2001). First, these employers tend to be heavily concentrated in labor- and skill-intensive work, with particular emphases on the construction and repair of offshore rigs and the ships that serve them. Second, because they cannot easily relocate this type of work to other locations, employers rely on local sources of labor by hiring residents and/or those laborers relocated to their region. Third, an oil-dependent economy dictates that employers have a flexible labor force. Because the price of oil fluctuates, profits are linked to how quickly employers expand or contract the size of their labor force. Fourth, onshore oil-related employers in southern

Louisiana are hostile to unionization. Most expressed a strong reluctance to accept unions in their workplaces.

Following the sharp downturn in the Louisiana oil economy during the mid-1980s, many local workers either left the region or, if they stayed, they sought other jobs for support. Ten years later, motivated by a shortage of skilled workers in the local labor market, many employers saw Mexican workers as the answer. They had the skills for the jobs employers needed to fill, they had a strong work ethic, and they were profitable in part because they were expendable. During periods of high productivity in the 1990s, employers hired as many workers as possible, but as the local economy loosened, they quickly scaled back their Mexican workforce by reducing either hours or employees to avoid affecting local workers and the community at large.[1] Finally, our interviews revealed that Mexican workers were paid less than their local counterparts. In some cases, this meant lower wages but in others inequality took the form of contract workers hired without benefits. Therefore, because Mexican workers were seen as expendable, temporary, and less costly, employers in southern Louisiana hired them more and more often, sometimes placing them at the very top of the hiring queue.

DIFFERENT FORMS OF IMMIGRANT ECONOMIC INCORPORATION: A TALE OF TWO CITIES

Given similarities in the economic makeup of Morgan City and Houma—their heavy reliance on the oil industry and demand for blue-collar labor—we expected to observe similarity in the economic incorporation of Mexican immigrants. Consistent with this idea was the expectation that immigrant workers in the two communities would not differ in their stock of human capital. In fact, from our immigrant interviews, we learned that most immigrant workers in Houma and Morgan City were born in Mexico. Unlike recent studies suggesting that Mexican workers are settling in new U.S. destinations because they are searching for areas where their entire family may live, the substantial majority of our sample, in both locations, were men who migrated without their families. However, most men had families—wives, children, and parents—living in Mexico. They reported maintaining strong connections to their origins—emotionally, financially, and socially. Most sent money home to their families and returned frequently to visit. Many expressed a strong desire to return permanently to Mexico once they had improved their financial well-being. In short, workers in both communities maintained their social and economic attachments to Mexico through remittances, frequent return trips, and other forms of communication.

With respect to education and work experience, most workers had only a few years of formal schooling. Some reported experience with welding and other jobs found in the oil industry in Mexico or Texas before arriving in southern Louisiana. On the whole most workers did not have papers certifying their experience. They were thus hired as assistants to welders or as other semi-skilled laborers. Immigrants without any prior experience in welding or oil-related jobs typically began as helpers. Our interview data therefore suggest no community differences in the human capital immigrant workers presented to their employers and no discernible differences in the goals of these immigrant workers.

Despite the similar profiles, we found significant community differences in the economic experiences of Mexican migrants. Differences in communities' contexts of reception, we argue, ultimately led to different incorporation profiles for the two groups of immigrants. As many researchers have shown, the process of immigrant incorporation varies widely and largely depends on the characteristics of the arriving immigrant group and the context within which the immigrant group is received. In one part of their new book, Alejandro Portes and Rubén Rumbaut (2001) describe how immigrant assimilation may be dramatically different for the same group of immigrants entering different social environments. In contrast to the idea that assimilation is a linear process where immigrant groups become more incorporated into the American mainstream as time progresses, the assimilation process of immigrants is segmented, not linear, and varies with the human capital brought by the group of newcomers and with the context of the receiving community (Zhou 1997).

Portes and Rumbaut (2001) describe three contextual factors that shape the process by which immigrants are incorporated into a particular community: government policies, societal reception of newcomers, and existing co-ethnic communities. Governmental policies in place at the time of migration shape the newcomer's experience and affect the ability to use human capital and skills. According to Portes and Rumbaut, government policies may exclude, passively accept, or actively encourage immigration. If immigrant groups are not allowed to enter the United States legally, they will not be offered any form of government protection or assistance and may be forced into an underground economy. In contrast, policies emphasizing passive acceptance may legally admit immigrants but do nothing to assist newcomers with incorporation. As a final governmental policy, active encouragement not only legally admits immigrants but actively encourages migration of a particular group and provides a variety of adaptation resources. This occurs either when the receiving country has a shortage of professional workers or when a particular group of immigrants are classified as refugees and participate in a government resettlement program. In both cases, the group is given special consideration and assistance that facilitates adaptation and possible upward mobility.

A second contextual factor affecting the economic and social incorporation of immigrant groups is the host community and its reception of newcomers. This refers to the extent to which newcomers are accepted by community members and employers. It affects the amount and quality of interaction between residents and newcomers and the willingness of the local community to provide valuable incorporation assistance (for example, social services such as assistance with housing, transportation, language, employment, and the like). Portes and Rumbaut (2001) point out that newcomers who are most similar to the community members are most likely to be favorably received, while those differing in appearance based on race-ethnicity, class, or some other attribute face greater barriers.

In addition, the extent to which a co-ethnic community has been previously established in the host community affects the newcomer's experience. Immigrants entering a community with well-established co-ethnic networks benefit by receiving invaluable assistance in finding jobs, housing, transportation, food and other immediate needs. Without a number of compatriots residing in the host community, migrants must often tackle their foreign community alone and often have more difficulty incorporating into the community.

Our focus on the contexts of immigration runs the risk of portraying immigrants as passive. Immigrant community formation and capacities for collective action depend on whether immigrants intend to settle in the United States or intend to temporarily work and later return to families in Mexico. However, as we will see, migrant intentions and their consequences are often reshaped by local opportunities. In both communities considered in the next paragraph, immigrant workers initially viewed themselves as sojourners rather than settlers. Nonetheless, the channels by which immigrants arrived and the opportunities they found affected the kinds of social relations they formed among themselves, with their employers, and with native-born residents.

TABLE 4.2   Immigrant Incorporation in Two Communities in
             Southern Louisiana, 1999

| | Mode | | |
Community	Government	Societal	Co-Ethnic
Morgan City	Neutral	Prejudicial	Working class; concentrated
Houma	Favorable-neutral	Neutral-prejudicial	Working class; concentrated

Source: Portes and Rumbaut (2001).

Table 4.2 places our southern Louisiana communities into the Portes and Rumbaut framework by describing the modes of incorporation of immigrant groups in each of the communities. We refer to this table to help us describe the economic and social incorporation of the Hispanic newcomers in Houma and Morgan City. We rely on data from conversations with employers, community leaders, and Hispanic workers to explain how varying contextual factors shaped these outcomes. Employers, community reception, and co-ethnic networks all played key roles in the incorporation of the Hispanic newcomers to southern Louisiana. We examine these as we describe the incorporation of immigrants in each of these two localities.

HOUMA: EMPLOYERS AS THE DOMINANT FORCE

The methods employers used to attract Hispanic workers to Houma directly influenced the incorporation outcomes of the newcomers. Employers tended to attract Hispanic workers by relying on an established system of recruitment and labor contracting that occurred outside of the firm. For example, one shipbuilding company relied exclusively on a separate contracting agency to provide labor, requesting only Hispanic workers. From another company making offshore platforms, the president told us that the year before he had employed "forty [Hispanic] workers and they were all contract workers" (Interview 03107, October 4, 1999). An official at a third company described the local Hispanic population as "mainly Mexicans in the contract labor force" (Interview 03103, September 28, 1999).

The use of contract labor agencies to find immigrant workers was an important contextual factor that shaped the way Latino workers were incorporated into the community and had far-reaching implications for the working conditions of these immigrants. In Houma, labor contractors recruited Hispanic workers by traveling to Mexico, gathering workers, completing all legal paperwork for H-2B visas, and returning to Houma with the workers. As one worker that we interviewed told us, "some contractors ... placed an ad in the newspaper in Tampico, they interviewed me, and I came here with them" (Interview 03304, December 3, 1999). Hispanic workers reported that recruiters promised them a certain number of work hours, a set pay scale, and room and board.

To some extent, immigrant workers reported these benefits. "You need to make enough money to invest in Mexico and then you can live very comfortable without having to come back here to work. It is worth the sacrifice of coming here to work and get that money" (Interview 03306, December 3, 1999). Benefits were even greater, however, for employers. "We tried all kinds of different systems looking for workers and we found that they had ... pretty much the skills we wanted. The only problem that we had was a language barrier which we worked out pretty well but ... and we spent twenty-seven months trying to see how we could get them into the country to help us because we lost probably about $20 million worth of revenue by not having them (Interview 03121, November 17, 2000).[2]

An important correlate of this system of hiring foreign-born workers was that immigrant housing was directly linked to the employer. As part of their agreement with employers, Mexican workers were required to live in company trailers on the job site. Payments for room and board were excessive and usually extracted from workers' paychecks each week.[3] Each trailer contained bedrooms and bathrooms, but never a kitchen. "Sixteen persons to a trailer, that has four rooms ... there are four persons to a room and ... two bathrooms. Eight of us have to use one bathroom and that is not enough bathrooms for eight persons" (Interview 03310b, February 13, 2000). Workers were also charged for food they reported to be inadequate, often forcing workers not only to pay for on-site food but then to purchase supplemental meals elsewhere. "We have very little food, sometimes you are still hungry after you eat. Sometimes the chicken is not well cooked and smells rotten" (Interview 03310a, February 13, 2000). The mandatory housing arrangement meant that employers had a large degree of control over their Hispanic work force. "We are at their mercy, we cannot ask for anything or say anything because they consider it an act of rebellion" (Interview 03310b, February 13, 2000).

Conditions of contract employment affected the social and economic incorporation of workers. First, because workers signed contracts that bound them to a specific employer for a given amount of time, they were legally obliged to remain with their employer even if they did not make the money they were promised. Second, as a special work force, these workers were required to work without breaks, whereas locals were given at least two fifteen-minute breaks through the work day. Third, they were often allocated to the dirtiest, least desirable jobs, but not always offered overtime hours. "I can see that there is discrimination because the Mexicans get the dirtiest and hardest jobs, but we came here to work. It doesn't bother me because I was used to even tougher jobs, but it really bothers me that when it comes to working overtime, they give Americans those hours first, and we only get them if there are some left" (Interview 03309, February 13, 2000). Finally, Mexican workers reported that the contract company held their passports and would not return them on request. This practice made it difficult, if not impossible, for workers to move freely away from the work sites, and many resented it. "I don't know why they do that. The passport is personal," were words that echoed the feelings of many (Interview 03310a, February 13, 2000).

One consequence was that the contract labor system became a source of entrapment and isolation for the workers, operating against any true social or community incorporation or chances for upward mobility of the newly arriving immigrants. Because housing was physically, legally, and geographically attached to the employer, workers were segregated from the existing community. They also had very limited autonomy, and employer control over workers was maximized. They were unable to seek out alternative employment or housing, and as a consequence, they were relatively invisible to most community residents. As the company president we cited earlier told us, "they [immigrants] were not out buying clothing, entertainment dollars and uh . . . eating out so . . . [their impact on the local economy was] minimal" (Interview 03107, October 4, 1999).

In short, the contract labor system had a direct effect on immigrant workers' economic autonomy and well-being. As we will see, compared to their counterparts in Morgan City, immigrant workers in Houma were much less satisfied with their housing or employment conditions and had considerably less autonomy to affect change in their current conditions. As a result, Hispanic workers in Houma reported a number of grievances. Having been rented out to secondary employers who were insulated from responsibility for labor conditions, immigrant workers had a number of complaints. These included: "Company Z makes the decisions about feeding us poorly, having us crowded in those trailers but they won't take the responsibility. Most of the bosses are Americans, they don't want to be involved in a racism problem, so they have this man (a Mexican foreman) as liaison between them and the workers" (Interview 03304, December 3, 1999).

The systemic barriers between workers and those who used their labor and between workers and the local community lent itself to some interesting local misreadings of the immigrant experience. While the workers felt that they were enduring hardship for the sake of their families in Mexico and for the sake of their futures, employers and local residents tended to view immigrants as basking in good fortune. A newspaper editor in the area said of the immigrant workers, "I mean they are loving it cause hell they are . . . making $3 or $4 an hour at home and they come over here and make $16 an hour plus overtime. They are sending back money . . . they are getting rich" (Interview 03215, October 11, 1999). In contrast to the grievances many workers voiced to our interviewers, an employer presented a sunny view of migrants. "They are happy with it [their living situation]. They are away from their family and all they want to do is work. . . . They want to work, want to work all the time" (Interview 03121, November 17, 2000).

Because Mexican workers spent most of their time on the job, and lived separate from the rest of the community, few residents reported feeling threatened in any way as a result of the newcomers. Most reported that levels of crime in the area were low and that these had not increased noticeably with the arrival of immigrant workers. When asked whether increased immigration had affected crime rates in the area, a law enforcement official replied, "I haven't noticed anything . . . The crime uh . . . our crime rate is pretty much stabilized. Our violent crime is pretty much down to a small, small percent" (Interview 03225, December 3, 1999). The newspaper editor gave similar views: "it wasn't like there was a big increase in crime because they started importing all these blue collar workers. . . . It wasn't anything like that. And actually a lot of the employers you talked to said these guys are working their butts off. I wish I had 100 percent of my work force like this, you know" (Interview 03215, October 11, 1999).

The positive views of immigrants held by local residents contrasted sharply with the negative experiences reported by the immigrants themselves. If residents in the region negatively viewed the immigrant labor system, they were suspicious that immigrants were providing cheap labor and, as a result, driving down the wages of (or taking jobs away from) U.S.-born residents in the region. But there appeared to be an element of self-contradiction in these fears. On the one hand, many we spoke with agreed with the chamber of commerce official who told us that Mexicans had been brought in because "There was no more work force. We were down to under three percent unemployment. That was because the oil industry had perked up" (Interview 03206, October 25, 1999). On the other hand, however, every time that Mexicans were perceived as such hard, eager workers it led some locals to believe that immigrants threatened the job opportunities of the U.S.-born. A white-collar professional and community leader complained that "I think it is ludicrous that we deny our workers the benefits of the free enterprise system . . . bring in foreign labor and so forth and they have done this on [numerous] occasions . . . foreign labor [keeps] local wages down" (Interview 03222, November 1, 2000).

Therefore, we describe Houma as a neutral-to-prejudicial immigrant receiving context (see table 4.2). Other than stereotyped opinions of Mexicans as people who love to work and do so for low wages, Houma residents had few strong opinions about Mexican workers. The contract labor system, segregated housing, and few existing immigration problems in the community meant little active engagement with the new arrivals, either in the form of strong opposition or support. And although community-based services targeted toward newcomers may help ease transition (for example, English language classes, referrals with housing and transportation, church services), the community offered few such services. Neither migrants nor employers reported knowledge of Spanish-speaking church services, English language classes, or stores in the area that assisted immigrants. No doubt, the separation and isolation of these workers from the local community explains part of the limited knowledge. But without these services, or knowledge of them, immigrants had no mechanism through which they may be introduced to the community and they were left to fend for themselves.

In theory, existing co-ethnic networks provide some of the same incorporation benefits that community groups provide. If there is an established network of compatriots in the receiving community, newcomers may benefit because members of the network provide food, housing, information, jobs, or other forms of assistance that facilitate successful incorporation. A strong co-ethnic community may therefore provide a buffer and sense of protection for the arriving newcomers. However, with the system of contract labor in place, development of, and access to, co-ethnic networks were limited. Most migrants did not know anyone in Houma until after they arrived, and newcomers could not easily access existing co-ethnic network ties in the community.

In sum, the system of contract labor was the dominant force shaping the economic and social incorporation of immigrant workers in Houma. Without the protection provided by a co-ethnic community or local community service agencies, Hispanic workers were left to fend for themselves. The result was a group of disenfranchised workers suffering mistreatment at the hands of employers, with no real opportunities to socially and economically incorporate into their new receiving community.

MORGAN CITY: HOW COMMUNITY RECEPTION AND CO-ETHNIC NETWORKS MEDIATE

Although the methods employers used to recruit and employ Mexican workers directly affect immigrant incorporation, the methods used by employers in Morgan City were significantly different from those in Houma. In contrast to Houma, where employers relied on a formal system of contract labor to attract immigrants, Morgan City employers used a loosely structured system of recruitment. Employers first contacted migrant workers by relying on co-ethnic network ties, either by providing incentives to workers already employed or by contacting an immigrant activist who had made her reputation by solving migrant problems in the community. Also in contrast to newly arrived immigrants in Houma, those in Morgan City did not live in housing provided by employers. These immigrant experiences emerged in Morgan City in large part because of its past history in recruiting foreign laborers, a point we begin with in the next paragraph.

Despite the proximity of Houma to Morgan City, and the former's success in formally recruiting many legal immigrants, Morgan City employers were not following this same path at the end of the 1990s. Not one employer reported they sought H-2B visas to obtain immigrant laborers. However, many told us about one employer's experience when he announced to the community he would provide housing for immigrant workers on the job site. Although the employer initially thought that his public declaration of the labor shortage problem and purchase of new mobile housing offer would temper any community resistance, local residents forcefully objected. The employer's actions had triggered memories of transient labor camps in Morgan City set up in the 1970s and early 1980s, when many U.S.-born workers from distant states were recruited to meet the industry's demand for labor. One employer described how, in those days, offshore work in the oil industry was a magnet for those seeking invisibility: "These guys could come in here ... get on a boat, offshore, and stay out there for three or four months, come into town and go get drunk, get in a fight or something and get put in jail, then they [would] check their history and they were wanted all over." Therefore, "at one time, per capita, Morgan City had more arrests than any city in the United States" (Interview 02121, January 7, 1999). A city official explained that "back in the 1970s when the labor camps were common here ... we had one fellow wanted for murder who was arrested here, he had ... been to the soup kitchens and ... around people who recognized him. Once he got arrested, people said, 'wait a minute, this guy was walking amongst us.'" Then, he explained, "there was a real brutal murder in one of the camps where a guy was beat with a concrete brick to death and set on fire," and another "guy ... who had lived in the labor camp here, had abducted three kids on different occasions and ... none of the three of them has ever been found" (Interview 02222, December 30, 1998).

These earlier transients were mostly white, non-Hispanic internal migrants from other parts of the United States, not from Mexico. Still, because of the murders and abductions that took place during this earlier period, community members developed deep suspicions of outsiders in general and tended to associate them with criminal activity. As a consequence, in the late 1980s the community passed a zoning ordinance that stated that labor camps, defined as temporary, high-density housing for workers provided by employers, may not be located within city limits. Given the experiences of the community with its internal migrant labor, the city council adopted the ordinance quietly and with little controversy. However, controversy arose with the arrival of the Mexican migrant workers.

The issue of nonlocal labor temporarily receded into the background during the mid- to late 1980s, when the domestic oil industry bust led to high unemployment. With respect to jobs tied to oil production, one employer in a shipbuilding business in Morgan City observed that "you can make a great deal of money doing this for a few months, but then you are likely to find yourself out of a job all of a sudden" (Interview 02117, February 2, 1999). Workers and employers alike agreed that many onshore occupations involving ship repair and the building of offshore platforms were physically difficult, dirty, and dangerous. Therefore, as the volatility of the oil economy and the types of jobs it supports became apparent, jobs in this field became less attractive to many Louisianans. One consequence was that once labor demand increased again, there were relatively few local workers prepared to enter these jobs.

As a result, in the mid-1990s employers in Morgan City faced a severe labor shortage. Many employers we interviewed complained that they had been unable to find enough workers. One Louisiana government representative said of the employer who sparked the local housing controversy: "his [the employer's] problem was that he was getting contracts that he just couldn't fill. It wasn't because he couldn't get the material or didn't have the space in the yard. It was because he couldn't get the skilled workers to perform the tasks necessary to fulfill his contracts. In desperation, he went and recruited and he found a source in south Texas" (Interview 02219, December 29, 1998). Having brought foreign workers to the area, he needed to house them. One immigrant worker remembered how the "company bought us [to live in] trailers and we stayed there," but "there was a problem and the owner moved us to _____, where we live now" (Interview 02315, August 31, 1999).[4]

The community official explained the development of the ordinance controversy as follows: "basically what happened was this ... [because of the lack of housing for workers recruited in South Texas] he needed to locate those trailers on his property. I had to tell him, no you can't do that because our ordinance doesn't allow it" (Interview 02222, December 30, 1998). The incident with this employer drew attention to cases of other companies who were attempting to house their workers in motels or in trailers. Activists within Morgan City began to demand enforcement of the existing ordinance.

The controversy over immigrant housing lasted several months, giving other residents time to articulate xenophobic attitudes. Some associated the newcomers with the criminal activity of earlier waves of transient labor. Others were opposed to any change in the cultural character of the city or to Mexican immigrants more specifically. One local political figure told us about a local group that usually opposes changes in the community because "its fear, at least it is what they reported to me, was that we were going to put all these people in close proximity to the general population of Morgan City.... I mean, I had one lady who was extremely vocal in this group tell me that she would not let her children play outside because of these people [the Mexican immigrants]. They were going to come and rape and kill her children is what she told me. I thought it was horrible that she made that judgment about these people" (Interview 02219, December 29, 1998).

The workers we interviewed described the apparent prejudices of some Morgan City residents. Asked about the relationship between

Americans and Latinos, one worker observed, "I guess we get along okay, although the Americans don't like the Latinos.... For example, my next door neighbor turns her back to me when she sees me" (Interview 02319, September 29, 1999). Prejudicial attitudes also appeared as residents articulated their opposition against the housing proposal. A local informant described the situation this way. "He [the employer of the immigrants] was not too far from a residential area ... in fact, right across the railroad track. That is the _____ area and most of the opposition came from that community. They didn't want that element living at their back door" (Interview 02121, January 7, 1999).

Although those favoring housing workers on the job site suggested that the ordinance be rewritten to allow trailers to remain but add certain protections for the workers, in the end community members rejected this amendment, unable to disassociate their previously established fears of outsiders from employer's current demand for labor. After the employer was forced to remove his trailers from the job site to a small community on the outskirts of Morgan City, community members were appeased.

Since that time, they have not publicly expressed concerns about immigrant workers. More and more immigrants established residence in a small barrio outside the city limits, as the demand for blue-collar labor continued and employers' preferences for immigrants grew. Many employers believed that Mexican workers were highly skilled, motivated, and comparatively low-cost laborers. Increasingly, these employers began to look to the Texas-Mexico border to find workers. As one of the employers explained, "in the past probably about two years, because ... the demand in the industry is so high that we haven't found local people. We couldn't get the black and white locals to do the work and like most other people around here we had to concentrate heavier on foreigners." Those foreigners, he went on, were chiefly recruited in El Paso, on the Texas-Mexico border (Interview 02113, November 10, 1998). Furthermore, the existence of a Mexican settlement outside of Morgan City meant that potential immigrants learned of these employment opportunities through relatives and friends already working in this small Louisiana city. One worker gave a fairly typical explanation of how he found work in Morgan City. "I was in Houston and I knew about this job in Louisiana, but I did not know anybody here. This friend brought me over here and now I have a job that pays me very well" (Interview 02305, April 3, 1999).

As in Houma, the Mexican residential settlement was first and foremost a labor settlement. "All we do is work, eat, and sleep," sighed one worker, "there is nothing to do for entertainment" (Interview 02317, September 18, 1999). Still, growth of a residential area separate from the workplace made the emergence of a multidimensional immigrant community possible in Morgan City. Although the majority of Latino immigrants were single men, some families moved to Morgan City. One resident of a trailer park in the small Mexican neighborhood explained that she and her four children had followed her husband to Louisiana. "My husband came first, he was here for a month, a month and a half. He started working and when he saw that he was doing all right he brought us. He called me and told me to get ready to come here" (Interview 02314, August 31, 1999).

Placing housing away from the job site affected immigrant incorporation in Morgan City in another important way. It reduced employers' control over workers, and with their autonomy, immigrants (often with the help of their co-ethnic network ties) moved from one employer to another. One part-owner and manager of a labor contracting company with a predominantly Mexican work force boasted to us. "I have taken over one hundred people from [another local company] . . . because they were making $8.50 per hour and over here they make $15 to $18 per hour" (Interview, January 14, 1999). Moreover, the housing controversy ironically publicized the use of immigrant workers to those employers that had not yet hired them. As one person explained, "I think there were some [employers] that were sensitive to . . . being accused of being anti-Mexican and they made an outreach to the Mexican community to make sure that there was no continuing allegation of that" (Interview, December 30, 1998).

Although immigrant workers in Morgan City were certainly isolated in a particular geographic space rather than living dispersed within the community, they were considerably less isolated than their counterparts in Houma. One important reason was the emergence of a key social actor, Mary, who reached out and assisted Spanish-speaking migrants. She did this in a variety of ways. She began by answering a call from her non-Spanish-speaking pastor to translate religious services into Spanish for the immigrant population. She did the translation at a weekly Saturday evening service and meal especially geared toward Spanish-speaking immigrants. There Mary met as many immigrants as arrived; on the evenings we attended, there ranged from thirty to sixty persons. During an ethnic dinner that usually consisted of chicken, tortillas, and beans, Mary and a few other more established migrants passed on information and advice about housing, food, and transportation to the newly arrived. Mary also offered assistance with grocery shopping, laundry services, and accompanied sick workers to the doctor whenever necessary.

Over time, as local employers heard that Mary had developed contacts with large numbers of immigrants in the community, employers sought Mary's assistance to recruit workers. Therefore, in addition to facilitating their social incorporation, she also guided immigrants in their economic assimilation as she matched employers with workers. She became a critical link, placing workers in jobs, accompanying them to the workplace to fill out the necessary paperwork, and periodically stopping by to check on "her boys." During one of our interviews with Mary, an employer called seeking workers and Mary offered to bring the two newest arrivals to the workplace that next morning. She did, and they were hired.

Through Mary, immigrants became aware of their surrounding community and what it had to offer. As a result, unlike in Houma, immigrants in Morgan City knew about and attended English language courses taught at a local school, they often attended church services and events, and they regularly gathered to play soccer at a public gym. In just a few years, Mary had become an important social actor in the social and economic incorporation of immigrants.

Existing co-ethnic networks provided an additional layer of protection for newcomers in Morgan City. Many Mexican workers we interviewed came to Morgan City because they had family and friends living in the community and were told of promising job opportunities in the oil industry. Some had arranged for the employment of their family and friends before they arrived. Once they arrived, many newcomers shared housing with their more established friends or family.

In effect, the community (its members and institutions) provided a buffer to protect newly arrived Mexican workers in Morgan City. Rather than depend solely on employers as did immigrants in Houma, those in Morgan City relied on existing co-ethnic networks to provide information and assistance with housing, transportation, and employment. With employers unable to completely control migrant newcomers, workers had alternatives and some autonomy over their lives. Therefore, in Morgan City, there was no one dominant force shaping the early assimilation experiences of immigrants. All three forces—employers, community reception, and co-ethnic networks—interacted to facilitate the incorporation of newcomers. The result was high levels of immigrant satisfaction, despite an initial public controversy over an employer's attempt to house immigrants on his work site. Immigrants in Morgan City reported being satisfied with their current housing and employment, happy to live in the community, saying it was a peaceful and pleasant place to live.

CONCLUSIONS

Our examination of immigrant workers in two small cities in Louisiana offers insight into the early process of social and economic incorporation of Mexican immigrants. Unlike the Europeans who immigrated early in the twentieth century, many recently arrived migrants no longer follow the old residence patterns and live only in urban centers of the United States. Also unlike their earlier counterparts, immigrants of the 1990s are filling nontraditional labor niches in the U.S. economy. Neither unskilled day laborers nor migrant agricultural workers, immigrants in Morgan City and Houma in the 1990s were semi- and highly skilled blue-collar workers. Despite this similarity, however, our examination illustrates the heterogeneous and at times paradoxical outcomes linked to immigrant incorporation. As Mexican migrants worked and settled in Morgan City and Houma, different social forces in each place influenced the reception of newcomers and the growth of ethnic communities. One consequence was unintended: the formation of an emerging immigrant settlement in Morgan City, a community that was initially hostile to immigrants and that contained a salient social actor who individually facilitated the social and economic incorporation of many Mexicans. Thus, by opposing the housing of immigrants within their city limits, yet at the same time providing a key social actor who influenced the institutions that served Mexican migrants, the people of Morgan City ultimately ended up contributing to the emergence of an immigrant community.

In theory, differences in the modes of immigrant incorporation across the two localities may have suggested that workers would find a more favorable environment for settlement in Houma than in Morgan City. After all, legal immigration through H-2B visas should have provided support for the arrival and settlement of Mexican workers. In fact, bringing immigrants to Houma did not produce the intense controversy and opposition seen in Morgan City.

Without controversy, the predominant characteristic of societal incorporation in Houma was employer control. This control was heightened by reliance on formal governmental avenues of immigration. In Morgan City, on the other hand, community opposition weakened employer control. Together with less government involvement in Morgan City (in the form of providing H-2B visas), co-ethnic networks played a greater part in bringing immigrants to this location than they did in Houma. The role of these networks was heightened when the controversy in Morgan City caused settlements to be moved off work sites. Furthermore, to some extent, community opposition created a reaction to itself, leading to more ties between local people and immigrants.

Despite the differences between the two localities, there were underlying similarities that make public awareness of immigration an important issue for both citizens and noncitizens alike. In both communities, immigrants were, to a certain extent, invisible outsiders. Although residential and social segregation took somewhat different forms, it remained a fundamental reality of new immigrant settlements. Therefore, the greatest problem facing Mexican immigrants in U.S. society may be that the parts they play occur off the public stage, unheard and unseen.

On the whole, our case study suggests two questions for future research to address. The first refers to the extent to which the three modes of incorporation—government policies, societal reception of newcomers, and existing co-ethnic communities—affect each other. Our findings suggest considerable interrelationships among the three in one community, but substantial independence in the second community. The second question must consider how power and control are distributed across the three dimensions. To what extent are immigrants arriving and leaving because of their co-ethnic network ties, and to what extent are they arriving under the direction of host country organizational actors? To what extent do we find conflict between communities and employers over immigrant issues and to what extent are employers left to do as they see fit with their workers? Finally, to what extent do individual actors offset employer power and affect community institutions that interface with Mexican immigrants? Ultimately, answers to these questions will help us fully understand differences in the early assimilation experiences of immigrant workers in the United States.

NOTES

1. One employer admitted to initiating a raid by the Immigration and Naturalization Service (INS) to reduce his workforce by approximately one-third just before the holiday season, when business is typically very slow and many fabrication yards close down for several weeks. By having the INS raid his workplace, the employer got the INS to do what he did not: to lay off workers. INS intervention ensured that the employer would not lose credibility with migrant workers, and as a result, when his company reopened that January, he had more than enough new applicants.

2. Immediately before collecting data for this project, the state of Louisiana

petitioned the U.S. government for H-2B visas on behalf of several Houma employers. This request was part of a growing demand for H-2B visas in the 1990s. By 1999, there were 35,815 H-2B visas, up from 17,754, the total in 1990 (available at http://www.ins.gov).

3. Immigrant workers reported that employers charged $350 a month, a figure that seems particularly high given the conditions described.

4. The first author witnessed the company's removal of the mobile homes from its job site, several days after the community declared that the company was in violation of the zoning ordinance.

REFERENCES

Borjas, George J. 1999. *Heaven's Door: Immigration Policy and the American Economy.* Princeton, N.J.: Princeton University Press.

Donato, Katharine M. 1998. "Labor Migration and the Deepwater Oil Industry." A proposal submitted to the Minerals Management Service, U.S. Department of the Interior.

Donato, Katharine M., Carl L. Bankston, and Dawn T. Robinson. 2001. "Immigration and the Organization of the Onshore Oil Industry: Southern Louisiana in the Late 1990s." In *Latino Workers in the Contemporary South*, edited by Arthur D. Murphy, Colleen Blanchard, and Jennifer A. Hill. Athens, Ga.: University of Georgia Press.

Durand, Jorge, Douglas S. Massey, and Fernando Charvet. 2000. "The Changing Geography of Mexican Immigration to the United States: 1910–1996." *Social Science Quarterly* 81(1): 1–15.

Escobar Latapí, Agustin, Phillip Martin, Gustavo Lopez Castro, and Katharine Donato. 1998. "Factors that Influence Migration." In *Migration Between Mexico and the United States.* Vol. 1. Washington: U.S. Commission on Immigration Reform.

Frey, William H. 1998. "The Diversity Myth." *American Demographics* (June): 39–43.

Grambling, Robert. 1996. *Oil on the Edge: Offshore Development, Conflict, Gridlock.* Albany: State University of New York Press.

Hernández-León, Rubén, and Víctor Zúñiga. 2000. "Making Carpet by the Mile": The Emergence of a Mexican Immigrant Community in an Industrial Region of the U.S. Historic South." *Social Science Quarterly* 81(1): 49–66.

Kniffen, Fred B. 1968. *Louisiana: Its Land and People.* Baton Rouge: Louisiana State University Press.

Lofland, John, and Lyn Lofland. 1995. *Analyzing Social Settings: A Guide to Qualitative Observation and Analysis.* Belmont, Calif.: Wadsworth.

Louisiana Migration Project. 2001. *Labor Demand and the Deep-Water Oil Industry.* Supported by the U.S. Department of the Interior, Minerals Management Service.

Massey, Douglas S. 1988. "International Migration and Economic Development in Comparative Perspective." *Population and Development Review* 14(3): 383–414.

Massey, Douglas S., Rafael Alarcon, Jorge Durand, and Humberto Gonzalez. 1987. *Return to Aztlan: the Social Process of International Migration from Western Mexico.* Berkeley: University of California Press.

Massey, Douglas S., and Kristin E. Espinosa. 1997. "What's Driving Mexico-U.S. Migration? A Theoretical, Empirical, and Policy Analysis." *American Journal of Sociology* 102(4): 939–99.

Portes, Alejandro, and Rubén Rumbaut. 2001. *Legacies: The Story of the Immigrant Second Generation.* Berkeley: The University of California Press.

Sassen, Saskia, and Robert C. Smith. 1992. "Post-Industrial Growth and Economic Reorganization: Their Impact on Immigrant Employment." In *U.S.-Mexico Relations: Labor Market Interdependence,* edited by Jorje A. Bustamante, Clark W. Reynolds, and Raul Hinojosa-Ojeda. Stanford, Calif.: Stanford University Press.

Smith, Robert C. 1996. "Mexicans in New York: Membership and Incorporation in a New Immigrant Community." In *Latinos in NY,* edited by Gabriel Haslip-Viera and Sherrie L. Baver. Notre Dame, Ind.: Notre Dame Press.

Stull, Donald, Michael Broadway, and Ken C. Erickson. 1992. "The Price of a Good Steak: Beef Packing and Its Consequences for Garden City, Kansas." In *Structuring Diversity: Ethnographic Perspectives on the New Immigration,* edited by Louise Lamphere. Chicago: University of Chicago Press.

U.S. Department of Justice. 1997. *Statistical Yearbook of the Immigration and Naturalization Service.* Washington: U.S. Government Printing Office.

Zhou, Min. 1997. "Segmented Assimilation: Issues, Controversies, and Recent Research on the New Second Generation." *International Migration Review* 31(4): 825–58.

PART II

LOCAL IMPACTS AND REACTIONS
FROM ESTABLISHED RESIDENTS

CHAPTER 5

✕

BRIDGING THE COMMUNITY: NATIVISM, ACTIVISM, AND THE POLITICS OF INCLUSION IN A MEXICAN SETTLEMENT IN PENNSYLVANIA

DEBRA LATTANZI SHUTIKA

"Migration changes things" is at once a truism and yet a vast understatement. Current estimates suggest that approximately 2.3 percent of the world's population consists of labor migrants (Andreas and Snyder 2000), a number so small that it is statistically insignificant, yet the influence these mobile laborers have on their sending and receiving communities is remarkable. Here we consider the ways changes in migration after the passage of the 1986 Immigration Reform and Control Act (IRCA) have transformed the local social and political structure of Kennett Square, Pennsylvania, and the response of the dominant English-speaking community to these changes. The reciprocal influence that settlers from western Mexico have had on Kennett Square, and Kennett Square on these settlers is immediately obvious. Migration has afforded a relatively underprivileged group of laborers substantial class mobility, and in return these women and men have transformed the culture and sense of place in Kennett Square. For many years, Mexicans living on the periphery of this prosperous farming community were scarcely noticeable; now they are one of the defining characteristics associated with Kennett identity.

In addition to the more obvious changes associated with Mexican settlement, there are a number of deeper issues that this substantial and rapid demographic shift has produced. Historically, the Kennett Square English-speaking population, consisting primarily of persons of Anglo European descent, has constituted the numerical majority and its membership has provided the direction and leadership in the community.

These residents pride themselves on being a socially progressive, inclusive community. However, as Mexican families began setting down roots and purchasing homes in local neighborhoods in the early 1990s, the limits of community tolerance were tested for the first time. What initially transpired in Kennett Square is not surprising: there were a series of community protests directed against Mexican settlement that exposed local nativistic sentiment. However, the protests themselves soon became a point of contention in the community, but not between Anglos and Mexicans. Instead, a marked division emerged within the English-speaking community. This division, characterized by active public debate, was prompted by a widespread fear that, in opposing Mexican settlement, the town ran the risk of being labeled a racist community. Ultimately, the discussions that ensued worked to persuade community members to work toward a social contract of inclusion that is consistent with the community's image of itself, which manifested in a new social movement called Bridging the Community (Bridging).

The events surrounding the formation of the Bridging movement are noteworthy because they provide an example of how embodied experience, specifically a widespread fear that characterized the early years of Mexican settlement, foments social action and reaffirms local identity.

KENNETT SQUARE: THE MUSHROOM CAPITAL

Kennett Square lies thirty miles southwest of Philadelphia and twenty miles west of Wilmington, Delaware, in Chester County, Pennsylvania's wealthiest county. It has been the home of the nation's largest commercial mushroom industry for the last century. Despite its rural ambiance and history as a farming community, Kennett Square is a sophisticated town that is home to a number of upscale boutiques and restaurants and maintains its own symphony orchestra. The village is approximately one-mile square, and home to some five thousand residents. Politically, Kennett Square, like surrounding Chester County, is known as a conservative community and Republican Party stronghold. Founded as a Quaker settlement in 1855, Kennett has a local reputation of being socially progressive, a point frequently emphasized by local residents. Locally produced histories of the town often emphasize the role the community played in the nineteenth-century emancipation movement, the Underground Railroad (Kashatus 2002; Taylor 1995/1999; 1976/1998).

The town is governed by an elected borough council, which in turn selects the mayor (a nonsalaried official).[1] Kennett Square is an aging town, with 75 percent of the population eighteen years or older (U.S.

Census 2000). Of the 3,621 students enrolled in the Kennett Consolidated School District in 2000 through 2001 (which includes all of the Borough of Kennett Square, Kennett Township, New Garden Township, and a small portion of East Marlborough Township), 68 percent were white, 24 percent Hispanic and Latino, and 5 percent African American. Kennett's diversity, a point of pride for many local residents, stands in stark comparison to the neighboring Unionville–Chadds Ford School District. In the same year that student body was 95 percent white, 2.89 percent Asian American, 1.3 percent Hispanic and Latino, and 0.76 percent African American (Pennsylvania Department of Education 2000–2001).

Like other communities in the United States that depend on migrant farm labor, the Kennett Square workforce has historically consisted of persons with few employment options. Mushrooming, like other forms of agricultural production, is a labor-intensive endeavor and requires a steady supply of able-bodied laborers willing to work all night in the dark dank buildings where mushrooms are grown. Thus it is not surprising that the workforce historically has drawn from recently arrived immigrants and the working poor: Europeans at the turn of the century, African Americans, low-income whites from Appalachia, Puerto Ricans, and—most recently—Mexican nationals from the state of Guanajuato (Bustos 1994).

Mexican migration into the community began when the first workers arrived as early as 1958 and evolved into a steady pattern of seasonal migration to the area between 1968 and 1972 (Shutika 2000). Since the late 1960s, Kennett Square and the surrounding area has seen a slow but steady increase in the population of Mexican men who have come to work in the mushroom industry through the mid-1980s. Then as today, the majority of Mexicans working in Kennett are from the industrial town of Textitlán, Guanajuato.[2] These single Mexican men first made their way to Kennett Square in significant numbers as Puerto Rican workers were beginning to move out of mushrooming and into industrial employment (Bustos 1994). Kennett residents accepted having men who would travel into Kennett during the peak mushrooming months between October and March[3] as an acceptable and desirable consequence of being the hometown of a thriving agribusiness. The majority of the laborers between 1968 and 1990 were men who could be housed out of sight on farm property in trailers or barracks, where they worked, ate, and lived together. While many of these men worked in Kennett for years, sometimes a decade or more, their families and lives remained in Mexico. While they were an essential part of the mushroom industry, most never considered Kennett Square "home." Oral histories from the earliest migrants to Kennett emphasize that their lives were entirely work centered. At times working twenty hours a day, seven days a week, these men accepted the hardships and poor working conditions as a matter of course. One migrant recalled his early years as an honguero (mushroom picker), "I worked hard, my life here was pure work, but I knew it would end. I could rest at home [in Mexico] and I would have money for my family" (Pedro Camacho interview, January 20, 2000.).

These seasonal migrants fit well into the hierarchical social structure of Kennett Square. In this sense, the local body politic has always situated the Mexican labor force in a liminal position in the community, a place in the community hierarchy that has been more or less rigidly fixed. Migrant workers were routinely excluded from community events, like the annual Mushroom Festival. "We knew our place well," said former honguero Joel Luna of his early years in Kennett Square on the fringe of the community (quoted in Alfredo Corchado, "Growing Together: Struggle for Pennsylvania Town, Mexican Immigrants to Accept Each Other May Signal Path for Other Agricultural Areas [The Reshaping of America Series]," *Dallas Morning News*, September 24, 1999, p. 1). Mexicans "belonged" to fulfill a specific purpose: picking mushrooms, but they were transients, and were never intended to be fully accepted members of the local community. Similarly, most of these men never intended to stay.

But the passage of IRCA in 1986 permanently altered the social and cultural landscape of Kennett Square. With a newly acquired amnesty and legal permanent residency, many then seasonal migrants elected to settle in Kennett Square and the surrounding county, and shortly thereafter were joined by their wives and children (Shutika 2000). Why did these seasonal workers decide to bring their families north? Settling in Kennett Square became an attractive option, and Mexican migrant workers throughout the United States, after the passage of IRCA and its associated regulations governing the 1986 amnesty and legalization. Jorge Durand, Douglas S. Massey, and Emilio A. Parrado (1999) note that IRCA offered these seasonal migrants the option of establishing a secure and legal family and work life in the United States at a time of severe inflation and unemployment in Mexico. Given the option of economic stability in the United States versus a potentially uncertain future in Mexico, many former migrants chose to settle with their families in the United States. Similarly, IRCA included several provisions that compelled former migrants to stay in the United States for extended periods, such as English and civics classes that were required in order to obtain their permanent legal residency papers (Durand, Massey, and Parrado 1999; Durand, Massey, and Charvet 2000). Given the fact that mushrooming also offered the possibility of year-round employment, these events coalesced to transform the long established seasonal migration pattern in Kennett Square into widespread settlement of former migrant workers and their families.

These changes are evident in the increase in the total numbers of Mexicans living in Kennett Square Borough between 1990 and 2000. Census figures for 1990 indicate that of the 662 Hispanics and Latinos[4] living in Kennett Square, only 374 were of Mexican origin. By 2000, the total number of Hispanics and Latinos had increased to 1,470, of whom 1,154 were Mexican[5] (U.S. Census 2000). These changes were also evident in survey data collected in Textitlán in December 1999. Figure 5.1 shows that between 1940 and 1965 only men were migrating from Textitlán. However, between 1965 and 1970, women began mi-

FIGURE 5.1   Textitlán, Guanajuato, Total First Trips to
              United States

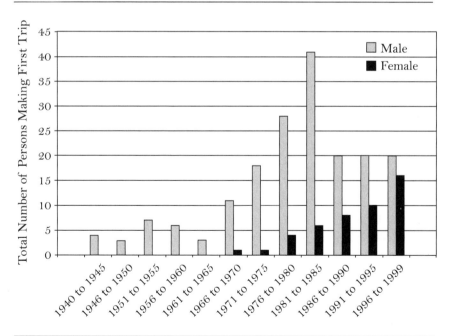

Source: Persfile, MMP71. Mexican Migration Project, Princeton University. mmp. opr.princeton.edu.

grating in small numbers, a trend that increased gradually through the late 1980s and 1990s.

By the early 1990s, what had been a barely perceptible seasonal workforce of Mexican nationals was now a conspicuous attribute of the area. Local public school enrollments bulged with Spanish-speaking students in need of English-language instruction and educational assistance. For example, in 1980, there were a total of 192 Hispanic students in the Kennett Consolidated School District (KCSD). This number increased to 299 by 1990, and by the start of the 2000–2001 academic year, the total number of Hispanic students enrolled in KCSD reached 890, raising the percentage of Hispanic students in the district from 8.2 to 24.5 percent in only two decades (Pennsylvania Department of Education 1980–2000). Similarly, the numbers of Mexican families seeking affordable, adequate housing found it difficult or impossible to locate residences. The number of women seeking prenatal and well woman health care doubled, and adults enrolling in English as a second language (ESL) and high school equivalency courses (GED) courses were turned away or placed on waiting lists (Iris Ayala, personal communication, April 17, 1999; Claire Russell, personal communication, April 20, 1999). In short, the need for educational and social services for families began to outpace the community's ability to provide them.

While their numbers were increasing, this once invisible population also initiated efforts to improve the working and living conditions for Mexican workers and their families. This was most evident when workers walked out on strike on April 1, 1993 at Kaolin Mushroom Farms, one of the largest producers in the area. With this action, Kennett residents quickly became aware that things were changing and that at a minimum Mexicans would not be the compliant workforce that they had once been (Corchado 1999). Within five years these changes forced long-term Kennett residents to take stock of their community: they could neither continue to ignore their Mexican neighbors nor the changes that they were producing. Between 1994 and 1997, these changes prompted a number of rancorous community disputes about Mexican settlement that were a reflection of the anxiety and fear associated with the changes taking place, and the unpredictable consequences Mexican settlers might have on the town long-term.

THEORETICAL FRAMEWORK: SOCIAL ACTION AS AN EMBODIED PROCESS

In framing my analysis around anxiety, I am following other social scientists who have explained the motivation to act collectively, whether the action is peaceful or violent, as a shared emotional response. Most often, these accounts cite an "anxiety" or a "fear" that results when there are perceptible transformations in the social structure. Notable examples of this include Neil J. Smelser's (1962) analysis of social movements where he frames collective action through notions of love-hate relationships, and Alberto Melucci's (1996) discussion of the function of identity and collective emotional response in social movements. Similarly, Douglas S. Massey and Nancy Denton's (1993) description of white flight from inner-city neighborhoods is characterized as prompted by fear of African Americans moving into previously all white communities.

Like these examples, many social scientists link emotional triggers to group action. Yet rarely do these descriptions go beyond straightforward statements that distinguish between biological anxiety, the neurophysiologic response that humans and other mammals experience in the face of a real or perceived threat, and social anxiety, which I define as the perceptible and reportable experience of dread or foreboding commonly associated with persons or social contexts that are uncertain. Although anxiety is apparently an individual emotion and derived internally, it is inherently relational, and exists as a phenomenon between a person or persons and their environment(s) (Spielberger 1972). For the purposes of this discussion, anxiety can be understood as an individual's or group's affective response to a specific social situation; it is initiated from contexts involving personal and social relations in which systems of shared meaning, or expectations of shared meaning, fail (Perin 1988).

In neurophysiologic terms, physical responses to anxiety (for example, palpitations, rapid breathing) occur when one perceives that their environment is in some way threatening. The threats that can trigger anxiety can be physical, such as the approach of an unknown person on a dark street; material, as might occur if one inadvertently steps out in front of a moving car; or cognitive, such as the apprehension experienced in anticipation of an exam. In all of these instances, anxiety is initiated by perceptions that appear to be threatening regardless of whether they actually are. In this sense, the contexts that trigger anxiety are not necessarily "rational" (that is, the unknown person may well be a friend you don't recognize from a distance) and anxiety can result from situations that would not be threatening to another person or to the same person in another context. In each case the individual's appraisal of a particular situation will greatly influence their reaction to it (Spielberger 1966; 1972; May 1950/1977). Massey (2002), writing of the significance of emotion in social life, notes that the biologic response to fear "unleash[es] a variety of somatic and emotional reactions that focus our attention on high alert before our rational brain has had a chance to act" (17). Even in circumstances when one has determined that there is no actual threat, the biochemical responses invoked continue to produce feelings of anxiety (Massey 2002). Further, anxiety is not merely an emotional response, but it invariably produces action on the part of the person experiencing it, typically expressed in terms of fight, flight, or freeze (Gray 2000; Perin 1988).

It is the classic responses of flight, flight and freeze that concern us here. Constance Perin (1988) insists that one can identify more or less anticipated patterns of behavior from groups who are subjected to ambiguity in social contexts. In this sense, Perin links uncertainty with the biologic responses of anxiety or fear so that what is physiologically the urge toward freeze, flight or fight "results in paralysis, avoidance, [or] attack" (1988, 9). This phenomenon is the focus of Perin's study of established suburban residents' responses to newcomers (who often share the same racial and class status of the established residents) moving into their neighborhoods. She notes that,

> "Intolerance for ambiguity" is not merely a personal trait. . . . When shared systems of meaning become unreliable, how to act becomes uncertain. With those meanings, we define our social expectations. Whatever is believed to dismantle meaning and thereby disable action evokes both curiosity and fear; whatever calls certainty into question comes under the heading of novelty, incongruity, confusion, sheer difference and discrepancy. On the one hand, humans socialize curiosity and arousal as learning and development and, on the other hand . . . humans socialize fear responses of freezing, flight and fighting as *social discrimination, stigmatization, and withdraw.* (Perin 1988, 9, emphasis added)

In this sense, the shared emotional response exemplified in social anxiety is an attributed cause of any variety of disconcerting actions, such as intolerance or hostility. I would also propose that social anxiety may produce collective behavior that appears progressive, and or inclusive, particularly in social contexts where there are compelling disincentives to act in a manner that suggests racist or discriminatory intent.

Under normal circumstances, Perin notes that human beings are most at ease and actually derive comfort from social settings that are familiar and commonplace, and will work to maintain distinct boundaries between what is known and unknown. Yet within the routine and familiarity of daily life, humans also desire novelty. As such, we seek new experiences that are stimulating and pleasurable, and as such will vary everyday routines. However, there are thresholds beyond which the novelty associated with pleasurable experiences and associated discovery or curiosity can lead to feelings of anxiety or fear. For example, while most would agree that meeting new people is often a pleasurable experience, the degree to which this occurrence is perceived as "pleasant" or "fun" depends on the context in which it takes place (Perin 1988).

Similarly, in her ethnographic analysis of the 1992 through 1993 riots in Bombay, Radhika Subramaniam (1999) argues that the construction of differential identity between "Muslim" and "Hindu" "acquires habitual forms and circulate as every day beliefs" which promote fear and as a consequence, collective action (97). These beliefs regarding the other coalesce in what she terms a "culture of suspicion," typified by "dread and unease that does not throb with overt hostility but is fleeting" (101). Although fleeting, these cumulative emotional responses form the basis of what would otherwise be implausible beliefs about the other, and ultimately encourages collective action, in this case, collective violence. Subramaniam argues that the culture of suspicion is grounded in experiences and encounters that are "located at the crossroads where memory and habit collide daily and where banal routine can momentarily render an experience *unfamiliar*" (101, emphasis added). Such unfamiliarity creates an emotional state that makes the implausible plausible, so that even unsubstantiated, fantastic rumors of social instability or violence will provoke fear, then group action. *"It is a fear* that comes of the knowledge that normalcy is utterly contingent, that the spaces that surround one, the streets that one inhabits, can become, suddenly and without warning . . . hostile" that precipitates collective behavior that is sometimes defensive, sometimes violent (Ghosh, quoted in Subramaniam 1999, 104, emphasis added).

I would also propose that organized social action prompted by the fear and anxiety of unfamiliar social contexts, such as a significant increase in Mexican settlement in a small Anglo community, can also incite action that is organized and peaceful, and ultimately has a political objective. Such action can reestablish the familiar comfort zone within the social context by securing one's position within the community hierarchy. This type of social action serves the dual purpose of affirming the identity of the social actors as a collective and also achieving a political objective through group solidarity. Commonly referred to as New Social Movements, these group actions offer a means of reestablishing control and asserting identity in what might otherwise be perceived as an uncontrollable situation.

Historically, social movements have offered people with common interests a way to join forces and work toward shared goals and assert political power. Academic examinations of social movement organizations generally group them into two broad categories. The first is termed either "old" or "ideology-based," where social action coalesced around shared grievances or perceptions of social injustice. Trade unions are the most salient example of these movements. Often members united around a common ideology, which determined the movement's course of action. Ideology-based social movements were common in the United States until the early 1960s when social scientists began to identify a perceptible shift in the basis of social movement membership. The second category, termed "New Social Movements" (NSM) were similarly directed toward improvement of the social milieu; but the basis of membership was no longer predicated on a shared ideological framework. Increasingly, social scientists noted that the factors driving these movements were based on less "objective" elements, such as "identity, status, humanism, and spirituality, and as such the link between mobilization and grievances became less compelling" (Laraña, Johnston, and Gusfield 1994, 8; Della Porta and Diani 1999; Johnston and Klandermans 1996). This is not to say that contemporary mobilization factors deny the fact that shared grievances continue to be a factor in group cohesion. However, in many cases, grievances are fundamentally linked to issues of identity. This is evident in movements where feminist, gender, or sexual issues are central. In these cases the grievances and political objectives of group members are inextricably centered on notions of identity for the activists. Still, the overwhelming emphasis in these groups and what hold them together are their shared experiences and common identity (Laraña, Johnston, and Gusfield 1994). Like their ideology-based counterparts, NSMs can be seen as a means of achieving or maintaining political power through collective action that can challenge or reaffirm the status quo.

When considering this in the context of new destination communities, anxiety and fear are precipitated by the unknown, and are a consequence of rapid community change. Unlike Mexican settlement sites in the gateway states of California, Texas, and Illinois, the new destination community is likely to be a place where Mexican settlement is a recent phenomenon, thus generally less prepared to adjust to the sometimes rapid changes afforded with large-scale settlement. In such cases, a large shift in the ethnic composition of a settlement area radically alters the local identity of the community, and as such produces a situation where fear of the changes taking place and the associated unknown consequences of these changes could lead locals to develop a systematic social action consistent with a New Social Movement to reassert their identity and by extension, political power. The founding of Bridging the Community in Kennett Square is an example of this process.

METHODOLOGY

I began my work in Kennett Square in the fall of 1995 and have continued to visit, interview, and participate in varied community activities through May 2002. I began with participant-observations in Kennett at a local social service provider for Mexican migrants. As my network of contacts expanded, I conducted in-depth interviews with some sixty Kennett residents, the majority of whom were Mexican settlers and the remainder with the English-speaking population. I also conducted three separate research trips to Textitlán, Guanajuato. One of these was a three-month stay to conduct survey research for the Mexican Migration Project at the University of Pennsylvania, where I completed one hundred and seventy household surveys on migration and work histories. This trip took place from December 1999 through March 2000, the time when most migrants and settlers return home for the holiday season. The other two research trips were shorter, to follow up on the previous work and to conduct in-depth interviews and participant observations.

As my work in the field expanded to focus on the larger community of Kennett Square, I also began research with Bridging the Community, attending public meetings and private planning sessions from December 1999 through June 2000. The data presented is derived from field observations of Bridging meetings, in-depth interviews with community members and Bridging leaders, as well as the collected documents that Bridging participants write and self-publish and distribute to one another. In addition, the Bridging leadership provided a detailed bibliography of books that have influenced the philosophical development of the movement. Within this extensive body of data, I have endeavored to present the organization and the philosophical perspective it brings to the community in a manner that replicates the ways that Bridging leaders present the organization to the Kennett Square community. In the account that follows I have been careful to distinguish between what the organizers say about their movement from my own critiques.

FROM YELLOW RIBBONS TO BRIDGING THE COMMUNITY: THE TRANSFORMATION OF COMMUNITY OPINION

While the passage of IRCA set in motion a number of factors that led to the social and cultural transformation of Kennett Square, change most keenly felt by residents centered on the fact that Mexicans were becoming more visible in the community. Local social services providers and advocates, who in the early 1990s began to take steps to challenge the status quo, only enhanced this visibility. This was most apparent with the development of the Alliance for Better Housing (ABH) in 1993. Affordable housing had long been scarce in Kennett Square. Sheila Druily, then the executive director of the local Latino social service organization, La Comunidad Hispana (LCH), Inc., founded a nonprofit organization, Alliance for Better Housing (ABH) to address housing needs for Mexican and other low-income residents in the area. Druily knew that there was a need for these services. Tenants in the Center Street Apartments and Scarlet Manor Apartments, both on the southern edge of town, had long complained that they were being overcharged for the run-down two bedroom units they were renting for $600 or more per month, but also recognized that they had few other options. Guillermo Rivera of ABH confirmed this, saying: "everyone knows that if a family moves out of one of those apartments, there are probably three more families waiting to move in" (Rivera interview, July 1, 1999).

In 1994 ABH, now under the leadership of executive director Howard Porter, initiated efforts to develop low-income housing in Kennett and the surrounding area, but his efforts met strong resistance. The first project that ABH initiated was the purchase and renovation of 420 and 422 Broad Street, an abandoned duplex situated three blocks from the center of town. The homes would be rented to two families, clients of LCH. When local residents got word of the planned renovation, several organized a flyer distribution and blanketed cars in town with notices that LCH-ABH had plans to house up to eight to twelve single men in each home. The borough council meeting in which Porter was scheduled to appear was flooded with local residents who had come to protest ABH's plans. The council passed a number of ordinances aimed to close down ABH. According to Porter, this included one ordinance that read, "the Borough will attempt to determine who is funding Howard Porter and to halt that funding" (Porter interview, August 9, 1999). Many of the ordinances passed that evening were illegal and immediately revoked at the following borough council meeting. The response of the citizenry was a visceral reaction to false information[6] (LCH-ABH had never intended to rent their units to single men), yet the incident is telling in that it indicates the level of anxiety related to Mexicans moving into town, and suggestive of the nativist sentiment at the time in Kennett Square.[7]

Housing, however, was not the only observable flash point in the community. From time to time, Mexican recreational or social spaces have emerged in the area and subsequently become sites of controversy. For example, the dinner theater The Big Apple, just outside of town, evolved into a Mexican dance club that regularly featured Mexican and Latin music and live bands. The club was a popular recreational spot for Mexican families for several years in the early 1990s. Although a profitable business, in November 1995 the owner decided to close the club, citing complaints from the English-speaking residents and ongoing disputes about zoning. Complaints centered on the club's alleged association with drug dealers, commercial sex workers, and brawls among patrons. The demise of The Big Apple came several months after a stabbing that resulted in a death near the club. Although the club owners (local Anglos) denied that the event took place on their property, according to a newpaper article by Clea Benson, they closed the club in response to the pressure of the township and local residents ("For Two Steppers, the Party's Over: A Popular Dance Spot Ceased Latin American Music Nights After Township Pressure," *The Philadelphia Inquirer*, November 28, 1995, p. W-1).

Similarly, as Mexican families have been reunited, many have begun to purchase homes in established neighborhoods, prompting small-scale protests and grumbling from the citizen residents who fear their new neighbors will devalue their properties. For example, in the spring of 1997, the residents of Stenning Hills, the majority of whom were Anglo European and U.S. citizens, began to notice that Mexican families were purchasing homes in their neighborhood. Most of these families were large by U.S. standards, typically with three to five children. Also common was the presence of other adults living in the home. Most often these were men who were members of the extended family, others were close family friends, and still others were acquaintances renting space from the homeowners.

With these adult males came additional vehicles, and in some cases homes had as many as five cars or trucks parked in driveways and on the street. It was the presence of these adult men and their cars that first prompted anxiety among Stenning Hills residents. Several citizen neighbors began complaining to the borough council that their Mexican neighbors were violating zoning ordinances, which prohibited more than two unrelated adults living in one household. Although acknowledged by the borough council, no action was taken in response. By midsummer, several residents began organizing a peaceful protest with their fellow citizen neighbors, as described by local reporter Mary

Hutchins, by attaching yellow ribbons to their mailboxes and front doors in what they described as a protest against overcrowding in their neighborhood ("Ribbons a Call for Unity Say Residents: Stenning Hills Reels Under Accusations that a Resident's Group's Symbolic Action Was Racist," *The Kennett Paper*, October 2–8, 1997, p. 1). The ribbons were nearly unnoticed until Hutchins's articles suggested that the yellow ribbon campaign was racially motivated (see Hutchins, "Ribbons," 1997; and Hutchins, "Yellow Ribbons Send Mixed Messages: Two Stenning Hills Residents Spoke Out on Charges that the Protest is Racist," *The Kennett Paper*, October 9–15, 1997, p. 1).[8] The citizen neighbors responded quickly and viscerally, clearly resenting the idea that their protest had been interpreted as an act of racism. "I was so upset when I saw the charges of racism," one anonymous organizer said. "Racism is not the issue. Overcrowding is" (Hutchins, "Ribbons," 1997, 1). To date, many of the organizers recall these events bitterly, believing their actions were wrongly interpreted (Corchado 1999; Joan Holliday, personal communication, June 3, 1999).

It is clear that as Mexican families began moving into Kennett Square in greater numbers, the population shift galvanized a reconsideration of the English-speaking population's understanding of what it meant to be a member of the community. What became an issue and what continues to be resonate as an issue in the Bridging movement was the identity of the community. In a letter to the editor of *The Kennett Paper*, Kenneth Roberts, then the Kennett Square Borough Council president, commenting on the state of Scarlet Manor apartments (an apartment occupied primarily by Mexicans) commented,

> It is a shame that billions of dollars are being spent for housing and an equal amount hasn't been spent on educating the people on how to live in *our culture* and lead full and productive lives. (Quoted in Hutchins, "Ambit Lal, Scarlet Manor Problems Won't Go Away," *The Kennett Paper*, June 9–15, 1994, p. 4, emphasis added)

Another concerned citizen, similarly distressed about the poorly maintained condition of Scarlet Manor Apartments and the changes he observed in Kennett said, "I was raised in Kennett Square, and this is *not* Kennett Square" (Patrick Donohoe, quoted in Hutchins 1994, 4, emphasis added).

As these statements indicate, it was clear that as Mexican families moved in, the English-speaking residents could no longer rely on the assumption that the family living next door would speak their language, share their aesthetic preferences, or hold the same cultural values. While in many cases the divide between Mexican and Anglos was not nearly as wide as that perceived, the presence of Mexican families also meant that neighborhood life was no longer familiar or predictable. Similarly, as the population of Mexican women and children increased, there was a concomitant fear that English-speakers were losing their advantage in the community, and as such these perceptions resulted in anxiety, which further led to protests against Mexican settlement (May 1950/1977; Perin 1988).

However, it would be a mistake to consider the English-speaking community as a unified collective opposed to Mexican settlement. Editorials and letters to the editor printed in *The Kennett Paper* reflect the opinions of a number of citizens who openly dissented to these actions, in some cases characterizing their neighbor's protests as racism, as local reporter Hutchins observed ("Yellow Ribbons," 1997). "When so much of life seems random and unpredictable," local resident Carol T. Ernst wrote in a letter to the editor,

> there are still some constants that we count on. Like stupidity and prejudice, for example. Kennett Square's borough council has once again demonstrated that bigotry is alive and well in Kennett Square. What else can one assume but massive brain damage and monumental small-mindedness from a group of people who would choose a boarded-up eyesore (420–422 South Broad St.) over a rehabbed dwelling that would cost the taxpayers nothing. ("Kennett Square's Soul is Dying," *The Kennett Paper*, February 16–22, 1995, p. A6)

These vocal opponents clearly influenced some local reactions and apparently have tempered much of the overt anti-Mexican sentiment once common in Kennett Square.

This has been evidenced in a number of venues. In addition to Mrs. Ernst's letter to the editor in *The Kennett Paper*, in an interview with the *Dallas Morning News*, Jane Perrone, one of the "yellow ribbon" organizers, expressed remorse about the campaign, but emphatically denied that her actions were in any way racist, insisting instead that she and her neighbors were opposing overcrowding and violations of the zoning laws. To demonstrate that she was repentant, when Mexican families began moving into their new houses in the Buena Vista Townhome complex, as Alfredo Corchado (1999) explained, Perrone and other members of the Four Seasons Garden Club presented the families with gardening equipment as a gesture of welcome and goodwill. Other Kennett residents have similarly spoken openly to me about the yellow ribbons and some of the incidents, with one of several explanations for the events. Some insist that racism was not involved with the protests and that the incidents were misinterpreted. Others suggest that while there may be members of the community who oppose Mexican settlement, those people are not representative of the larger community. Finally, others have suggested that while there were problems associated with Mexican settlement in the past, community sentiment has now changed.[9] The significance of these multiple interpretations of community opinion and action is that there has been a decided shift away from openly discouraging Mexican settlement. More important, this shift took place after insensitive actions toward Mexicans were publicly criticized by other members of the community and transmitted in the local press.[10]

Correspondingly, accusations of racism and general disapproval from within the community coincided with a shift away from protest and toward community development, from a focus on the "problems" associated with Mexican settlement and toward one emphasizing the "potential" benefits that these newcomers could contribute to community.[11] In this instance, the move away from Mexican settlement as a "problem" to a community asset appears to be, at least in part, a response to dissenting Kennett Square residents who were unhappy with the community action against settlement. In this sense, the discriminatory action was interrupted through the interplay of emotion and behavior. This association is expounded in Norbert Elias's (1939/1978) *The Civilizing Process.* Here Elias argues that there is a discernable relationship between human emotion and behavior in complex societies, which he argues can be employed as a means of social control. In this sense, the basis of social control rests in the relationship between emotion (the impetus to action) and behavior (the bodily expression of the emotional pull). Thus the maintenance of behavioral norms and complex cultural values is accomplished when the consequences of stepping outside those norms provokes feelings of embarrassment or shame. To avoid these emotions and the negative associations they inspire, individuals are motivated to restrain their behavior and maintain social norms to avoid the emotional consequences. In short, the avoidance of shame can be a powerful motivation to act appropriately (Elias 1939/1978). Roger Abrahams (1983) argues that gossip fulfills a similar purpose in a small West Indian community, claiming that the fear of being the subject of gossip is an effective means of maintaining certain social mores. To avoid the shaming associated with gossip, community members are cautious in their behavior, and community norms are held in check.

In the case of Kennett Square, those who continue to be unsatisfied with Mexican settlement are compelled to express displeasure in a manner that is more socially acceptable to the broader community and to possible outside observers (such as journalists and ethnographers).[12] In fact, in some cases this did indeed happen. For example, the key opponents to the ABH renovation of 420 and 422 Broad Street sought positions in the next borough council election, and were successful (Porter interview, August 9, 1999). Similarly, there were others who were not involved with the protests, but nevertheless wanted to actively direct the course of social relations in Kennett Square in a way they believed would be positive and socially inclusive. Many of them found their place in Bridging the Community, a new social movement intended to foster mutual aid and ethnic integration, but simultaneously minimized Mexican influence in the community.

BRIDGING THE COMMUNITY: A PLACE FOR EACH AND ALL

The racial and ethnic tension that centered on housing and recreation issues was a response to the growing visibility of the Mexican population some local residents saw as a threat to their community. The anxiety prompted by these changes in Kennett, along with the disorganized, often rancorous protests exemplified in the yellow ribbon campaign and the ABH protests, prompted Kennett activist and community health nurse Joan Holliday to initiate community-based conversations that she hoped would heal the growing divide in Kennett Square. In the spring of 1997, a group of Kennett area citizens, under Holliday's leadership, began meeting to discuss "the Kennett community." These meetings were designed to strategically unite a cross-section of the population, looking for a means to increase local participation in community events and service.

When Holliday called Kennett Square residents together in 1997 to reflect on their community, it was commonly acknowledged that the town was not known for communal participation, particularly across racial and class lines. This did not deter Holliday, a Chester County Health Department nurse, from trying to transform this reality. Holliday had begun working in Kennett Square in 1982, and since that time had been a discerning observer of the social relations in the area. She arranged these early meetings to initiate dialogue around the idea of community development, working specifically to create a process by which community members from all parts of the area could come together. Through her position in the county health department, Holliday was intimately familiar with the cultural and economic diversity in Kennett Square and surrounding communities. Writing of her observations, Holliday notes that during home health visits she was "struck by the lively spirit of the struggling poor as well as by the comfort of the other segments of the community. Although this community is small, the varied 'worlds' seem to know very little about each other" (Holliday 2001a, 11). The fact that Kennett residents from different racial, social, and economic groups were not interacting in any meaningful way seemed both unfortunate and unacceptable. She writes that the Kennett community,

> holds a diverse representation of life.... I sadly experience a lack of unity and crossing over of the different cultures, economic groups and age groups. In essence, I see that the community has no way to meet in the middle—where human spirit and potential become significant and differences drop away. (Holliday 2001a, 11)

Drawing on her extensive social network and a firm conviction that community participation could overcome the differences that isolated Kennett residents, these early conversations that Holliday initiated grew into Community Bridging Generations,[13] later renamed Bridging the Community. The concept was simple: to create a community-based forum that would facilitate volunteer efforts in Kennett Square, provide networking opportunities for local activists, and in turn integrate all members of the community.

The importance of the Bridging movement in the understanding of social life in Kennett is fundamental in that the timing of the initiation of the movement corresponds with eruption of communal anxiety and the associated fear that the English-speaking community was losing control of the town. In this sense, the Bridging goals of minimizing the differences associated with race, class, age, and ethnicity are fundamental to the long-term success of the movement because these perceptions of difference ignited the protests, which today most Kennett residents agree were divisive and counterproductive.[14] Part of the Bridging focus was a decided shift away from characterizing people or groups within the community as "problems" to one that emphasized the "potential" that these people can contribute to the local community. In this sense, those who might be stigmatized for any number of reasons (teenage mothers, for example) are reconceptualized as nevertheless having a vital role in the overall functioning of the community. In its most idealistic moments, Bridging endeavors to find a place for those residents who might not otherwise "fit in" to the ideal vision that many local residents have (and have had) of Kennett Square.

Although initially conceived as a modest community effort to minimize differences and increase volunteerism in Kennett, Bridging the Community has transformed into a structured social movement that is unique in its organization and implementation. Bridging is conceived entirely as a local effort. Its leadership refuses to establish its position in the community through a bureaucratic structure, and as such does not conform to the conventions of standard nonprofit or public service organizations. Rather, the activities of the group are based on a short list of guiding principles that endeavor to keep the movement perpetually "in process." For example, there are no by-laws, board of directors, or elected officers. The group has no official "home" or office space, but meets bimonthly in rotating locations around the Kennett area, such as the public library, churches, or community centers. In addition, Bridging the Community organizers refuse to accept funding from sources outside the community, insisting that outside money can be a direct path to outside influence. Participants are also exhorted to "come from the heart," and to avoid participating in activities and projects they do not have a strong commitment to seeing through. The group holds firm that Bridging projects should be by and for Kennett Square residents and supported locally through volunteer efforts or by local financial support. The organizers are quick to point out that this is not simply a community improvement club or social organization, but rather an association they see as a vehicle to regenerate and subsequently transform the community.

The intention of this "structure-free" framework is to illustrate, by example, that the organization is an outgrowth of the broader community (as opposed to the interests or desires of a small percentage) and that the organization is always evolving. Despite this goal, the meetings consistently follow a standard format and lack neither form nor organization. While there is a stated commitment to processes that are fluid and evolving, the objectives and superficial workings of the organization belie the fact that there is a distinct structure and leadership. For instance, although there are no elected officers or board of directors, Holliday has been the initiator and main overseer of the group, and her efforts ensure that the process moves forward.[15] She is responsible for making the logistical arrangements for each meeting, such as finding a meeting space, making announcements in local papers, and recruiting new participants to attend. Holliday also prepares a list of volunteer opportunities and contact information that is distributed at each meeting. There is a group of ten to fifteen people who regularly attends most meetings, but there is also a steady stream of newcomers who come to enlist volunteers for their projects or are there to expand their social networks. During the time of this study Bridging meetings were well attended, with some forty to sixty participants present at each meeting, with ethnic and racial composition consistent with the English-speaking population of the area, with approximately 80 percent to 85 percent of the participants white and 15 to 20 percent of the participants African American.

The community projects that Bridging participants have undertaken have been striking, considering the modest resources of the organization. These accomplishments include a mentoring program for elementary students, a tutoring and homework assistance program organized through local churches, and an after-school program for middle-school-age children. The organization has been praised for its youth outreach programs, all of which have attracted the attention of Kennett residents and neighboring communities. The chief of the Kennett police attributes the significant decrease in juvenile crime in the first three years of the organization's existence to Bridging youth programs, and organizers from the neighboring city of West Chester have considered replicating the Bridging process. In all, the English-speaking community considers Bridging the Community an unqualified success, and a reflection of the Bridging motto that Kennett Square is each day is a "better place to grow up and grow old" (Holliday interview, June 3, 1999).

PHILOSOPHICAL FOUNDATIONS: ENVISIONING KENNETT AS A UNIFIED PLACE

These community-based efforts are significant in that in a relatively short period, Bridging has developed a program of sustained community volunteerism. But at the same time, the group's successes are diminished by the fact that in nearly five years they have not effectively recruited Latinos into their organization. When asked about this, Holliday acknowledges that this is not so much a deficiency in the group itself, but a reflection that Bridging is a process. She believes that as the group demonstrates itself as a positive force for community change, more people will want to become involved, and in time this will encompass all members of the community, including Latinos. Moreover, Holliday also insists that advocates of Latino interests (such as social workers and health care professionals) are valid representatives of Mexican or Latino interests in the movement, although they themselves are not Mexican or Latino[16] (Holliday 2001b).

The reasons why Bridging is more appealing to the English-speaking community than to Latinos can be found by examining the foundational principles of the group, which are embedded in a structured philosophical process not readily apparent from the open community gatherings. The guiding principles of Bridging are developed and elaborated in regular meetings of a smaller core group of some eight to ten participants identified as the Each and All group.

Each and All meets bimonthly to conduct in-depth intellectual discussions regarding the fundamental principles of the Bridging organization. The membership of this group stands out from the standard Bridging members in a number of ways. For instance, participants in these meetings have to be identified as a member of the Kennett community, a stipulation that is interpreted broadly, as a number of key members, including Holliday and two of her co-organizers, do not live in Kennett Square. The other members of Each and All include a number of distinguished Kennett citizens, who live or work full-time in Kennett Square, and are thus considered community members. They include schoolteachers, a dentist, and the current executive director of LCH, a mushroom farm owner, housewives and employees of the Kennett Borough, among others. Notably, members of this group are all highly educated, Anglo, and either middle or upper class.[17]

The principles developed by the Each and All group are rooted in a shared belief system reminiscent of contemporary New Age and Judeo-Christian philosophies, although the group members uniformly dismiss associations with New Age thinking.[18] Central to this belief system is the notion that to be effective, group members have to be willing to set aside their personal agendas and come together to participate in "reflective dialogue," a process in which the group works toward a new model or vision of the community. The group insists that the basis of discovering the untapped community potential is found through a thoughtful consideration of Kennett as a unique place.

Drawing on local history and legend, the Each and All meetings emphasize that the land Kennett occupies has historically been home to peaceful inhabitants: the Algonquin Indians, the Society of Friends (Quakers), and now a larger, more diverse population that is nonetheless peace loving. Based on this history and reflective thought, the group determined that this history is an expression of the "socioecosystem" within which the community is located. In much the same manner that different ways of life evolve differently in distinct regions of the United States in relation to the local environment (such as by the sea or in the mountains), participants agree that the history of Kennett is intimately linked with their local environment. As such they believe that the history of the area is a result of the natural process of living in harmony with the land. The land itself is associated with identifiable spiritual and vital qualities that attract and maintain specific human activity that will correspond with the local socioecosystem.

The notion that the self, or by extension, the authentic nature of a community is revealed through an interaction of the place it inhabits is also the central idea in Gaston Bachelard's (1964/1969) *The Poetics of Space*. Here Bachelard argues that the life of the mind is given form through experiences in the places and spaces it inhabits so that place actually shapes and influences human memory, feeling, and thought. Accordingly, the mind and the world, which he distinguishes as distinct but intercommunicative inner and outer realms, are conceived of as entities transformed by one another. In this sense, the inner space (or mind) is externalized and outer space (or world) is incorporated within. Similarly, Jeffrey Edward Malpas (1999) argues that while most people would acknowledge that landscapes reflect human existence, technology, and culture, he sees this as a two-way relationship. Beyond the obvious ways that environment determines thought and actions, such as local topography influencing where one decides to build a home, Malpas insists that "there are other less straightforward and perhaps more pervasive ways in which our relation to landscape and environment is indeed one of our own *affectivity* as much as of our ability to *effect*" (1999, 1, emphasis in original). The significance of these perspectives regarding the relationship between humans and their environment is not so much that that they influence one another, which is fairly obvious, but rather how such notions work to naturalize specific types of human activity. There are a number of possible consequences of locating the philosophical foundations of a social movement within a theoretical frame that maintains human behavior *naturally* evolves as an interrelated experience with the environment. To take this position is to recognize the logical extension of specific human activity taking place within distinct physical surroundings, but it can also serve as a tool to legitimize group action.

In the case of the Each and All group, by reflecting on their community and local history, they have determined that the underlying authentic nature of Kennett Square is "peaceful progressive inclusion." By this, the group acknowledges that Kennett has evolved as place of perpetual immigration over the last two hundred years and has become a welcoming home to the area's newest arrivals, all of whom have eventually been accepted into the larger community. Although Kennett is viewed as a naturally peaceful place, participants insist that inclusion is a process, and one that often occurs slowly, but is always advancing. This philosophical foundation for the movement is the basis of the Each and All meetings as well as the Bridging the Community meetings.

Like many New Age groups, much of the visionary thinking that supports Bridging and Each and All is based on the shared understanding that, as community members, this small nonrepresentative group has the ability to visualize the whole community in its ideal form. In this respect, Each and All members believe that they can work together to develop a process that will move the community into an idealized future. Group participants are cautious to point out that in this context they are not limiting this process to their own human understanding or experience, although many of their reflections are grounded in personal experience and/or knowledge of local history. Instead, they are drawing upon spiritual knowledge that is accessed as they become "instruments of a higher power." While the higher power purposefully is not identified as any particular religious deity, there are strong associations with the Judeo-Christian god and the humanistic principles associated with this religious tradition. The higher power is acknowledged to be a universal source of life and truth. It is believed that when the group comes together in the correct state of mind (that is, putting aside personal agendas and seeking what is best for all) they will be able to make decisions about the community and its direction with the assurance that they have the Truth.

THE PROBLEMATICS OF "US": EMBODYING COMMUNITY PROCESS

The idea that Each and All members can come together and project their vision, inspired by a higher power, is central to many New Age groups. Paul Heelas's (1996) study of New Age spirituality writes that "self-spirituality," or viewing humans as a vehicle for determining divine Truth, is a hallmark of New Age thinking. However, while some groups like Each and All value reaching consensus for determining their guiding principles, there is also room for "epistemological individualists" who mediate the established authority of group experts by way of inner experience (Heelas 1996, 21). In this sense, the Each and All ideals evoke a recognized New Age principle in order to reconcile the individual versus group authority in the process of making group decisions. In a similar fashion, there is a strong affiliation in New Age movements to value "intuition," or an "inner voice" as a reliable source of information in the decision-making process of everyday life.

Each and All participants are following spiritual principles that are indeed consistent with other contemporary New Age movements. The fact that they trust in their ability to fairly and equitably envision the "whole" of the Kennett Square community without the participation of a substantial portion of that community is consistent with the (limited) visionary framework of the community they have created. While Bridging promotes the idea of unity in the community, communal inclusion is predicated on a marked degree of assimilation to the values and expectations of the English-speaking community. This is obvious in the meeting formats: all meetings are conducted in English, and emphasize positive New Age philosophies that strongly oppose anyone criticizing events or people in the community while encouraging the membership to be prepared to give something back to the community, through volunteer work or financial support. Bridging leaders presume that all community members have a similar ability to engage and participate in community events, and as a result the group attracts well-established residents who have the time and resources to dedicate themselves to community projects.

By limiting the development of the philosophical work of Each and All to designated "intellectuals" (regardless of where they live) it essentially guarantees that the majority of the Mexicans living in Kennett (who do not speak English) cannot participate in the Each and All process. However, when I raised this issue with Each and All members, they maintained that their membership has to be able to read the same books, write about the community, and engage in deep intellectual discussions that follow the philosophy of the organization. However, this reasoning does not explain why other area Latinos who might fit these criteria, such as Puerto Ricans and Mexicans who live in Kennett Square, speak English fluently, and have degrees in higher education, have not yet participated in this aspect of the organization.

So while the group has had some remarkable accomplishments and appears well intentioned on many fronts, it is also clear that the organization is a vehicle that perpetuates the cultural and political status quo. These groups provide a vehicle for the English-speaking community to "make a difference" through good works such as mentoring programs, after-school events and family activities—all of which reflect the values and priorities of the English-speaking population. This is not to suggest that Mexican families have distinct or opposing cultural or moral values. Rather, by not taking active steps to recruit Mexican or Latino participation, Bridging has developed into a social movement that effectively excludes anyone not already part of the historic "mainstream" of this community.

CONCLUSIONS

In Kennett Square the transformation from unorganized, insensitive protests to an organized social movement suggests a concerted attempt to restructure the community and find a place for all members, recent and long-term. The fact that the Bridging organizers have fallen short of this mark is not to say that the movement is ineffective, but suggests that there are many obstacles on the path toward integration, and even well-meaning social actors can have significant difficulty as they become accustomed to local change.

When examined as an NSM, the purpose of a movement like Bridging the Community can be viewed two-fold:[19] to allow a small group within the community to promote change and to define what it means to be a community member in Kennett Square. In this sense, Bridging offers an opportunity for community members to influence the community in a manner beyond their actual numbers. As a relatively small group of participants (even with the largest estimates of participation being around one hundred to one hundred and fifty members, this would represent only 2 percent to 3 percent of the town's population), the group has succeeded in making a substantial change in volunteer efforts and community services. Similarly, the group has also done much to promote their vision of local history and identity, and in doing so has linked volunteerism, community participation, and maintaining a general positive attitude as a natural by-product of the Kennett socioecosystem, and by extension, Kennett identity. Thus, by naturalizing an interdependent alliance between "the Kennett community" and the land through the concept of the socioecosystem, the group has in effect defined what it means to be a community member. In this context, those who do not come into line with the notion of "peaceful progressive inclusion" are simply not living in harmony with the true nature of the community. In addition, because the group is convinced of its ability to visualize the true potential of the community, those who fail to fall into line with this accepted vision of the community risk becoming perennial outcasts.

However, one could similarly interpret the activities of the Bridging movement as an effort to permanently stall Mexican integration. Looking closely at the movement's emphasis on community potential, it becomes obvious that while there is unlimited possibility for momentous achievement, this philosophy similarly enables the group's membership to interpret their movement as a success even if nothing is ever accomplished. The movement has helped regain, or perhaps has even exceeded, the community's reputation as a progressive place, and in the process has created a much more hospitable community for Mexican settlers. In the process, it has allowed its participants to maintain their central role in leading the community despite their diminishing numbers as Mexican families move into town. In this sense, the Bridging movement is well intentioned. But as it is currently conceptualized, Bridging the Community seems unlikely to further integration and mutual understanding in Kennett Square.

NOTES

1. The previous and current mayors are African American, although the 2000 Census indicates that only 10.3 percent of the town's population is African American.
2. Textitlán is a pseudonym derived from the Nautil meaning "place of textiles."
3. While October to March is the peak season, Dr. David Beyer of the Pennsylvania State University School of Agriculture indicated that growers have used air conditioning in mushroom houses since the late 1960s and early 1970s to extend the growing season year-round. Nevertheless, in the warmer months (particularly April through September), crop yields are much lower, as is the labor demand (Beyer, email correspondence, April 30, 2002).
4. I am using the terms "Hispanic" and "Latino" together to reflect the changes in the U.S. Census Bureau's terminology for this group of people. In 1990, the term "Hispanic" was used, but "Latino" was adopted for the 2000 census.
5. In comparison, the number of persons of Puerto Rican descent, the other major Latino ethnic group in Kennett, remained stable: in 1990 and 2000, 238 and 222 Puerto Ricans were counted respectively (U.S. Census Bureau 2002).
6. False information was distributed by unidentified members of the community who printed flyers and placed them on car windshields around the borough (Porter interview, August 9, 1999).
7. LCH-ABH were granted approval for the renovation project, and the duplex is currently rented to two Mexican families. However, Porter en-

countered similar resistance in his attempts to develop Buena Vista, a low-income townhouse community in Toughkenamon, a borough adjacent to Kennett. That community was completed in 1999, and is home to twenty-four families, of whom twenty-one are Mexican, two Puerto Rican, and one African American. Porter has also attempted to develop similar properties in neighboring West Grove, but was unable to obtain zoning approval. ABH is currently developing another low-income project within Kennett Square Borough, and has received permission to build on property in town.

8. Corchado's 1999 article in the "Reshaping of America" series in the *Dallas Morning News* places the timing of the yellow-ribbon campaign four years prior to the publication of his series, in 1995. However, the events in Stenning Hills are chronicled in *The Kennett Paper* in October 1997.

9. Please be aware that the purpose of this discussion is not to evaluate whether or to what degree individuals have had a sincere change of opinion regarding Mexican settlement. What is at issue here is the particular process that was engaged in this transformation, and how this process relates to embodied experiences.

10. Lois Maharg, a reporter for *The Kennett Paper* from 1998 to 2001, confirmed these observations. In an interview and electronic correspondence she stated that when she was able to report on the positive aspects of community the response of "people in the white community—at least the ones who spoke to me about my articles—liked seeing them in the paper because they showed evidence that Kennett was a diverse and inclusive community" (Maharg interview, January 20, 2002; Maharg, email correspondence, January 24, 2002).

11. This is the exact terminology employed by Bridging the Community leaders to explain their particular emphasis in community development. However, the focus of the movement is not solely focused on Mexican settlers. Teenage motherhood, for example, is no longer referred to as a community problem; rather teenage mothers are viewed as community members who still have the potential to make positive contributions to local life (Holliday 2001b).

12. I have no doubt that in my presence, many in the community were cautious about what they said about Mexicans and Mexican settlement.

13. The initial name of the organization is telling, as Bridging was not conceptualized as a multi-ethnic community integration movement. This fact may be indicative of the trajectory of the movement since.

14. There are still, of course, people in Kennett who are unhappy about Mexican settlement. However, most of the residents involved in the protest, particularly the yellow-ribbon campaign, now say they regret their participation.

15. Although Joan Holliday's contribution to Bridging the Community is central, she often distances herself from her vital role in the organization.

For example, after reading a draft of my description of the organization, Holliday telephoned me to encourage me to re-write this section to emphasize Bridging as a community effort and not dependent on any one person. At the same time, she shifted the format of the bimonthly meetings so that other community members now lead the forum. Despite these changes, during the eighteen months that I observed the group and its activities, it seems obvious that Holliday is the driving force behind the movement. It is understandable, given the principles of the movement, that her role as "leader" would be problematic since the movement is thought of as a "community" initiative rather than one driven by "individual" interests.

16. I shall return to this issue, and address it in detail, later in the chapter.
17. It should be noted that the composition of this group has changed over time. While members may come and go, the demographics of the group have remained consistent in the four years of the organization.
18. While the membership resists this characterization of their group, I will demonstrate exactly how this group articulates contemporary New Age thought and specific instances where their position differs from New Age thinking.
19. Actually, there are multiple ways to interpret a movement like Bridging the Community, here I am offering two possibilities that I believe are supported by my observations and the writings the movement's membership has produced (see Anderson 2000).

REFERENCES

Abrahams, Roger. 1983. *The Man-of-Words in the West Indies. Performance and the Emergence of Creole Culture.* Baltimore: Johns Hopkins University Press.

Anderson, Terry. 2000. "From Migrant to Immigrant." *Path of Potential: A Bimonthly Reader of the Dignity Movement,* Paper 2, 1(November/December): 1.

Andreas, Peter, and Timothy Snyder, eds. 2000. *The Wall Around the West: State Borders and Immigration Controls in North America and Europe.* Oxford and Lanham, Md.: Rowman and Littlefield.

Bachelard, Gaston. 1964/1969. *The Poetics of Space.* Translated by Maria Jolas. Boston: Beacon Press.

Bustos, Sergio. 1994. "Mushroom Workers Strike in Pennsylvania." *The Progressive* 58: 14.

Della Porta, Donatella, and Mario Diani. 1999. *Social Movements: An Introduction.* Oxford and Malden, Mass.: Blackwell Publishers.

Durand, Jorge, Douglas S. Massey, and Fernando Charvet. 2000. "The Changing Geography of Mexican Immigration to the United States: 1910–1996." *Social Science Quarterly* 81(1): 1–15.

Durand, Jorge, Douglas S. Massey, and Emilio A. Parrado. 1999. "The New

Era in Mexican Migration to the United States." *The Journal of American History* 86(2): 518–36.

Elias, Norbert. 1939/1978. *The Civilizing Process.* Translated by Edmund Jephcott. Oxford: Blackwell Publishers.

Gray, Jeffrey Alan. 2000. *The Neuropsychology of Anxiety: An Enquiry into the Functions of the Septo-hippocampal System.* New York: Oxford University Press.

Heelas, Paul. 1996. *The New Age Movement: Celebrating the Self and the Sacralization of Modernity.* Oxford and Cambridge, Mass.: Blackwell Publishers.

Holliday, Joan. 2001a. "Leading a Heart-Felt Community Process Through Principles." *Path of Potential: A Bimonthly Reader of the Dignity Movement* 1(2): 11–15.

———. 2001b. *Presentation for Folklore 290: Ethnicity and Migration.* Philadelphia: University of Pennsylvania (February 17, 2001).

Johnston, Hank, and Bert Klandermans, eds. 1996. *Social Movements and Culture.* Minneapolis: University of Minnesota Press.

Kashatus, William C. 2002. *Just over the Line: Chester County and the Underground Railroad.* State College, Penn.: Pennsylvania State University Press.

Laraña, Enrique, Hank Johnston and Joseph R. Gusfield, eds. 1994. *New Social Movements: From Ideology to Identity.* Philadelphia: Temple University Press.

Malpas, Jeffrey Edward. 1999. *Place and Experience: A Philosophical Topography.* Cambridge, U.K.: Cambridge University Press.

Massey, Douglas S. 2002. "A Brief History of Human Society: The Origin and Role of Emotion in Social Life." *American Sociological Review* 67(1): 1–29.

Massey, Douglas S., and Nancy Denton. 1993. *American Apartheid: Segregation and the Making of the Underclass.* Cambridge, Mass.: Harvard University Press.

May, Rollo. 1950/1977. *The Meaning of Anxiety.* New York: Norton.

Melucci, Alberto. 1996. *Challenging Codes: Collective Action in the Information Age.* Cambridge and New York: Cambridge University Press.

Pennsylvania Department of Education. 1980–2000. *Pennsylvania Department of Education Statistics.* Harrisburg: Pennsylvania Department of Education. Available at http://www.pde.state.pa.us/k12statistics/site/default.asp (accessed October 26, 2004).

———. 2000–2001. *Pennsylvania Department of Education Statistics.* Harrisburg: Pennsylvania Department of Education. Available at: http://www.pde.state. pa.us/k12statistics/site/default.asp (accessed November 3, 2004).

Perin, Constance. 1988. *Belonging in America: Reading Between the Lines.* New York: St. Martin's Press.

Shutika, Debra Lattanzi. 2000. Ethnosurvey data collection of the Mexican Migration Project. Philadelphia: Population Studies Center, University of Pennsylvania.

Smelser, Neil J. 1962. *Theory of Collective Behavior.* New York: Free Press.

Spielberger, Charles D. 1966. "Theory and Research on Anxiety." In *Anxiety and Behavior*, edited by Charles D. Spielberger. New York and London: Academic Press.

―――. 1972. "Anxiety as an Emotional State." In *Anxiety: Current Trends in Theory and Research*, edited by Charles D. Spielberger. New York and London: Academic Press.

Subramaniam, Radhika. 1999. "Culture of Suspicion: Riots and Rumor, Bombay, 1992–1993." *Transforming Anthropology* 8(1 and 2): 97–110.

Taylor, Frances Cloud. 1976/1998. *The Trackless Trail: The Story of the Underground Railroad in Kennett Square, Chester County, Pennsylvania, and the Surrounding Community*. Kennett Square, Penn.: Graphics Standard Printing.

―――. 1995/1999. *The Trackless Trail Leads On: An Exploration of Conductors and Their Stations*. Kennett Square, Penn.: Graphics Standard Printing.

U.S. Census Bureau. 2000. *American FactFinder*. Available at: http://www.census.gov (accessed November 3, 2004).

―――. 2002. *American FactFinder*. Available at: http://www.census.gov (accessed November 3, 2004).

CHAPTER 6

✕

"LATINOS HAVE REVITALIZED OUR COMMUNITY": MEXICAN MIGRATION AND ANGLO RESPONSES IN MARSHALLTOWN, IOWA

MARK A. GREY AND ANNE C. WOODRICK

Marshalltown, Iowa, is a typical new destination community for Mexican migrants in the United States. This midwestern community of twenty-six thousand has been fundamentally transformed and revitalized by rapid growth in its Mexican population over the last ten years. In 1990, there were only 248 people of Hispanic origin in Marshalltown, or 0.9 percent of the total population. In 2000, there were 3,265 or 12.6 percent of total population. The 2000 census figure is probably low because of the reluctance of many undocumented immigrants to complete U.S. census forms. Many Latinos and Anglo community leaders believe the actual number of Mexican and other Latinos in Marshalltown is between four thousand and forty-five hundred.

Rapid growth in Marshalltown's Mexican population mirrors that of Iowa and many Iowa communities. The state experienced 153 percent growth in its Hispanic and Latino population between 1990 and 2000. Numbering 82,473 in 2000, Hispanics and Latinos are now Iowa's largest minority population, and outnumber African Americans by more than 20,000. Seven Iowa counties experienced ten-fold increases in their Hispanic and Latino populations in the 1990s, including Marshall County, of which Marshalltown is the county seat. In 1990, Marshall County had 292 Hispanic residents, of whom 201 (69 percent) were from Mexico. In 2000, there were 3,523 Hispanics in Marshall County, of whom 3,115 (88 percent) were from Mexico.

Marshalltown makes an interesting case study for understanding the transformation of rural communities with rapid influxes of Latinos.

133

First, the experience of Marshalltown parallels that of many U.S. communities because the main draw for Latinos has been the availability of jobs in a large meatpacking plant. Although most migrants arrived to take jobs in this plant, newcomers have slowly but surely begun working in other sectors of the local economy. They also opened their own businesses, bought homes in growing numbers and their children have bolstered sagging school enrollments. Second, most of the newcomers hail from the same village in Mexico. This gives us an opportunity to present what we call the "unofficial sister city" relationship between a single sending community in Mexico and a single receiving community in the United States. Third, the interesting and important aspect of the Marshalltown experience is the sustained and enthusiastic efforts of Anglo leaders to welcome Latinos and successfully bring the community through an often difficult period of demographic, social and cultural transition. In many respects, Anglo leaders in Marshalltown serve as models for their colleagues in other Iowa and midwestern communities that are dealing with similar influxes of Latino migrants.

METHODS AND ACTIVISM

The data used in this chapter came from our joint and separate projects in Marshalltown. Mark Grey started working in Marshalltown in 1996. Anne Woodrick started in 1997. Grey conducted ethnographic research in Marshalltown's meatpacking plant from 1997 to 1999. Research in the community has focused on changing relations between Mexican newcomers and established resident Anglos (Grey 2000; 2001). This research has involved interviews and participant observation. In addition, Grey has performed a number of consulting activities with Marshalltown schools (Grey 1997a; 1997b), community leaders, packing plant managers, and the Marshalltown Diversity Committee.

Together we have been particularly active in working with Anglo community leaders to help them understand and address the new Latino population. This assistance not only took the form of sharing our research findings but also involved actively taking these leaders through a personal discovery process concerning how they as leaders and individuals can try and make the New Marshalltown "work." We have done so primarily by taking Anglo leaders to Villachuato, the Mexican village we call Marshalltown's "Unofficial Sister City" (Grey and Woodrick 2002). We share some of the results of these journeys below.

Our work in Marshalltown has not simply been based on the traditional academic research model. We did not simply go into Marshalltown, collect our data, publish our findings, and move on. Quite the contrary. We have maintained close working relationships with many community leaders, established resident Anglos, and Latino newcomers and plan to continue to do so. This continued relationship also fits well with our work in the New Iowans Program. Our task in the New Iowans Program is to work with communities and employers to make immigration in Iowa "work." That is, to assist communities and employers as they struggle with learning to accommodate immigrant newcomers in their communities and workplaces. Rapid influxes of Mexicans and other immigrant newcomers in small-town Iowa have been difficult for established residents and newcomers alike. In Marshalltown, we have tried to help both groups understand each others' background and perspective. We have also sought ways to bring members of both populations together. Thus our journeys to Villachuato, which we plan to continue.

Our activism in Marshalltown and other Iowa communities also reflects the reality that even though influxes of Latinos have occurred relatively quickly, it will take years for the affected communities to work through the process of mutual accommodation (Grey 2000; Woodrick and Grey 2002). It will also take patience on the part of Anglos and Latinos. However, we are convinced—as are many Marshalltown leaders—that successfully accommodating the newcomers is essential for the community's long-term economic and social health.

WHAT BRINGS MEXICANS TO MARSHALLTOWN?

Marshalltown is home to the third largest pork-packing plant in the world. The plant is owned and operated by Swift and Company. The Marshalltown Swift plant is capable of slaughtering and processing up to sixteen thousand hogs each day and approximately 3.6 million hogs each year. The plant employs about twenty-one hundred people, of whom approximately eighteen hundred are production workers who work "on the line" slaughtering, gutting, and cutting up hog carcasses. This elaborate and labor-intensive process is often called "disassembly" by the packing industry. The Marshalltown plant often slaughters and disassembles one thousand hogs each hour. Typical annual output is one hundred million pounds of pork products with annual sales of $800 million. The Swift plant also provides Marshalltown's largest payroll. In 1998, the plant paid out $51 million (Grey and Woodrick 2002).

The Swift plant began hiring Mexicans in early 1989 (Grey and Woodrick 2002). At first the number of Latino workers remained small, but over the course of eight years Mexicans and other Latinos became the predominant population in the plant. In the early part of 1997, which was a pivotal year, the percentage of Anglo production workers (48 percent) was slightly more than that of Latino workers (45 percent). By May 1997, the numbers were the same, with the number of Latino workers increasing and Anglo workers decreasing. Since that time, Latinos have been the largest group in the workforce. Indeed, by the end of 1998, Anglos made up only 38 percent and Latinos 55.5 percent. Smaller groups included Southeast Asians, African Americans, and Sudanese refugees. In 2002 Latinos made up approximately 75 percent of the Swift production workforce.

As the Marshalltown plant indicates, Mexicans and other immigrants and refugees have become critical to the midwestern meatpacking industry. Hiring Mexicans solves a number of problems for packing plants. First, hiring outsiders compensates for the loss of local Anglo working-age populations. During the 1980s, Iowa suffered a tremendous loss of population. This was particularly the case in rural Iowa. In addition to out-migration, rural Iowa has also experienced dramatic declines in birth rates and rapid aging of the working population. Between 1990 and 2003, the state's average birthrate dropped from 14.2 live births per one thousand to 13.1. Birthrates as low as 6.9 per one thousand were recorded in some rural counties in 2000. The state's birthrate fell even further in 2002, to 12.8 live births per one thousand.

Iowa's Anglo population is aging rapidly. In 2000, for example, 20 percent were age 60 or older. The median age in Marshalltown rose steadily between 1980 and 2000—was 31.1 in 1980, 36.8 in 1990, and 38.4 in 2000. In 2000, 21.7 percent of the town's population was age 60 or older and represented 28.8 percent of the adult population (Grey et al. 2001).

By contrast, the Mexican population is significantly younger. In Iowa, only 4 percent of Latinos in 2000 were age 60 or older. The median age among nonwhite Hispanics in 2000 was 22.6. The median age for Anglos was 37.9. Hiring Mexicans made up for the shrinking Anglo workforce. Population loss in rural areas has continued and in many communities like Marshalltown, the 2000 census would have shown further population decline if it were not for the in-migration of Mexicans.

Throughout most of the 1990s, packing plants like Swift also faced trying to hire sufficient numbers of workers during a thriving economy. Low unemployment rates meant that few applicants were available from an already shrinking local workforce. The Marshalltown average unemployment rate was 2.7 percent, well below the U.S. average of 4.0 percent. In 2000, applicant-to-opening ratios averaged 0.75:1 for all job categories in the Marshalltown office of Iowa Workforce Development,[1] meaning that on average there were fewer than one applicant for each job opening. Applicant to opening ratios in agriculture averaged 0.51:1 and in processing the average ratio was 0.78:1 in 2000. A 1998 survey of Marshalltown employers found that finding qualified employees was "almost impossible" (Grey et al. 2001).

Wages in the packing industry and Swift plant rose during the 1990s and early 2000s. In 1997, the average hourly wage rose from about $7.50 to $9.55. In 2002, it was about $10.50. However, in addition to a shrinking local workforce and low unemployment rates, meatpacking jobs carry a stigma that discourages many Anglo and other applicants (Fink 1998; Grey 1999). The work is distasteful and physically demanding.[2] Because of the highly repetitive nature of the work, and the presence of knives, slippery floors, and dangerous machines, meatpacking has the highest injury rates of any industry in the United States. The difficult nature of the job combines with high injury rates to create a tremendous stigma about the work. This stigma prevents many local potential workers from even applying.

Hiring Mexicans also helps packing plants overcome high worker turnover rates of typically more than 80 percent per year. Even higher rates of more than 100 percent per year have been noted (Kay 1997). Turnover reflects the difficult nature of the work and relatively low pay as well as high injury rates. Workers often quit or are forced out of the plant because of injuries. High turnover also benefits the plant by keeping aggregate wage and benefit costs low, lowering the number of workers eligible for health benefits after six months on the job, and replacing injured and exhausted workers on a continuing basis. Unstable workers are less likely to become active members of unions (Stull and Broadway 1995; Grey 1997c). Although hiring Mexican migrants helps to maintain worker rolls despite large turnover, newcomers are not passive victims. There is research that indicates Mexicans have also learned how to use turnover to their advantage by tapping income and wealth in the United States and using it to its fullest potential in home communities. A fact that was often underappreciated by Anglo bosses (Grey 1999).

Packing plants and other employers in Iowa also find Latino workers attractive because of their relatively marginal status in the job market. For the most part, Mexican migrants come to towns like Marshalltown and take jobs like meatpacking because they are unqualified to take jobs in other sectors of the economy. This fact is certainly not lost on the packing plants. Their recognition and recruitment of immigrant and refugee workers because of their limited opportunities in the job market is well documented (see Stull, Broadway, and Griffith 1995).

MARSHALLTOWN AS A TRANSNATIONAL COMMUNITY

Recruiting Latino migrants also means that the Swift plant is taking full advantage of its place in the global labor market. The majority of Latino workers and their families in Marshalltown migrated from central Mexico. In some cases they migrated directly. Others came via other communities in the United States. Depending on these workers meant that the Swift plant successfully tapped into a labor pool well beyond local and even the national markets. Of course, there is nothing new about the establishment of migrant worker streams from rural Mexico to the United States. However, the important experience for Marshalltown was that when Swift tapped into Mexican labor sources, and those workers began to arrive, Marshalltown became a transnational or postnational community (Hackenberg and Alvarez 2001). Through the years, not only has the local workforce taken on characteristics of the new migrants, so have Marshalltown institutions. Certainly the primary sending community in Mexico has taken on characteristics of Marshalltown, but Marshalltown looks more and more like Mexico. Indeed, these communities have developed a very deep interdependence, regardless of the geopolitical border that separates them (Grey and Woodrick 2002).

Along with dramatic growth in the Mexican population, Marshalltown has experienced rapid growth in the number of businesses that are owned by or service Latino newcomers. In 2001, the Marshalltown Chamber of Commerce counted thirteen different Latino-owned businesses. These included tiendas, restaurants, auto repair shops, clothing stores, bars, tortillerias, laundromats, and bakeries. With names like La Michoacana and Tacos de Jalisco, they certainly reveal the origins of their owners and customers. On the same block, one can now buy Mexican tacos that bear little resemblance to the Taco Bell variety and certainly contrast with such traditional Iowa fare as pork tenderloins and Maid Rites, ground beef on a hamburger bun. Many operations like Latino Auto Repair started out providing service to Latino customers, but through the years their Anglo customer base expanded as well, often leading to expansions or movement to larger locations. Latino entrepreneurs also offer construction and roofing services. To the consternation of many established Anglo companies, Latino roofing firms often provide services at substantially lower prices.

The Mexican presence has also had a tremendous impact on school enrollments. In the 1991 to 1992 school year, there were 75 students classified as limited English proficient (LEP) in Marshalltown public schools, or 1.6 percent of the total enrollment. Of the LEP students, 55 (73 percent) spoke Spanish as their first or "home" language. In the 1995 to 1996 school year, the LEP count grew to 249, or 5.1 percent of total enrollment. Spanish speakers numbered 229, or 92 percent of LEP students. In the 2001 to 2002 school year, 782 students were classified as LEP, or 16 percent of district enrollments. Spanish was the primary language of 756 (97 percent) of these students.

The dramatic growth in the Spanish-speaking student population presented opportunities and challenges to school administrators. Influxes of Latino students helped Marshalltown schools buck the trend of declining enrollments experienced in most rural Iowa school districts. Indeed, the Marshalltown school district was one of the only 30 percent of Iowa districts that experienced net increases in enrollments in the 2001 to 2002 school year. School administrators openly acknowledge that if it were not for immigrant students, two of Marshalltown's six elementary schools would have closed.

There have been challenges. English as a second language (ESL) instruction began in the 1970s and was aimed toward small influxes of Southeast Asian refugees. However, with the arrival of more Latino students in the 1990s, ESL and related offerings mounted rapidly. At Woodbury Elementary, the school located near the Swift plant, Latino enrollments grew particularly quickly. In 1990, the majority of students were Anglo. By 1996, 57 percent of students were minorities, mostly Hispanics. In the 2001 to 2002 school year, the percentage of minority students at Woodbury grew to 69 percent.

Marshalltown schools also experience high enrollment turnover. High worker turnover in packing plants manifests itself in a variety of ways in the larger community. Typically, employee turnover contributes to high rates of transience, rising crime rates, more homelessness, and inadequate housing. Turnover is also reflected in school enrollments. As parents move into and out of the community, their children often move with them. This is certainly the case in Marshalltown, particularly in the two elementary schools with high enrollments of Mexicans and others with parents who work in the packing plant. In an analysis of the 1995 to 1996 enrollment data in the two schools associated with the packing plant, these schools had 33 percent of the district's elementary enrollments and 54 percent of parents who worked in the Swift plant, but they had 48 percent of the elementary students who transferred into or out of the district during that school year. At Woodbury School alone, 29 percent of students moved into or out of the district in the 1995 to 1996 school year. An analysis of kindergarten cohorts also showed the effects of enrollment turnover. For the kindergarten cohort of 1990 at Woodbury school, the average annual loss of this cohort by 1996 was 18 percent (Grey 1997a).

Combining rapid growth in enrollments of LEP students and high enrollment turnover poses tremendous challenges to teachers and administrators. They do so because they challenge the underlying assumptions of schooling. There is no continuity in student cohorts or the learning experience and traditional ways to determine student progress become meaningless. This challenge to teachers is compounded by the limited or poor schooling newcomers often received in Mexico. In addition to not speaking or reading English well, and the high degree of mobility, many Latino students come inadequately prepared for age- and grade-appropriate academics even in their primary language.

ANGLO REACTIONS

Anglo reactions to the Mexican influx have been mixed. In our work in communities, we have discovered what we call the "20-60-20 rule." In any rural Iowa community, about 20 percent of the people actively welcome immigrant newcomers or they are at least open to making it work. At the other end of that spectrum, we usually run into about 20 percent of the population that is dead set against immigrant influxes. Motivated by any number of concerns or biases, they have made up their minds that newcomers are bad for their community and nothing will change their perspective. The large 60 percent of the population is not sure about newcomers. They are not actively welcoming immigrants, but they are also not actively working against their arrival either. This portion of the population is ambivalent and often fearful of change. Most take a wait-and-see attitude. Many are open to learning more.

The ambivalence most Iowans feel about immigration is reflected in state-wide polls. A 2000 poll in the *Des Moines Register* reported on by Jonathan Roos and John McCormick showed that 59 percent of Iowans believed immigrants "do jobs that might otherwise go unfilled." Another 32 percent believed immigrants "take jobs from Americans." However, 58 percent disapproved of any state policy to encourage immigration to the state ("Majority: Don't Foster Immigration," September 3,

2000, p. 1A). Similar findings were found in another survey. When asked how Iowa should improve and grow its future workforce, encouraging recruitment of workers from other countries was ranked last of five options. Yet, this option still received support from 60.9 percent of respondents. In the same survey, a full 76 percent of Iowans said that immigrants "take jobs other Iowans don't want." In terms of how they perceived the impact of immigrants on the quality of life in communities, 68.6 percent said immigration "improves quality of life" (Lutz et al. 2001).

The 20-60-20 rule certainly applies to Marshalltown. The 20 percent that try to make immigration work in Marshalltown are already quite active as we will discuss below. The anti-immigration 20 percent are often just as active. Their voice is usually heard in two outlets: editorials and letters in the Marshalltown *Times-Republican* newspaper and the weekly publication *MarshallTimes*, or by calling in questions for a column in the newspaper called "After the Beep." "After the Beep" provides opportunities for people to make comments, ask questions, or even make accusations anonymously. Many of the anonymous comments and questions are about the Mexican influx.

Three issues related to the Latino influx sparked the most interest in the local press: English, illegal immigration, and drugs. Language is always a hot topic in rural Iowa communities. Many Anglos complained bitterly and openly about the lack of spoken English among Mexican newcomers. Their ancestors had to learn English so why don't the Latinos? America is a melting pot, so why aren't the Mexicans melting? Of course, these kinds of arguments are spurious and take a rather narrow and ahistorical view. They leave out, of course, the amount of time it took previous generations of immigrants to learn and use English in their daily lives. That learning English was a priority for most Mexicans, but doing so came after work and taking care of their families. These arguments also conveniently left out information about growing attendance at adult ESL classes throughout the community.

Nonetheless, the backlash against Mexicans and their language came to a head in 2000. In that year, the Veterans of Foreign Wars chapter submitted a petition to the Marshalltown County Supervisors to make English the county's official language. The commissioners did so, stating to do otherwise would show disrespect for the veterans. However, one bitter irony was that many veterans survived World War II because of the ability of Navajo and other American Indian "code talkers" to speak languages other than English. Despite the fact that English was made the official language of Marshall County, the leadership of

Marshalltown objected, noting that such a move sent a message to new-comers that they were unwelcome. The Marshalltown city council passed their own resolution that English may have been made the official language of Marshall County, but not Marshalltown.

Undocumented or "illegal" immigration has also been a hot topic in Marshalltown and other rural Iowa communities. The presence of un-documented workers and their families was rumored for years. But their presence was confirmed by a 1996 Immigration and Naturalization "raid" on the Swift plant in which 148 Latinos were arrested and de-ported. The raid confirmed what many Marshalltown residents already suspected: the Swift plant hired illegal workers. The INS raid contrib-uted to a conspiracy theory among many working-class residents that hiring undocumented workers was part of a larger scheme to undermine unions and wages. This theory remains popular among many union leaders in Marshalltown today.

In addition to issues of labor and wages, "illegal aliens" were crimi-nals because they were breaking the law by simply being in the country. In the newspapers, the arguments became deeply polarized. "Liberals," "leftists" and the "politically correct crowd" argued the anti-immigra-tion sentiment was "racist" and "intolerant." "Conservatives" and "the mean spirited" on the other hand, insisted that their concerns about "diversity," illegal immigration, and making English the official lan-guage, were not a matter of bias or discrimination, but "lawlessness." Immigrant advocates were accused of naïveté and creating—rather than healing—division in the community, with some arguing, "we don't need diversity, we need unity" (Conte 2002, 32).

One issue about which immigration advocates were accused of being "naïve" concerned the connection between the Mexican influx and drugs. Crime rates began to rise in the early 1990s and many established resi-dents blamed the Latinos. Central to the rising crime rates were grow-ing problems with illegal drugs. Marshalltown became a major distribu-tion center for methamphetamine, a distinction that was highlighted in *U.S. News and World Report* in 1998 (McGraw 1998). A similar exposé was published by reporter Jeff Zeleny in the *Des Moines Register* ("Meth's Long Road to Iowa: Drug is Funneled via I-80 Pipeline," February 27, 1998, pp. 1A, 4A). Both articles exposed the transportation of metham-phetamine from Mexico to Marshalltown through California. The *U.S. News* article played on stereotypes about small-town Iowa versus the international drug trade. The same author "implied that the Mexicans, fearing that sooner or later they will be deported anyway, decided to make quick cash by 'selling meth to crazy gringo tweakers.' He claimed that although a few of the Mexicans were outright agents of Mexican drug gangs, most who ended up selling drugs had simply fallen into the job because 'it is easier to sell meth than to cut up hogs for $7 an hour'" (Grey 2000, 97; McGraw 1998, 34).

In an essay entitled "How Far Have We Fallen in Marshalltown?" (*Marshalltown Times-Republican*, March 26, 1998, n.p.) anti-immigration author Biff Dysart pondered "a community that allows a 'diversity' committee to roll out the red carpet to those who run what *U.S. News and World Report* calls a 'methamphetamine pipeline from Mexico to Marshalltown.'" "Previous migrations of transplants, such as the infamous tramps and yeggs of a century ago and the more familiar gypsies and 'bums' of the Great Depression," he observed, "were not accepted in Marshalltown back then any more than the Mexican drug runners are accepted today" ("No Racism or Intolerance Here," *Marshalltown Times-Republican*, April 5, 1998, n.p.). Such rhetoric fed stereotyped perceptions of a homogeneous, monolithic and crime-ridden Latino community. However, there were counter attacks. "Don't lump Hispanics into One Group," wrote one citizen: "Yes, there are Hispanics involved in bad things. But that is true among the Anglo community too."

Despite the condemnation of publications that linked Latinos with drug trafficking, stereotypes about Marshalltown and other meatpacking communities often prevailed and they became part of widespread efforts against the location of a new meatpacking plant in Iowa in 2000 and 2001. Excel, Inc., in cooperation with the Iowa Cattlemen's Association, proposed building a new $100-million beef-packing plant in central Iowa that would employ one thousand. A few small communities and Des Moines were proposed as possible sites. However, in community after community, opposition to the plant mounted. In some cases, the expressed concern was the potential environmental impact. The trade magazine *Meat & Poultry* noted that opposition to the packing plant often came from residents who expressed concerns about environmental and traffic issues. However, a representative of the Iowa Department of Economic Development said that vocal opponents, who really harbored an "unspoken but very real fear—significant immigrant relocation," often used these issues as "smokescreens" (Crew 2001, 25–26).

Citizens in Iowa Falls did not want their town to become another Marshalltown and experience an influx of Latino newcomers. To those opposing the Excel plant in Iowa Falls, as reporter Lisa Smith wrote on the subject, it was a matter of "quality of life" ("Protestors Want to Send Cattle Plant Packing," *Waterloo-Cedar Falls Courier*, April 23, 2000, p. C2). In that community, signs appeared on front yards showing crime and other statistics—including tuberculosis statistics—from meatpacking towns in Iowa. In protests against city leaders and their efforts to recruit the plant, Smith continued, activists carried signs that read "With Excel we all lose."

The Mexican influx in Marshalltown has not always been met negatively. Nor has it always spurred stereotypes about declines in the quality of rural life. As we will discuss in detail below, Marshalltown has greatly benefited from the positive and proactive response of many Anglo community leaders who embrace the Latino influx as key to the community's long-term social and economic health. Before we describe their efforts, more background on the Latino population in Marshalltown will be helpful.

UNOFFICIAL SISTER CITIES

Most Latinos in Marshalltown come from Mexico. The 2000 census found smaller groups from Honduras, El Salvador, Cuba, Puerto Rico, and other countries. A survey of Latino members of St. Mary's Catholic Church indicated Guatemala and Panama as well. In the church survey, Mexicans came from eighteen different states and the Federal District. In 2001, approximately three thousand Latino residents came from the same rancho in Michoacán, Mexico—Villachuato. The first known Villachuaton to arrive in Marshalltown was hired at the Swift plant in 1989. He was part of an initially small group of Latinos in the plant that eventually grew over the 1990s. There were already thousands of migrants from Villachuato living the United States. In the 1970s and 1980s, most of them lived in Merced, California. A smaller group lived in Yakima, Washington. Villachuatons moved to both communities as migrant farm workers and many settled. Small groups of Villachuatons continue to live in both towns. However, with the rising cost of living in California, and the attraction of packing jobs in the Midwest, many Villachuatons migrated to Marshalltown, Grand Island, Nebraska, Lexington, Nebraska, and Postville, Iowa. The largest group moved to Marshalltown.

After the initial group of Villachuatons established a "beachhead" in Marshalltown, many of their relatives and friends followed (Cantu 1995). Today, Villachuatons insist that even though the village has a total population of about eight thousand, fewer than one thousand live there year round. Indeed, throughout most of the year, there are more Villachuatons living in Marshalltown than in Villachuato.

The well-established connection between Villachuato and Marshalltown has benefited both communities. Several hundred workers in the Swift plant and other businesses in Marshalltown hail from Villachuato. Losing these workers would be devastating to Swift in particular. Villachuato benefits most from the remittances to families and development of local infrastructure. Some of the streets are now paved. Electricity became available to every house in the village in 1999, and running water is also available to every household. Individual families also invest in building homes.

Besides the economic interdependence, there are also important social connections. For the last six years, one of four Villachuato majordomos has actually lived in Marshalltown and was a Swift employee.[3] This person's primary task is to organize the annual fiesta and collect money for infrastructure and to renovate Villachuato's church. In 2001 more than $25,000 was raised in Marshalltown alone (Grey and Woodrick 2002). Central to the spiritual and social life of Villachuato is their saint El Señor de la Salud. El Señor is the patron of the rancho and the annual holy week fiesta is held in his honor. Most Villachuatons have tremendous faith in his ability to provide safe crossings into the United States without apprehension by la migra. Villachuatons in Mexico regularly make mandas (promises) to El Señor for such things as good health, work in the United States, and good schooling for their children. One way to pay one's manda is to travel to the annual fiesta and pay respects to El Señor.

Perhaps more important, the annual fiesta brings together Villachuatons from across the United States. The fiesta and saint provide a common spiritual focus for Villachuatons and helps them maintain a sense of community despite their wide physical dispersion in the United States (see Fortuny Loret de Mola 2000; Wellmeier 1998). La Virgen de Guadalupe provides a similar role for Mexicans in Iowa and elsewhere, but El Señor de la Salud provides a spiritual and social focus for Villachuatons specifically.

Villachuato is a former hacienda. According to Villachuatons, hacienda land was divided among residents in 1936. Today, families with land hold between two and eight hectors. Many residents rent out their land to other families. Crops are typically cash crops such as strawberries and garbanzo beans. Some land is used for subsistence purposes. In either case, agriculture is generally a losing proposition in Villachuato. The experience of one farmer we met seemed typical. He planted two hectors of land with wheat. His inputs of seeds, fertilizer, pesticides, and herbicides—not to mention his labor—totaled nearly ten thousand pesos, but his crop fetched only two thousand.

These conditions are made worse by the lack of water. An extensive irrigation system was built under the hacienda and the main canal runs right through the heart of Villachuato. Before the 1970s, Villachuatons and others along this irrigation system enjoyed ready access to water but things changed in 1972 with completion of a large dam on the Rio Baja. This dam diverted control of irrigation away from local communities and placed it in the hands of federal water officials. This particular dam was built as part of the huge Rio Lerma-Chapala Basin project that diverted water to Mexico City and large commercial agribusiness operations. All of the Villachuatons we have interviewed have pointed to the construction of this dam, and their subsequent loss of control over access to irrigation water, as the beginning of Villachuato's demise. Residents must now apply and pay for water through federal authorities who may or may not provide adequate supplies and usually don't. Everyone we talked to agreed: the limited water provided to the rancho is inadequate to sustain viable agriculture. With limited access to water, and the higher costs of other inputs like seed and fertilizer, Villachuatons were forced to look elsewhere for jobs and income. For hundreds of Villachuatons and their families, the primary source of income became Marshalltown and the Swift plant. In one interview with a man from Villachuato, we asked, "What would Villachuato be without Marshalltown?" He shrugged his shoulders and without hesitation responded, "nada [nothing]" (Grey and Woodrick 2002).

ANGLO COMMUNITY LEADERS REACT TO THE VILLACHUATO CONNECTION

The interdependence of Villachuato and Marshalltown is not lost on Anglo community leaders. As researchers, we recognized this connection in 1996, but Anglo leaders were unaware of the connection until we made them aware of it in 1998. Since that time, we have been able to help Marshalltown leaders develop a deeper understanding and appreciation for Marshalltown's unofficial sister city, and, more important, the economic, social, and political conditions that brought these two communities together.

The Mexican influx in Marshalltown has presented a number of challenges. It has often been a difficult transition for established Anglo residents and newcomers. However, Marshalltown benefits from the dedication of many key Anglo leaders to make the new Marshalltown work. For example, as early as 1990, local churches provided Latino ministries. Initially, church services in Spanish were provided by a Lutheran pastor, then by a newly established Hispanic Ministry by the Catholic Church in 1992 (Grey and Woodrick 2002). The ministry office also opened an immigration service.

In 1996, the Marshalltown newspaper published a Spanish language newspaper, *La Voz de la Comunidad.* The publication lasted only seven months and lost about $10,000. The publisher publicly blamed the lack of advertising revenues and the paper's demise on the biases of Marshalltown merchants against Latinos (Grey 2000).

The same year also marked the formation of the Marshalltown Diversity Committee. A Hispanic Task Force had been formed in 1991 and in many respects the new Diversity Committee picked up that role and expanded it. The committee is made of citizens, school district leaders and teachers, city administrators, the president of the chamber of commerce, a representative of the police department, and others. Right out of the chute this committee provided a valuable service in smoothing over relationships between Mexican newcomers and established residents. Two months after the committee was formed, on August 24, 1996, the INS raided the Marshalltown Swift plant. Among the 148 Latinos arrested were several people from Villachuato. The Swift plant fully cooperated with the raid by providing the names of undocumented workers and providing a pretext for coming to work on a Saturday morning. Most arrested workers were immediately deported to Mexico. Some were deported without the opportunity to see their spouses and children. Some children experienced losing both parents in the raid and friends scrambled to shelter and feed them.

The raid sent a shock wave through the Latino community. For many of them, life in the United States was already a stressful ordeal. The INS raid sent the message that life in Marshalltown and working at the Swift plant did not guarantee things would be any easier. However, the Diversity Committee quickly pulled together forums to smooth over some of the apprehension between Mexicans and Anglos caused by the raid. The first forum brought together Mexicans and other Latinos, Anglos, police officers, city leaders, social service providers, and others to talk about the experience. Participants brought their own perspectives on the raid and were given an opportunity to express their anger and personal pain. The Marshalltown police helped with the INS action, but some officers attended the forum to hear the concerns of Mexicans. City officials assured Mexicans in attendance that despite the INS action, they were still welcomed in Marshalltown.

The second post-raid event brought the regional director of the INS to a public forum. More than one hundred people attended, including several Latinos, city officials, Anglo citizens, and others. The director gave a brief review of the raid and the federal immigration law that made it possible. He was very careful to point out first, the full cooperation of the Swift plant, and, second, that the human and civil rights of those arrested were assured by the presence of members of the Iowa Commission on Latino Affairs. Both Mexicans and Anglos expressed anger. Even union officials who represented workers in the Swift plant confronted the INS director about discrimination against Mexicans because many workers were pulled from the line for questioning based on their physical appearance (Grey 2000).

Hard feelings on the part of Latino newcomers were certainly understandable. For those in the United States without documents, the INS action shook their already tenuous position. For Anglos and community leaders who wanted to welcome newcomers, the INS raid was a major setback because it increased the already great suspicions Mexicans had of Anglo citizens and authority figures.

The aftermath of the 1996 INS raid also set back Anglo-Latino relations because it highlighted the presence of undocumented Mexicans and other Latinos in Marshalltown. For a time, even the diversity committee—whose mission statement was "to strengthen the community of Marshalltown by recognizing and embracing diversity"—was willing to make distinctions between deserving and undeserving newcomers. That is, there was no defending the presence of undocumented workers because they were, technically, breaking the law. But, newcomers in the United States legally deserved their help and were welcomed. Many diversity committee members were willing to excuse INS and police actions against undocumented workers (and their families), as long as the human and civil rights were covered.

In subsequent years, even that perspective changed among Marshalltown's Anglo leaders. The 1996 INS raid brought home the fact that the geopolitical border between Iowa and Mexico was effectively meaningless in terms of the flow of people and labor. This point was brought even closer to home for Anglo leaders when they realized the close connection between Marshalltown and Villachuato. Realizing this connection put a more personal face on Mexican migration and, as a result, on the question of illegal versus legal immigration.

We actively made Anglo leaders aware of the Villachuato-Marshalltown connection, but facts about migration and money flows between the two communities could not make the connection meaningful. We realized only a radical solution would help them understand the complexity of this situation. The educational experience we created was to take Marshalltown leaders to Mexico. In the summer of 2001, we took the Marshalltown mayor and police chief to Mexico to see and experience the sending communities of Latino migrants, including Villachuato. In February 2002, we took six other leaders on the same visit—the president of the Chamber of Commerce, the Woodbury School principal, the local director of adult education (including adult ESL), the chair of the Diversity Committee, a religious sister from the Hispanic Ministries Office, and the marketing and public relations director of the Marshalltown Medical and Surgical Center.

In general, the experience made participants fully aware of the economic conditions in Villachuato and Mexico that work to "push" people elsewhere to make a living. Or, as one participant said, Villachuato does not so much push people out, but rather gives them very few reasons to stay. The second lesson involved realizing the extent of the family connections between Villachuato and Marshalltown. Many of the participants met people from Villachuato who lived in Marshalltown Then, in Villachuato, we lived with or visited the relatives of those Villachuatons we had met in Marshalltown. Many participants continue to maintain relationships with the Villachuatons they met in Iowa and Mexico.

More important, the Marshalltown leaders have used the Villachuato visits to inform their own efforts back home. The mayor, for example, was already convinced of the need to welcome Mexicans and other Latinos to Marshalltown. He told *Governing* magazine that he went to Villachuato to understand the migrants' situation to encourage them to stay in Marshalltown. "I was being self-serving," he admitted. "We need people" (Conte 2002, 32).

Villachuato's poverty, lack of power, and lack of opportunities, left deep impressions on the Marshalltown leaders. As Mark Grey and Phyllis Baker (2002, 8–9) wrote in a magazine essay, the police chief said, "no water for irrigation and no industry revealed that Marshalltown is the primary source of income for the entire village.... That tells me that both Marshalltown and this village are somewhat dependent on each other.... Both towns would suffer without the support of the other." The trip also helped him understand Mexicans' inherent distrust of the police and other authority figures. The key in Marshalltown is to build up that trust. "Until I can establish a trust that has not been part of their culture," the police chief explained, "they will not share information with me to help make their own lives better" including crimes against Mexicans that go unreported. He is developing a videotape in Spanish to welcome Mexicans and other Latinos, explain local laws, and encourage them—even the undocumented—to report crimes to his department without fear of being turned in to the INS.

The Woodbury School principal posted photos of Villachuato in the hall. Children and parents from Villachuato recognized relatives and places in the village. Some parents pointed out the teachers who taught them when they were children in Villachuato. The Woodbury principal was moved by his visit to Villachuato schools. The village schools were in poor physical condition and underfunded; teachers lacked teaching aids. Understanding that education did not necessarily lead to a better life in ranchos like Villachuato, he developed a deeper appreciation for the Mexican students in his school and has expressed this in his policies and projects. Beginning with the kindergarten class of 2003, for example, his school has become a two-way bilingual education magnet school. Students become bilingual and biliterate in English and Spanish. Already, a waiting list of both Spanish- and English-speakers has formed that includes children from outside the Woodbury attendance zone.

The Anglo leaders who have visited Villachuato express their new appreciation of the conditions that bring Latinos to Marshalltown in a variety of ways. As the Catholic nun said in her homily two weeks after the journey, "I believe that during the short pilgrimage . . . we were all changed; our eyes and hearts were opened in a new way." The hospital representative developed a new appreciation for migrants' perspectives on health care when he visited the government clinic in Villachuato. The "doctor" was an indifferent third-year medical student. Supplies and diagnostic equipment were limited. Medical records were nonexistent. There was no telephone. To the Marshalltown health leader, the alarming state of the Villachuato clinic represented intentional denial of health care and sent a very clear message to encourage migration to the United States: "Leave or you are going to die." This same leader was instrumental in developing free and low-cost health clinics in Marshalltown to service Marshalltown's growing Mexican and larger Latino population.

Some members of the community accused visitors to Villachuato of "recruiting" more migrants to live and work in Marshalltown. Rumors spread that the Anglo leaders went to Mexico on behalf of the Swift plant to encourage more illegal immigration to Iowa. Some tried to accuse trip participants of using city or other public funds for the trip. But this argument was easily dismissed because the trip was funded by a private Marshalltown foundation. The people who visited Villachuato countered rumors about their journey in public presentations and newspaper reports. The president of the Marshalltown Chamber of Commerce explained the trip this way, as Bryan Shultz ("Local Group Visits Mexican Town," *Marshalltown Times-Republican* April 8, 2002, pp. 1A–2A) explained in an article on the visit: "'The best way to know who they are is to know where they come from'" (1A). "When asked why a trip was required to Mexico instead of simply asking the Marshalltown Hispanics their questions, the answer was universal: 'We wanted to see for ourselves and draw our own conclusions'" (2A). The participants all emphasized the positive nature of their journey. "'We have made one-on-one personal connections with families there and right here in Marshalltown. That's an opportunity I wouldn't have had otherwise'" (2A). We have taken about thirty different Marshalltown leaders on these journeys and more are planned.

CONCLUSION

In many ways, the last ten years have been difficult for Marshalltown. Established residents found themselves experiencing rapid influxes of Mexicans and other Latinos and their language, cultures, and migration patterns. Mexican newcomers moved to a predominantly Anglo community that was not also sure about whether the newcomers were welcome. The barriers between these parallel communities are many. Language, culture, and religious practices get in the way, but the differences are also class based. By and large, Mexican newcomers have low incomes because they earn relatively low wages, whether in the Swift plant or elsewhere. Also contributing to their lower status is the fact that many are undocumented, although a growing number are gaining permanent residence or even citizenship. Many Anglos, however, continue to lump all Latinos together and assume they are in the country illegally.

As we showed, many Anglo community leaders are willing to break down the cultural and language barriers between themselves and Mexican newcomers. Their leadership has gone a long way to make the new migration "work" as much as it has. As leaders, they readily recognize the important role Mexicans have in the long-term economic and social health of Marshalltown. However, class differences still exist between themselves—and other Anglos—and Mexican newcomers. There is still suspicion on both sides. Even among the most active and well-meaning, sustaining relations with Mexicans are often difficult. Attendance at the Marshalltown Diversity meetings for example, comes and goes, but generally few—if any—Latinos attend even though interpretation is provided.

Two factors will probably lead to the development of a more integrated Marshalltown: children and time. Mexican children in growing numbers are graduating from Marshalltown schools. They are fluent in English, have grown up in the United States, and consider themselves "American." For many of them, visiting Mexico is fun and an opportunity to see their grandparents, but their long-term goal is to stay in the United States. Many parents have told us they want to eventually move back and live in Mexico, but their children don't want to. Parents also recognize the lack of opportunities for their children in places like Villachuato. As children pull to keep their parents in the United States, cross-border migration seems to slow down somewhat. More Latinos are buying homes in Marshalltown, a definite sign of the desire to settle down.

Time will also integrate Marshalltown. Mexicans and Anglos already work together and there are mixed marriages. The children are also growing up in mixed ethnic situations. Woodbury school prides itself on the number of bilingual birthday parties it holds. However, it will take several years for the Anglo and Mexican children growing up together to become adults and translate those relationships into the neighborhoods and community institutions.

The long-term prospects for Marshalltown are positive because there is a strong commitment to making it work among Anglo community leaders. Slowly but surely, key institutions are also playing their part, like the schools, police department, and health care. The majority of Mexicans we interviewed over the years were very positive about Marshalltown. It's safe. Their children receive high-quality education. There are jobs. The cost of living is relatively low. Of course, the success that Marshalltown has in integrating Mexicans comes at the expense of sending communities like Villachuato, which seems to be well on its way to becoming another dwindling central Mexican community.

NOTES

1. Iowa Workforce Development is equivalent to Job Services found in other states.
2. For vivid descriptions of the work on the packinghouse floor, see Deborah Fink (1998) and Donald D. Stull (1994).

3. The other three lived in Merced, California, Grand Island, Nebraska, and Villachuato.

REFERENCES

Cantu, Lionel. 1995. "The Peripheralization of Rural America: A Case Study of Latino Migrants in America's Heartland." *Sociological Perspectives* 38(3): 399–414.

Conte, Christopher. 2002. "Strangers on the Prairie." *Governing* 15(January): 29–33.

Crew, Joel. 2001. "Not in My Backyard: Community Resistance Hinders New Plant Construction Projects." *Meat & Poultry* (February): 24–26, 28–30.

Fink, Deborah. 1998. *Cutting into the Meatpacking Line: Workers and Change in the Rural Midwest.* Chapel Hill: University of North Carolina Press.

Fortuny Loret de Mola, Patricia. 2000. "Religious Festivities in Reinforcing the Houston/Guadalajara Connection in a Transnational Church." Paper presented to the annual meeting of the Society for the Scientific Study of Religion, Houston (October 19–22, 2000).

Grey, Mark A. 1997a. "Secondary Labor in the Meatpacking Industry: Demographic Change and Student Mobility in Rural Iowa Schools." *Journal of Research in Rural Education* 13(3): 153–64.

———. 1997b. *Open Enrollment Survey. Marshalltown Community Schools.* Cedar Falls: University of Northern Iowa Center for Social and Behavioral Research.

———. 1997c. "Storm Lake, Iowa and The Meatpacking Revolution: Historical and Ethnographic Perspectives on a Community in Transition." In *Unionizing the Jungle: Essays on Labor and Community in the Twentieth-Century Meatpacking Industry,* edited by Shelton Stromquist and Marvin Bergman. Iowa City: University of Iowa Press.

———. 1999. "Immigrants, Migration and Worker Turnover at the Hog Pride Pork Packing Plant." *Human Organization* 58(1): 16–27.

———. 2000. "Marshalltown, Iowa and the Struggle for Community in a Global Age." In *Communities and Capital: Local Struggles against Corporate Power and Privatization,* edited by Thomas W. Collins and John D. Wingard. Athens: University of Georgia Press.

———. 2001. "Welcoming New Iowans: A Guide for Citizens and Communities. Building Respect and Tolerance for Immigrant and Refugee Newcomers." Cedar Falls: University of Northern Iowa New Iowans Program.

Grey, Mark A., and Phyllis Baker. 2002. "Positive Exposure: Immersion in Latino Culture Brings Positive Changes." *Cityscape* [Iowa League of Cities] February: 8–9.

Grey, Mark A., and Anne C. Woodrick. 2002. "Unofficial Sister Cities: Meatpacking Labor Migration Between Villachuato, Mexico, and Marshalltown, Iowa." *Human Organization* 61(4): 364–76.

Grey, Mark A., with Andrew Conrad, Maureen Boyd, and Anne C. Woodrick. 2001. *Marshalltown New Iowans Pilot Community Assessment: A Report to the Marshalltown New Iowans Pilot Community Steering Committee.* Cedar Falls: University of Northern Iowa New Iowans Program, University of Northern Iowa Institute for Decision Making.

Hackenberg, Robert A., and Robert R. Alvarez. 2001. "Close-Ups of Postnationalism: Reports from the U.S.-Mexico Borderlands." *Human Organization* 60(2): 97–104.

Kay, Steven. 1997. "The Nature of Turnover: Packers Attempt to Reverse a Financial Drain." *Meat & Poultry* (September): 30–34.

Lutz, Gene M., May E. Losch, Melvin E. Gommerman, and Aaron Maitland. 2001. *Iowa 2001: State Government Survey: Workforce Shortage.* Cedar Falls: University of Northern Iowa Center for Social and Behavioral Research.

McGraw, David. 1998. "The Iowa Connection: Powerful Mexican Drug Cartels Have Hit Rural America." *U.S. News and World Report* 124: 33–36.

Stull, Donald D. 1994. "Knock 'Em Dead: Work in the Kill Floor of a Modern Beefpacking Plant." In *Newcomers in the Workplace: New Immigrants in the Restructuring of the U.S. Economy,* edited by Louise Lamphere, Alex Stepik, and Guillermo Grenier. Philadelphia: Temple University Press.

Stull, Donald D., and Michael Broadway. 1995. "Killing Them Softly: Work in a Modern Beef Plant and What It Does to Workers." In *Any Way You Cut It: Meat Processing and Small-Town America,* edited by Donald D. Stull, Michael Broadway, and David Griffith. Lawrence: University of Kansas Press.

Stull, Donald D., Michael Broadway, and David Griffith, eds. 1995. *Any Way You Cut It: Meat Processing and Small-Town America.* Lawrence: University of Kansas Press.

Wellmeier, Nancy J. 1998. "Santa Eulalia's People in Exile: Maya Religion, Culture, and Identity in Los Angeles." In *Gatherings in Diaspora: Religious Communities and the New Immigration,* edited by R. Stephen Warner and Judith G. Wittner. Philadelphia: Temple University Press.

Woodrick, Anne C., and Mark A. Grey. 2002. *Welcoming New Iowans: A Guide for Christians and Churches.* Cedar Falls: University of Northern Iowa New Iowans Program and Ecumenical Ministries of Iowa.

CHAPTER 7

✕

RECENT MEXICAN MIGRATION IN THE RURAL DELMARVA PENINSULA: HUMAN RIGHTS VERSUS CITIZENSHIP RIGHTS IN A LOCAL CONTEXT

TIMOTHY J. DUNN, ANA MARÍA ARAGONÉS, AND GEORGE SHIVERS

The isolated peninsula containing Delaware and the Eastern Shore (of the Chesapeake Bay) portions of Maryland and Virginia saw an explosive growth in Mexican and other Latino immigrant residents from 1990 to 2000. The Latino immigrant population grew several hundred percentage points in key counties and more than 1,000 percent in several towns, increasing from tiny absolute numbers to hundreds and thousands in those towns and counties, respectively (see tables 7.1 and 7.2). The largest portion of the broader Latino and Hispanic category regionally is Mexican, followed by Guatemalan. The expanding Mexican presence as settler-residents follows several decades of experience as seasonal, migratory farm workers and is preceded by early 1990s waves of Guatemalan and Haitian immigrants as political refugees who settled in the area. That Mexican and other Latino immigrants would settle here is somewhat remarkable, as the region is relatively isolated and had until now seen little immigration since the colonial and slavery periods. In addition to newness on the receiving region, many Mexican immigrants settling here also originate from a new immigrant-sending area within Mexico, the state of Veracruz. This is all creating a new and visible form of international integration for the long-isolated Delmarva region.[1]

The influx of Mexican immigrants as longer-term residents on a significant scale, rather than seasonal ones, is still in the early phase here. Their presence presents an opportunity to see from the initial stages how Mexican immigrants impact such an unlikely new settlement area

155

TABLE 7.1   Hispanic and Other Town Populations in Three
Delmarva Counties, 1990–2000[a]

	1990	2000	Percentage Change
Sussex County, Delaware			
Total Hispanic	1,476	6,915	369
Mexican origin	708	3,108	339
Other Hispanic (included Central American)	330	2,687	714
Central American[b]	ND	1,610	NA
Guatemalan	ND	1,426	NA
Puerto Rican	399	1,029	158
Hispanic percentage of county population	1.3%	4.4%	
Wicomico County, Maryland			
Total Hispanic	610	1,842	202
Mexican origin	155	664	328
Other Hispanic (included Central American)	255	595	133
Central American[b]	ND	99	NA
Guatemalan	ND	30	NA
Puerto Rican	177	519	193
Hispanic percentage of county population	.8%	2.2%	
Accomack County, Virginia			
Total Hispanic	452	2,062	356
Mexican origin	246	1,364	455
Other Hispanic (included Central American)	149	620	316
Central American[b]	ND	420	NA
Guatemalan	ND	388	NA
Puerto Rican	52	72	38
Hispanic percentage of county population	1.4%	5.4%	

Source: U.S. Census (2002a; 2002b).
Notes: ND = no data; NA = not applicable.
[a]These three counties have the bulk of the Hispanic population on the portion of Delmarva of interest to our study (from Sussex County southward). The other three counties in our region of interest had from 596 to 334 Hispanic residents in 2000, and fewer still in 1990.
[b]Data for Central Americans as a category, including specific member countries, were available for the 2000 census, but not for the 1990 census. In the latter, Central Americans were placed in the "Other Hispanic" category.

and how a variety of local actors and organizations are responding to newcomers. In this context, we are especially interested in how immigrants' rights are affected and constructed through immediate, local practices, rather than distant policies. This topic is rooted in a larger debate between two competing paradigms on rights—citizenship theory versus the human rights perspective, with contradictions between the two especially evident in immigration (Turner 2002). In general, citizenship theory views rights as conditional and nation-state defined—that is, dependent on state recognition, fulfilling duties, and following states guidelines (Marshall 1950; Barbalet 1988; van Gunsteren 1978; 1998; Turner 1990).[2] In contrast, the more nascent human rights perspective postulates that rights are unconditional—that is, people have rights qua humans (Sjoberg 1996; Sjoberg, Gill, and Williams 2001; Turner 1993; 2001; Feagin and Vera 2001). Citizenship theory and ideas dominate the literature on international migration and those works drawing on them portray immigrant rights as a problem for the nation-state.[3]

Drawing on Gideon Sjoberg (1996, 276–79), we claim that the citizenship theory approach represents a form of ethical relativism based on systems-maintenance and nation-state commitment, and a nation-state oriented morality on immigration matters (Eschbach, Hagan, and Rodriguez 2001). In contrast, as Bryan S. Turner notes (1993, 178), "the point about the concept of human rights is that they are extragovernmental" and that they are typically used to fight repressive state actions. Gideon Sjoberg, Elizabeth Gill, and Norma Williams (2001, 25) broaden the focus beyond the state in defining human rights as "claims made by persons in diverse social and cultural systems upon 'organized power relationships' in order to advance the dignity (or, more concretely, equal respect and concern for) human beings." The human rights perspective has begun to be taken up by other immigration scholars.[4] We build on such perspective by providing qualitative data from specific local cases and analyze such data using the above competing conceptual views of rights.

Before proceeding to our own research, we briefly review census data, the regional economy, and a Guatemalan case for comparison. As noted previously (see tables 7.1 and 7.2), the rate of Hispanic and Latino population growth was extraordinary from 1990 to 2000, though absolute numbers remain small overall.[5] The three counties and seven towns shown in the tables are the main Hispanic population centers in the region. Note that Mexicans were the largest Hispanic group regionwide by 2000, in all three counties and in six of the seven towns (except

TABLE 7.2   Hispanic and Other Town Populations in Delaware
             and Maryland

	1990	2000	Percentage Change
Georgetown, Sussex County, Delaware			
Total Hispanic (percentage of town population)	75 (2%)	1,473 (31.7%)	1,864%
Mexican origin	32	191	497
Other (including Central American)	30	1,238	4,027
Central American[a]	ND	1,018	
Guatemalan	ND	1,003	
Puerto Rican	13	42	
Selbyville, Sussex County, Delaware			
Total Hispanic (percentage of town population)	25 (1.9%)	347 (21.1%)	1,288
Mexican origin	20	267	1,235
Other (including Central American)	3	70	2,233
Central American[a]	ND	34	
Puerto Rican	2	10	
Frankford, Sussex County, Delaware			
Total Hispanic (percentage of town population)	1 (.17%)	148 (20.7%)	14,700
Mexican origin	0	134	
Other (including Central American)	0	14	
Central American[a]	ND	9	
Puerto Rican	1	0	
Bridgeville, Sussex County, Delaware			
Total Hispanic (percentage of town population)	63 (5.2%)	239 (16.6%)	279
Mexican origin	39	173	344
Other (including Central American)	12	26	117
Central American[a]	ND	5	
Puerto Rican	12	39	225

TABLE 7.2   Hispanic and Other Town Populations in Delaware
and Maryland (*Continued*)

	1990	2000	Percentage Change
Milford, Sussex County, Delaware			
Total Hispanic (percentage of town population)	225 (3.7%)	594 (8.8%)	164%
Mexican origin	120	280	133
Other (including Central American)	32	138	331
Central American[a]	ND	74	
Guatemalan	ND	50	
Puerto Rican	73	168	130
Seaford, Sussex County, Delaware			
Total Hispanic (percentage of town population)	74 (1.3%)	285 (4.3%)	284.5
Mexican origin	18	171	850
Other (including Central American)	27	52	93
Central American[a]	ND	8	
Puerto Rican	28	55	96
Salisbury, Wicomico County, Maryland			
Total Hispanic (percentage of town population)	252 (1.2%)	806 (3.4%)	220
Mexican origin	60	251	318
Other (including Central American)	124	305	146
Central American[a]	ND	47	
Puerto Rican	54	222	311

Source: U.S. Census (2002a; 2002b).
Note: ND = no data.
[a]Data for Central Americans as a category, including specific member countries, were available for the 2000 census, but not for the 1990 census. In the latter, Central Americans were placed in the "Other Hispanic" category.

Georgetown, Delaware) and a majority in four of seven towns shown. However, Mexicans are also more dispersed in pockets of several hundreds in various locations, making them less visible, while Guatemalans in contrast are overwhelmingly concentrated in Georgetown. In five of the seven selected towns and cities the growth of the Hispanic portion of the population is striking, especially in the smaller communities, as Hispanics have gone from a tiny presence of 5 percent or less in 1990 to anywhere from 8.8 percent to 31.7 percent in 2000. This represents a very visible demographic shift quite apparent to local natives.[6] The rapid growth in the Hispanic population in smaller communities has remade the demographic landscape. In fact, total population in two of the seven localities (Georgetown and Frankford, Delaware) is now majority-minority (African American plus Hispanic) and the population makeup in two more towns (Bridgeville and Selbyville, Delaware) is nearly so (U.S. Census 2002a; U.S. Census 2002b).

The regional economy obviously plays a central role in the region drawing Mexican and other Latino immigrants to Delmarva. It is dominated by the poultry industry, but other key facets are coastal beach tourism, seafood and timber industries, agriculture (fruit and vegetable crops as well as that related to the poultry industry), healthcare services, construction, extensive retail and service activities, and some small non-poultry manufacturing (BEACON 2002). Our research has found Mexican immigrants in nearly all of these sectors, but especially poultry processing. Delmarva is one of the leading poultry producing regions in the country, with three of the nation's top twenty counties in broiler production. Six firms operate thirteen processing plants locally, including four firms that are headquartered in the region, three of which are among the top seventeen poultry firms in the nation (http://www.dpichicken.org).

The region's thirteen poultry processing plants employ approximately twenty-one thousand people (Horowitz and Miller 1999). There is a chronic need for new poultry processing workers—a need fueled by very high annual labor turnover rates and the increasing reluctance among native workers to take poultry jobs with their prevailing relatively low wages ($6 to $9 per hour) and demanding and sometimes dangerous work conditions. This is especially the case among the younger generation of African American residents, long the backbone of the area's poultry processing work force. Thus Mexican and other Latino workers are filling the poultry labor gap. By the early 1990s the labor shortage was so acute that at least one local poultry company offered cash bonuses to any workers who recruited colleagues (Borland 2001). Meanwhile, extensive demand growth for poultry products in recent years has fueled the need to ever increase production (Horowitz and Miller 1999). Another key regional economic feature in recent years is strong growth in the various services in beach resort areas and in construction (BEACON 2002). These industries have strong labor needs, if not shortages, particularly seasonal, in spite of relatively high local unemployment levels, and provide ample opportunities for immigrant employment outside the poultry industry.

Before proceeding, we should note the well-established and visible Guatemalan immigrant community in Georgetown, Delaware, the region's first large-scale Latino settler-residents, because their presence and experience shaped local responses to Mexican immigrants, especially among service providers. The Guatemalans established themselves in Georgetown beginning in the early 1990s. By 2000, they accounted for nearly one-third of the Sussex County seat's population. They flocked here to work in the local poultry plant; at least some were initially seasonal, migratory agricultural workers and "settled out" or were "recruited out" of that to work in poultry. The Guatemalans are mainly indigenous Maya, for whom Spanish is often a second language, and many of the earlier arrivals in particular are political refugees who have applied for asylum at some point (Horowitz and Miller 1999). Compared to Mexican immigrants, Guatemalans are less educated, have some sort of legal immigration status, and have built more of a supportive immigrant enclave (see Borland 2001). At the same time, Guatemalans are concentrated mainly in a single town and receive an impressive local nongovernmental organizational assistance.

METHODOLOGY

We conducted dozens of site observations in housing, work, and assorted community facilities and interviews with some ninety individuals (sixty-two immigrants, sixty of whom were Mexican, and the rest local resident social service providers and activists working with immigrants), from 2000 through 2002 in wide-ranging, ongoing fieldwork. The geographic focus of such fieldwork has been Sussex County, Delaware's southernmost county, as well as neighboring Wicomico and Somerset counties in Maryland, a rural area with only one town with a population of more than twenty thousand.

We identified a series of characteristics that provide a basic profile of Mexican immigrants we encountered during our research. It should be noted that this profile is based on snowball and convenience sampling procedures, which do not allow us to say how widespread the characteristics of our sixty Mexican interviewees are. We focused on working-class and working-poor settled Mexican immigrants staying for longer time periods, rather than those explicitly here temporarily for seasonal agricultural and seafood industry work. The gender and age composition was largely young (under thirty-five) and male, but there was a significant presence of young females and some children and families as well. By far, the largest portion of the immigrants we encountered in the region were from the rural areas of Veracruz state, many from the village of Huachín and surrounding environs.[7] We also encountered people from the states of Tabasco, Hidalgo, Chiapas, Morelos, Nuevo León, Tamaulipas, Mexico City, and, most recently, Oaxaca. Most were from rural areas, had previously been engaged in agricultural work at some point in Mexico, and had medium to low levels of education, ranging anywhere from a few years of primary school to completed middle school. A small portion were members of Mexican indigenous groups. Some had been skilled laborers in Mexico (for example, electrician) or small business owners, and a few were highly educated professionals (for example, a lawyer and an agricultural engineer).

Nearly all had come to the United States since 1995 and most since 1998 (many just in the last year or two). For most, the Delmarva region was one of their first settled residences in the United States. Nearly everyone said they left Mexico due to a lack of work and economic opportunity, especially in rural areas, which they reported had worsened in recent years. The mid-1990s Mexican economic crisis, ongoing neo-liberal economic reforms, and NAFTA combined to hit the rural sector particularly hard. Nearly all respondents were undocumented immigrants using false papers to obtain work, and most reported significant difficulties in crossing the U.S.-Mexico border, which in turn tended to discourage regular back-and-forth migration, leaving some even feeling trapped here. Social networks appeared to be the main means of arranging arrival to this region, though we encountered some use of recruitment by labor contractors, both those with and without legal visas for workers.

The types of jobs in which we found Mexican immigrants engaged are quite varied. At the same time, we discerned a strong sense of occupational progression up and out of poultry processing, most often within a few months to a year of arrival. While the largest share of the settler-residents we spoke with had worked in the poultry processing industry initially or early in their time here, most found it to be highly undesirable. They used it as a first step on an employment ladder leading to work with better working conditions or pay. In yet another pattern, some poultry workers are recruited from the seasonal, migratory agricultural workforce locally during the summers, but then leave poultry processing to return to agriculture, according to a union official (fieldnotes, March 14, 2002). More typically, we found Mexican immigrants moving from poultry processing on to work in landscaping, construction, hotels and restaurants, laundry and linen service, lumber industry (for example, saw mill). A few have even started their own small businesses, and not solely enterprises to serve immigrants. For example, a Mexican immigrant from Veracruz, who has lived in Delmarva since 1995, left his first job at a poultry plant to eventually start a tile construction business; he now employs half a dozen fellow immigrants during high summer season ("Miguel" interview, March 20, 2002).[8]

From here forward, we present research findings on the labor, social services, housing, and interethnic experiences of Mexican immigrants in this region and the impacts and local reactions to their presence. We conclude with a summary and then brief interpretation of these findings in light of the contrasting view of people's rights under the competing citizenship and human rights paradigms.

LABOR UNIONS AND OTHER LABOR ISSUES

As noted previously, the poultry industry is a principal employer in Delmarva and its labor needs attract increasing numbers of immigrant workers. Of the peninsula's thirteen poultry processing plants, five are unionized and represented by the United Food and Commercial Workers (UFCW). Until the 1990s, the bulk of the workforce was black; however, younger African Americans have been increasingly reluctant to take these jobs. Latino immigrant workers did not start appearing in the area's poultry plants until approximately 1987, according to one federal official who has frequented area poultry plants for two decades (fieldnotes, July 21, 2001). By the late 1990s, approximately half of the area poultry plant workforce was made up of immigrants, mainly Mexican and Guatemalan (Horowitz and Miller 1999). UFCW officials estimate that 70 percent of its members are Latinos, overwhelmingly immigrants, in the five plants it represents in the area. This varies widely by plant and shift—for example, Latinos account for 90 percent of the workers at the Mountaire Corporation's plant in Selbyville, Delaware (Joseph Cacchioli, "Poultry Activist Instigates Arrest" *Salisbury Daily Times*, February 14, 2001, p. 1), but only 10 percent of Perdue's nonunion Salisbury, Maryland, plant (fieldnotes, July 19, 2001). UFCW officials note that Latinos are the vast majority of the workers at the three larger plants the union represents, but only a minor fraction at the two smaller plants.

Latino immigrants are now recognized as a key force by the union, though with difficulty initially, and a Mexican immigrant has risen to be a vice president of the union local representing workers in five plants. Immigrants, particularly Mexicans, have been crucial to union revitalization in the poultry plants. The experience of one local unionized plant stands out, the Mountaire plant in Selbyville, Delaware. The union had a very low profile among Latino immigrant workers until a 1996 wildcat strike by Latino immigrants, mainly Mexicans, at the plant. Prior to this time, the now UFCW-local vice president reports that Latino workers generally had no idea there was a union presence at the plant, though they recognized dues were withheld from their checks. In actuality, there was only one shop-floor steward (for a plant of 800 workers), an older African American woman, who did not speak Spanish and made no effort to reach the Latino immigrant workers—several hundred of the plant's workers by the mid-1990s (Martinez interview, July 23, 2001).

Management's gross mistreatment of a Mexican immigrant provoked an uprising of previously largely passive Latino workers that caught both management and the union off-guard. In 1996 a teenage Mexican immigrant worker in the Selbyville Mountaire plant had a finger cut off at work. Officials from the plant's personnel office came to him at the hospital and said he was fired, because they knew he was an illegal immigrant (Martinez interview, July 23, 2001). This would have made the company less vulnerable to a worker's compensation claim and other expenses. Word of the injustice spread rapidly, and two days later, Latino workers launched a wildcat strike, starting with one hundred and later growing to two hundred (Lewis interview, July 12, 2001). Not a single American worker, black or white, joined them, nor did some Latino workers, who were afraid of being fired and were vulnerable as undocumented immigrants (Martinez interview, July 23, 2001). Nonetheless, several hundred Latino immigrants, including many undocumented workers did walk out or refuse to go to work. The now-union-local vice president, then a worker at the plant, said, "Many had fear, but many had more courage than fear because they said, 'Today it's him; tomorrow it could be any of us they will do the same thing to'" (Martinez interview, July 23, 2001).

Company personnel officials fired all the workers en masse on the spot. At the same time, a local Episcopal priest, Reverend Jim Lewis, sympathetic to the immigrant workers, offered a nearby church as a refuge for the strikers to use, and many remained there overnight. Local police were visible throughout and regional media covered the strike. The strikers were very fearful of not only the loss of jobs but also of being deported, as most were undocumented and using false papers. The union local was not supportive of the strike initially and tried to get the striking workers to return to work. However, Lewis interceded with the union, contacting regional UFCW officials in Baltimore to explain the situation as new rank-and-file activism that could be capitalized upon. Regional UFCW staff came out to assess the situation and the next day the union quickly switched to backing the strikers and was able to get all reinstated, while also providing a lawyer to seek redress for the teenage worker whose mistreatment provoked the strike (Lewis interview, July 23, 2001).

This wildcat strike became the basis for a rejuvenated rank and file union membership at the Mountaire plant, and the beginning activism for an immigrant, Maria Martinez, who would become the local vice president within four years. She was unique in having spoken to the media during the strike, because she was one of the few strikers who knew some English and was less vulnerable because she was a legal U.S. permanent resident. With Lewis's guidance, regional union officials recruited her to serve as a shop steward. She became a strong advocate for workers, cooperating with the African American shop steward to present a united front to management on key issues. This led to greater employee awareness of rights, grievance filing and negotiation, and as she got results, more Latino immigrant workers came forward. Within several years she was elected to become vice president of the UFCW local 27, which represents workers in five unionized plants on Delmarva. As the union became revitalized in the plant, the number of shop stewards increased to seven, three African American and four Latino. By 2001, there were fifteen very active shop stewards, fourteen of whom were Latinos, for some 980 workers at the plant (Martinez interview, July 23, 2001).

Meanwhile, Lewis aggressively used the episode as a "wake-up call" to educate the UFCW and AFL-CIO leadership on the growing importance of immigrant workers in their unions. In his view, the union was not prepared at all for the Latino immigrant influx, in terms of language skills or cultural knowledge, but that with much prodding the organization changed and responded constructively (Lewis interview, July 12, 2001). One innovative response of the UFCW to such prodding has been to place three bilingual Latino social workers and organizers at local union offices to serve the Latino immigrant community (for example, referrals, advocate with other agencies in immigrant case management), and do outreach for plant organizing. Recently, this UFCW effort was expanded to include classes on immigrant rights, adult literacy, and ESL (fieldnotes, September 6, 2002, March 2, 2001, and November 15, 2000).

Thanks in large part to Mexican immigrants, the UFCW is very active in this plant and in 2001 beat back a management-led union decertification effort by prevailing in the final vote by a margin larger than two to one. In this instance, management once again used the immigration status issue against Latino immigrant workers to try to intimidate them, which once again backfired. According to union officials and Lewis, a personnel department administrator at the plant was telling the mostly Mexican workers that he knew some were illegal immigrants and that if they voted for the union he would report them to the INS for deportation. Management strenuously denied this charge (Lewis interview, July 12, 2001; Martinez interview, July 23, 2001; Cacchioli 2001).[9]

Two days before the decertification election two union officials and Lewis went to the Mountaire Selbyville plant and attempted to confront the manager identified by workers as having made this claim and asked to debate him. Company officials refused the request and instead asked Lewis to leave, which he refused to do, and the personnel director eventually called the local police to remove him. In rather dramatic fashion, Lewis committed civil disobedience, refusing to move. The police arrested him for trespassing and hauled him away, with reporters looking on. It was a big local news story that shortly after received national exposure, including a National Public Radio report (Cacchioli 2001; Martinez interview, July 23, 2001; Lewis interview, July 12, 2001). According to union official Martinez, the arrest had a galvanizing effect in outraged workers, spurring a greater vote for the union in the election the next day. She characterized the Latino immigrant workers' reaction as something like "'if this is what they will do to a priest, to an American, what will they do to us?!'" (Martinez interview, July 23, 2001). On the day of the election, union activists handed out flyers to workers with a photo of Lewis being arrested and a letter from him asking them to support the union. The union won the vote by a margin of more than 2.5 to 1 (581 to 216), an 81 percent voter turnout of the plant's 980 workers. According to Martinez, the campaign served to unify Latino immigrant and African American workers (Martinez interview, July 23, 2001). More recently, the UFCW included two new immigrant protection clauses in the new 2002 contracts it negotiated for its members in five area plants.[10]

Beyond the Selbyville labor organizing case, in which Mexican immigrant workers figure so prominently, a more broad-based coalition effort has emerged in the area to address multiple types of grievances against the poultry industry from many social actors, including Mexican and Central American immigrant workers. The Delmarva Poultry Justice Alliance (DPJA) was formed in 1996, bringing together the union and other poultry industry workers, such as chicken catchers, contract farmers who raise the companies' birds, environmentalists, religious activists, and consumers in order to take on the poultry companies (Lewis interview, July 12, 2001). This very broad coalition has its roots among immigrant advocates working with Guatemalan immigrants in Georgetown, Delaware, the dominant component of the local poultry labor force. The DPJA had generated a great deal of publicity, including a March 1999 public meeting with a visiting federal congressional delegation, at which many of the speakers were Mexican and Latino immigrants, who spoke out despite fears of retaliation for publicly airing their grievances. Since then, the DPJA has also gained the attention of the *New York Times* and TV news show "60 Minutes," among other national media, focusing on worker treatment and injuries, both for native workers, mainly African Americans, as well as immigrant workers, notably Mexicans among them.

While there have been notable innovative and positive responses to the influx of Mexican and other Latino immigrant workers by labor and advocacy organizations in the region, there are many more problematic responses in the local economy. In our interviews, many immigrants reported either receiving less than the minimum wage or, more commonly, a lack of overtime wages for long hours in a variety of industries, especially for undocumented immigrant workers. Often though, our interviewees were not aggrieved about either issue, as most knew little of wage and overtime regulations and instead measured success in their ability to earn and save money and send much back to family members in Mexico. However, several area Mexican immigrants interviewed were quite aggrieved about a more serious matter—being entirely cheated out of wages. This came through from those working not only in some small-scale enterprises (for example, small farms), but also at companies such as McDonald's. Several undocumented Mexican immigrants working for the company in a resort area reported being regularly cheated out of pay for one shift (six to eight hours) per pay period, and occasionally an entire pay period (Ana and Marisol interview, July 25, 2001).

There has also been significant exploitation in the use of temporary and seasonal Mexican immigrant workers in the seafood and poultry industries, many brought in under INS visa temporary worker visa programs. To meet labor shortages and undermine union strength, the local poultry industry is now using the same INS visa programs and increasingly turning to temporary contract labor services, both of which make extensive use of Mexican immigrant labor. Union official Martinez indicated that a number of local plants were bringing in many Mexican workers under the INS visa program as temporary workers. In addition, Martinez noted that many area poultry companies were also increasingly obtaining workers by contracting with a temporary labor service. This was especially the case at the Mountaire Selbyville plant following the February 2001 union victory, where Martinez estimated the portion of such workers had grown to 10 percent to 20 percent of the plant's workforce by that summer. Having talked to some of those workers, her sense was that many were recently arrived Mexican undocumented immigrants, often without even false papers. It is unclear how widespread these practices are in this area, but the implications are ominous for unionization, and the empowerment and well being of any Mexican and other immigrant workers more generally.

Finally, it should be noted that there are a few Mexican immigrant-owned businesses in the area that play important and sometimes contradictory roles. They often serve as gathering points for social contact, support, and service provision for immigrants, but some also have very exploitative labor practices. New immigrants that begin their regional employment careers there often quickly leave for better prospects (fieldnotes, November 15, 2001).

SOCIAL SERVICES

In the past, one of the main points of contact for county social service departments with Mexican immigrants was the food stamp program, with one local county making an especially concerted effort to reach seasonal, migrant agricultural workers, employing bilingual outreach workers to assist and expedite client enrollment. In the early and mid-1980s, this county enlisted more than one thousand immigrants per summer season, but following federal law changes passed in 1996 to bar even most legal immigrants from the program, they have seen fewer than one hundred enrollees. One veteran social worker attributed this to the high proportion of undocumented workers in the targeted audience, who were thus ineligible. In addition, this county social service office checked every immigrant applicant's immigration papers with a new automated INS record system in order to screen out those with false documents, which they felt was necessary in light of the 1996 law (fieldnotes, July 18, 2001). Given such measures, it is no surprise that few immigrants, Mexican or others, enrolled in the program, even though this county social service department made a meaningful effort to work with them.

Medical care providers have responded to the growing Mexican and other Latino immigrant population with a mixture of indifference as well as inclusion and outreach. Data from immigrants and various service providers suggest that area hospitals, ambulance services, and the "regular" medical clinics in the region have done little to adjust to the growing Latino population in the region. For example, they have few if any Spanish speakers on staff, let alone for all shifts. When possible, volunteer translators from the community are called upon. One main local clinic receiving federal funds to serve low-income clients in several counties, including specifically migrant agricultural workers, has done little to reach or serve Mexican immigrants. Until very recently, they employed no one who spoke Spanish, and advocates who dealt with them reported they were largely unsympathetic and bureaucratic in dealing with immigrants. (It should be noted that federally funded grants and programs exclude undocumented immigrants from non-emergency care, generally.) Consequently, local immigrant advocates have instead taken people forty-five miles to a small clinic with a more friendly and sympathetic staff (fieldnotes, August 15, 2001).

In spite of barriers, a number of local organizations and advocates, often religious-affiliated, are finding creative ways to secure at least some of the medical care needed by Mexican and other Latino immigrants, including the undocumented. The staff of one small, Catholic Charities branch office, Seton Center, in Princess Anne, Maryland, has been especially determined in prevailing upon medical caregivers for undocumented Mexican and other Latino clients in need of assistance, often with great success (fieldnotes, August 16, 2001). La Esperanza immigrant assistance center in Georgetown, Delaware, has even succeeded in establishing a clinic for uninsured residents of their county, with bilingual staff, transportation help, and oriented especially (but not exclusively) toward serving Central American and Mexican immigrants. La Esperanza has also worked with a small local hospital in Seaford, Delaware, to better accommodate Latino immigrant clients and has persuaded the county social service department to hold a few regular office hours at La Esperanza's offices. The latter has made more accessible enrollment into Medicaid for low-income Latino immigrant expectant mothers (fieldnotes, March 2, 2001). Another faith-based organization, Delmarva Rural Ministries, has a mobile healthcare facility and bilingual staff that targets farm workers in two Delaware counties, including Sussex (see http://www.1drm.com). The health department in another local county has recently begun to enroll undocumented immigrant expectant mothers in a new program it devised to provide prenatal care for expectant mothers who are otherwise not eligible for medical public assistance prior to the birth (fieldnotes, March 14, 2002). Much more medical care access and cultural awareness on the part of medical institutions are needed, but these measures indicate a growing willingness among local residents and organizations to provide at least some meaningful health care assistance to Mexican and other immigrants.

Several legal service providers in the region have responded to the new presence of Mexican and other Latino immigrants in the region by expanding what is still limited legal assistance. It is worth noting that over the past three years two private immigration attorneys with at least a working knowledge of Spanish have set up practice in Salisbury (fieldnotes, September 27, 1999, February 5, 2002). More recently, La Esperanza center hired a bilingual immigration attorney (fieldnotes, May 15, 2003). In doing so, they have filled a wide gap by being nearly the only three such specialists south of Wilmington, Delaware. In addition, one bilingual private criminal attorney in Salisbury specializes in taking the cases of Mexican and other Latino immigrants. Similarly, several paralegal and other legal assistants working for Catholic Charities offices in three towns plus those at La Esperanza center are now providing very extensive, free to very low cost, bilingual legal assistance to hundreds of local Latino immigrants each year (fieldnotes, November 15, 2000, March 1, 2001). However, given the generally narrow parameters of U.S. immigration law, several of the above legal service providers expressed frustration that they can offer only limited access to immigration relief for Mexican immigrants or their Central American counterparts who have arrived in recent years (fieldnotes, March 1, 2001, March 2, 2001).

Funding restrictions limit the ability of a principal legal resource for low-income people, the Legal Aid Bureau, to work with Mexican and other Latino immigrants. The organization receives federal funding, and once again federal guidelines prohibit it from taking undocumented immigrants as clients. A local branch office has an active program with bilingual staff specifically designed to do outreach to seasonal, migrant farm workers, but the staff report being very frustrated because they can do very little for the great many workers they encounter who are undocumented immigrants (an estimated 80 percent). Most of these workers are Mexican, but increasingly Central American (fieldnotes, August 20, 2001).

The foremost provider of social services for Latino immigrants in the region is the La Esperanza center in Georgetown, Delaware, whose work has been aimed mainly at Guatemalans and other Central Americans and Mexicans to a lesser degree. La Esperanza is a faith-based organization formed in late 1996 by several Spanish nuns, a retired World Bank official from Chile, and an Episcopal priest, all newly arrived in the area for different reasons (fieldnotes, March 2, 2001; see also Borland 2001). They recognized the burgeoning Guatemalan immigrant community there was in dire need of help and woefully underserved, so they resolved to begin providing legal services as many of the early Guatemalan residents were political asylum applicants. The organization began by operating out of the nuns' house, and long operated on little resources, but last year they opened a new large, two-story building for the center (fieldnotes, August 5, 2001). They provide an array of services to approximately one thousand persons per month, including English and citizenship classes, housing assistance, transportation, family programs, in addition to the legal and medical service noted previously. The organization has become a place of first contact and referral for Latino immigrants for virtually any issue (fieldnotes, November 15, 2000, March 2, 2001). In addition, La Esperanza has spawned other services for Latino immigrants, including a Latino cultural arts center, and bilingual children's daycare and domestic violence programs. Other Latino immigrant services and organizations have also emerged in Georgetown, including a regional Latino soccer league, Spanish language radio station and monthly newspaper. Again, most of this is oriented around or inspired by the large Guatemalan community there, but Mexican immigrants in the area are also served, and may be more so in the future if their presence continues to become more preponderant there.

The La Esperanza center has yet to be replicated elsewhere in the region, where typically Mexican immigrants are more prominent, though there are steps in that direction. In early 2001 Catholic Charities expanded its immigration work from its Georgetown office to a part-time office in Salisbury. In addition, Bienvenidos a (Welcome to)

Delmarva was launched in spring 2001 by Salisbury University to bring together interested social service providers and others to try to better reach and serve Latino immigrants in the Maryland portion of Delmarva (fieldnotes, April 18, 2001, and August 16, 2001). Recently, Bienvenidos has been coordinating a series of outreach sessions of area service providers at a local Latino immigrant housing complex and is also developing a plan to provide much needed and requested cultural competency training for local organizations working with Mexican and other Latino immigrants (fieldnotes, May 16, 2002, August 15, 2002).

Beyond conventional social services, several religious institutions provide Spanish religious services aimed at Latino immigrants, which stand out as an important space for social support and networking for Mexican immigrants, as well as religious observance, (fieldnotes January 15, 2001). The regional Catholic Church diocese sponsors a semiroving Spanish-speaking priest to conduct mass and outreach to Latino immigrants in several locations in three area counties in two states. Several Protestant groups in the Salisbury area also provide Spanish religious services or other outreach, including a small Pentecostal Spanish-speaking congregation (fieldnotes, January 15, 2001), a Baptist church (fieldnotes, July 16, 2001), and recently a Methodist church in the heart of an African American neighborhood (fieldnotes, June 12, 2002). The number of churches doing such outreach to Spanish speakers seems to grow monthly.

Area educational institutions and others interested in education have responded to the increased presence of Latino immigrants in a variety of ways, generally presenting fewer barriers. (In part this is the case because unlike other programs receiving public funding, a 1982 Supreme Court decision ruled that public schools could not use immigration legal status as a criterion for admission.) Area school systems are adapting to an influx of Mexican and other Spanish-speaking immigrant students, although their numbers are relatively small thus far, with the exception of Georgetown, Delaware, where they are concentrated in the primary school level. Consequently, the need for teachers of English as a Second Language (ESL) is on the rise. Over the past several years Salisbury University developed an ESL teacher-training program. However, program staff found a wide range of degrees of willingness among public school officials in the region to accommodate Latino immigrant students (fieldnotes, June 2, 2000).

There is a small but growing response among area organizations to meet the need for English (ESL) classes for Mexican and other Latino immigrants working full time. La Esperanza center has filled the void in Georgetown and its classes are routinely full, though the center generally lacks formally trained teachers (fieldnotes, November 15, 2000, March 2, 2001). As previously noted, the UFCW is also beginning to offer such classes. Area community colleges have also responded with more ESL classes, especially in Delaware. Salisbury University's ESL program and its Bienvenidos a Delmarva program have drawn on ESL trainee teachers to set up small, informal English evening classes at a variety of community locations more accessible to immigrants (fieldnotes, February 14, 2002). However, public school districts offer very few ESL classes for working adults or teens. For example, the Wicomico County (Maryland) school district offers just few classes and the entire effort is coordinated by one volunteer (fieldnotes, August 16, 2001).

One notable very positive example of education made available to some immigrant children is the Migrant Children Summer Education Program (part of East Coast Migrant Head Start) at Princess Anne (Maryland) elementary school for children of seasonal farm workers, ranging from infants to early teens. It runs for four weeks in July, during the peak of the high tomato harvest season, each year and runs from 7:00 a.m. to 6:00 p.m. to accommodate parental field work schedules, with mainly African American women caring for and teaching Latino immigrant children—some 125 during summer 2001 (fieldnotes, July 16, 2001). Yet another educational development is that local public library officials are recognizing the growing Latino immigrant presence and responding by expanding their collections of Spanish language materials (fieldnotes, January 15, 2002, May 16, 2002) and conducting an extensive needs-assessment of Latino immigrants (fieldnotes, September 15, 2003).

Finally, arguably related to social services, law enforcement agencies have also responded to the growing presence of Mexican and Latino immigrants. Several informants view some local police agencies as targeting Latino immigrants in traffic stops, trying to write up extensive violations with large fines because most undocumented immigrants cannot get state driver's licenses or auto insurance (Martinez interview, July 23, 2001; fieldnotes, February 7, 2002). Still, the Delaware state police posted a bilingual Latino agent in Georgetown, Delaware, specifically to work with Latino immigrants in the area. The officer in question has a reputation among advocates for sensitivity and constructive engagement with immigrants (fieldnotes, November 15, 2000).

HOUSING

The response of housing providers to the growing presence of Mexican and other Latino immigrants has been one of the more problematic issues we encountered in our research. Lack of affordable housing and deterioration of the existing older, insufficient housing stock in the area is a primary concern for immigrants, advocates, and employers (Borland 2001, 16), as well as for working class and poor residents in the area generally. According to officials of the poultry industry, this issue greatly complicates its labor recruitment efforts (fieldnotes, June 20, 2002).

Religious-affiliated or faith-based groups have once again responded actively to the housing needs associated with increasing presence of Mexican and Latino immigrants. The Delmarva Rural Ministries secured federal funds to build and run three well-maintained apartment complexes specifically for low-income, legal visa holders and/or permanent resident immigrants or U.S. citizens engaged in agricultural work (fieldnotes, March 2, 2000; DRM complex manager interview, October 4, 2001). They are located in Salisbury, Maryland; Bridgeville, Delaware; and Eastville, Virginia (see http://www.drm.com). This housing resource has two significant restrictions, however. This first is that, once again due to federal funding guidelines, only legal status immigrants or citizens may live in the complex. In fact, the manager checks all household residents for their immigration papers, including nonworking children and employed adults (DRM manager interview, October 4, 2001). The second is that at least one member of the household must be engaged in agricultural work, which ranges from temporary seasonal work in tomato and other fruit harvesting to ongoing work in plant nurseries, forestry and timber, landscaping, and the poultry industry (only those working with live birds, however). Thus, due to the criteria imposed by the federal government as a condition for funding, the bulk of local Mexican and Latino immigrants are ineligible to live at the DRM housing complex. More recently, immigrant residents and their advocates have begun to lodge grievances against the complex's new managers (also Latinos) for overzealously and arbitrarily enforcing these guidelines (fieldnotes, September 11, 2002).

The nonagricultural and undocumented Mexican and Latino immigrants are left to fend for themselves and are not surprisingly vulnerable to great exploitation by landlords. We found that a number of our informants were living in overcrowded, subdivided apartments, old houses, and trailers that were not well maintained and typically overpriced (for example, $700 per month for run-down trailers). One of the most notorious cases is also the site of one of the largest Mexican immigrant residential areas on Delmarva, a three-building apartment complex with some five hundred residents, known locally as "Little Mexico," in a rural area of Sussex County, Delaware. Our informants said that nearly all the residents were undocumented immigrants and from the area around Huachín, Veracruz. Conditions were crowded in the two-bedroom apartment units; we found a range of four to sixteen people per unit, including children, teens, and most prominently young to middle-aged adults. Residents worked a variety of shifts, enabling rotating sleep schedules (fieldnotes, July 25, 2001). Besides overcrowding, this large apartment complex had been long plagued with the lack of safe, potable water for its residents (fieldnotes, July 25, 2001). Knowing that nearly all residents were undocumented immigrants and fearful of reporting him to the authorities, the landlord has simply refused to do anything about the problem, despite repeated requests from residents (Ana interview, July 25, 2001).

While there are a number of profound problems in the response of housing providers to the growth of Mexican and Latino immigration in the area, it is also the case that many of these immigrants are making progress. We found that over time some undocumented Mexican immigrants have been able to move out of the poorest housing conditions and into much better lodging arrangements, a few even becoming home owners. Still, we cannot say how widespread this progression is, although it is indicative of the efforts of undocumented Mexican immigrants to improve their housing circumstances in spite of significant obstacles.

INTERETHNIC RELATIONS AND REACTIONS FROM THE POLITICAL ESTABLISHMENT

The distinct yet related issues of interethnic relations and the reactions of the political establishment to the growing Latino population merit at least brief attention. It should be noted that the substantial recent immigration of Mexicans and other Latinos as year-round rather than seasonal residents to this long isolated region has broadened concerns beyond black-white relations, which had been the dominant intergroup issue.

The focus here is on relations between Latinos and African Americans. Mexican and other Latino immigrants are moving into poorer, predominantly black neighborhoods and thus far there does not appear to be visible, large-scale tension, though some friction is clearly present. For example, during the summer of 2001, one of the authors noted that the presence of Latino households in one of the main African American neighborhoods in Salisbury increased from approximately 3 percent to 10 percent. Residents of both groups shared public space with little obvious signs of discord (fieldnotes, summer 2001). At the same time, informants reported some street crime victimization and harassment of Mexican and other Latino immigrants by African Americans, but not of a serious nature (fieldnotes, January 15, 2001, September 11, 2002; Lewis interview, July 12, 2001). In a more divisive vein, poultry plant management sometimes fuels tensions between the two groups. One veteran immigrant and labor advocate noted: "The owners of the plants and the supervisors of the plants will let people know that the Latinos are better workers. . . . Whereas the black worker knows what they [management] can do and can't do to them, their rights, and they'll speak up. Whereas Latino workers won't; so they [management] use that." This observer also noted tensions outside the work place: "And we've also had community tensions, among social service providers. . . . The local community action people tend to be black social workers. . . . They see the problems the black community has, and now there's this Latino community coming in here, and they are getting a lot of attention. And blacks are saying, 'What happened to us?'" (Lewis interview, July 12, 2001). This local interethnic rivalry for services was also echoed by an immigrant advocate from La Esperanza center in Georgetown (fieldnotes, March 2, 2001). On the whole, it seems to us that there is a great deal of mutual ignorance and misunderstanding among local residents, African Americans, whites, and immigrants, which could lead to greater problems. Language barriers as well as lack of cross-cultural knowledge are divisive issues in this area.

The reactions of the local political establishment and various political actors to the growing presence of Mexican and other Latino immigrants has tended to be fairly positive of late, which is a good sign for interethnic relations given the generally conservative nature of local culture and politics. One landmark event in this regard was the conference entitled "The Changing Face of Delmarva" on June 2, 2000, which was sponsored by the three U.S. congressmen representing Delmarva districts, all of whom were Republicans. One has also hired a Latina specializing in assisting Latino residents as well as employers with immigration and government service issues. She was in fact the main force behind the conference. The event was essentially a series of panels and speakers recognizing the many contributions of new immigrants to Delmarva—Mexican, Haitian, and other Latinos—and their needs and the policy-related obstacles they face. The approximately two hundred and fifty attendees consisted mainly of community activists working with immigrants, a broad range of local, state, and federal governmental officials, and a few immigrants. The event also crossed various ethnic boundaries as several local and regional African American activists and elected officials linked the plight of Haitian and Latino immigrants and spoke of the need to assist both. One African American activist even said "We're going to form a chapter of LULAC (League of United Latin American Citizens), because we formed the NAACP to overcome discrimination against us, and now we see Latinos facing the same problems" (fieldnotes quote, June 2, 2000).

However, there are periodic public expressions of hostility and insulting ignorance by area political officials against Mexican and other Latino immigrants, yet the negative reaction against such sentiment is swift and strong. For instance, at the otherwise largely pro-immigrant conference noted above, the mayor of Bridgeville, Delaware, in fine good-old-boy fashion swore he had nothing against the rapidly growing population of mainly Mexican immigrants in his small town, but then exclaimed: "Those people need to learn English!" (fieldnotes, June 2, 2000). His remarks generated a storm of controversy and protest from many others, nearly all from established residents rather than immigrants, and he eventually toned down his statement.

A similar bigotry-renunciation cycle was triggered by the more widely reported prejudiced comments by the mayor of Georgetown, Delaware, in February 2001. The mayor claimed that the growing number of Guatemalan and Mexican immigrants in southern Delaware and specifically their living conditions were "lowering the region's standard of living." In that statement he also said "it is their job to bring themselves up to our level, not bring our society down to their level" (Associated Press, "Remarks on Del. Hispanics Spark Anger," *Daily Times* [Salisbury, Md.], March 1, 2001, p. 1). The remarks generated rapid and widespread controversy and were quickly criticized throughout the region. La Esperanza staff led this criticism but shortly thereafter established a dialogue with this official to reduce hostility. By June 2001, the mayor was present at the ribbon-cutting opening of La Esperanza's large new building (fieldnotes, August 20, 2001). In the spring of 2002, the same Georgetown mayor said, "Thanks to our new relationships with Hispanic community leaders, we have been able to gain and develop a sense of trust. Some barriers have come down." The town manager also made similar and more extensive comments recognizing Latino immigrants and the need to establish good relations. He said, "even though our resources are limited we cannot ignore that one third of Georgetown's population is an immigrant community . . . they are part of Sussex county's economy and they pay taxes. We altogether . . . must continue joining efforts in order to find a better understanding between Anglo American people and Hispanics" (Quoted in "Rompiendo las barreras del idioma, raza y religión, atraves del intercambio cultural [Breaking down barriers of language, race and religion, through the promotion of cultural exchange]," *Hoy en Delaware*, May 2002, pp. 9, 21). Further, even the governor of Delaware weighed in as an ally of La Esperanza center by presenting one of its founders and leading staff volunteers, a seventy-one-year-old Catholic nun, with the Delaware Governor's Volunteer Award for Social Justice ("Reconocimiento a la labor del voluntario [Recognizing the Volunteer Labor, Governor's Volunteer Awards]," *Hoy en Delaware*, May 2002, p. 10).

CONCLUSION

Mexican and other Latino immigrants have had varying but significant local impacts and made important gains on labor issues and union activity, social services, housing, interethnic relations, and the political establishment, with local organizations and actors often responding constructively to their growing presence. This is rather remarkable given the widespread undocumented immigration status among Mexican immigrants residing in this area, and the generally conservative nature of the region. Undocumented immigrants are, legally speaking, not even supposed to be here, and thus have severely circumscribed formal rights—that is, their rights are conditional upon their legal status. And we certainly have indications of that view being reinforced. Poultry industry managers have used it to intimidate Mexican and other Latino undocumented immigrant workers and to play them off as a more pliable workforce against African American workers. It also makes them more vulnerable to abuses in housing conditions, even the denial of potable water (!), as well as cutting off access to a plethora of federal government-funded social services.

Despite the formidable barrier posed by the lack of formal legal status, and in marked contrast to national policy, there have also been many important gains for the human rights of undocumented Mexican and other Latino immigrants at the local level on Delmarva. As the presence of these groups has grown in recent years, more local actors have become aware of their contributions to local communities and basic humanity and needs, and more have sought to provide some sort of assistance or at least recognize the immigrants as community members, regardless of their immigration legal status. Thus, access and rights for immigrants have been expanded in the areas of labor, education, legal assistance, and other areas, in part due to the informal recognition of mutual humanity at the local level. This recognition and assistance is coming from a diverse range of actors: especially faith-based NGO activists and union officials, but also political officials, educators of all types, health care providers, other more mainstream NGOs, and increasingly employers. The agitation and agency expressed by Mexican and Latino immigrants, together with the vibrant, innovative work of a tenacious group of advocates, has been instrumental. The relatively small size of the area's communities makes for more direct, personal contact between immigrants, their advocates, and a range of social actors; this in turn has heightened the responsiveness and accountability of the latter to the former. Federal policy changes, even minor ones, could greatly expand this process by opening more political space for such efforts to flourish.

In the future, we expect an increasing presence of Mexican immigrants as settler-residents on Delmarva, though this prediction is subject to national and binational policy and economic shifts. The 2000 census showed Mexicans as the largest Latino group in the area, and our research suggests that their presence here has likely grown since then. We also expect to see further labor progression of Mexican immigrants out of the poultry industry as Mexicans become more established and fill other labor needs in the region, especially construction and services, though poultry work will probably remain a vital early stop for newcomers. Given these factors, we anticipate that the interest in recognizing and assisting Mexican immigrants will grow among social service providers and local political actors. However, housing problems will likely continue, as they typically plague working class and poor residents of all types. Also, labor activism prospects have been greatly dimmed by a recent Supreme Court ruling, effectively denying union organizing rights to undocumented immigrant workers (see Charles Lane, "Court Denies Back Pay to Fired Illegal Immigrants," *Washington Post*, March 28, 2002, p. A-13).

The future for interethnic relations is open-ended. On the one hand, if things play out as a zero-sum competition among subordinated groups, then there will likely be increasing hostility, especially between

African Americans and Latinos. This tendency has been present, but not dominant, thus far and it can best be avoided by enhancing opportunities for all subordinated groups in the area—an admittedly large task. On the other hand, the increasing interest among local actors in intercultural exchange with Mexican and Latino immigrants should help improve interethnic relations. Also, we expect local political and social activism by Mexican and other Latino immigrants, which has only recently begun to emerge, to develop as immigrants become more well-established. This should contribute constructively to interethnic relations, and enhance immigrant rights as well as local civic life and the expansion of participatory (if not formal electoral) democracy.

We would like to thank Leila Krause, Myra El Assal, Janitzio Ouattara, Amy Liebman, Julia Foxwell, Al Snyder, Memo Diriker, Gonzalo Martinez, Niklas Robinson, and Suzy Benedict, among others, for their assistance in our research. We are also very grateful to all interviewees who were otherwise willing to speak with us and share their insights, experiences and time. Thanks as well to Gideon Sjoberg and Rubén Hernández-León for their helpful comments during the writing process. We are also grateful for the support we received that enabled our research from the Fulton School of Liberal Arts at Salisbury University, the U.S. Fulbright Visiting Scholars Program, and Washington College.

NOTES

1. Delmarva is separated from the rest of the East Coast by geography, surrounded by water on three sides; the only bridge to the west over the Chesapeake Bay was built in 1952, after three hundred years of European and African settlement. There are still only two bridges now, one bridge west and one bridge-tunnel south, plus a land route to the north. While the region is within about one hundred miles of four major metropolitan areas, it is rural, conservative, and culturally very distant from those metropolises.

2. The various dimensions of rights have been conceptualized in Thomas H. Marshall's (1950) classic work. Civil, political, and social rights have been won in succession over centuries by the working class and then other subordinated groups within society (with the British case as the prototype). Other citizenship theorists generally build on this view. We should note that several have specifically critiqued the concept of human rights and seem to take issue with the unconditional view of rights (Turner 1990, 190; Barbalet 1988, 6).

3. These works tend to pose immigrants and their rights as a threat to the well-being and sovereignty of the nation state, the value of citizenship, and even the physical security of nation states (Jopke 1998; Jacobson 1996; Weiner 1995; Soysal 1994; Sassen 1998; Brubaker 1989; Shuck 1998).

4. There is a growing literature at least implicitly preoccupied with the human rights and well being of immigrants rather than with the preservation of state power (see Eschbach, Hagan, and Rodriguez 2001; Eschbach et al. 1999; Heyman 1995; *International Migration Review* 1991; Goodwin-Gil 1998; Baubock 1994; Jonas 1996; Hernández-Truyol 1997; and Nickel 1983). However, it is far less developed conceptually than citizenship theory, relying instead on international law and often failing to link data to ideas and general guidelines. In that sense, like the citizenship literature, this emerging body of work is also very preoccupied with the state.

5. Many local observers view the census data as grossly undercounting the Hispanic population in the region, particularly the undocumented immigrant portion typically anxious to avoid detection by government representatives. It also seems that many seasonal, migratory farm laborers were not counted, especially in Somerset County.

6. The two exceptions from this list of seven are Salisbury, where the Hispanic proportion of the population remained low at 3.4 percent in 2000, and Seaford at 4.3 percent Hispanic. We included them on the list because they each have Hispanic populations of several hundred people, which while small in relative terms in each town, it makes them significant centers of Hispanic population in the region.

7. This is consistent with the findings of Mexican researchers, that Veracruz has become a large-scale migrant sending state since the 1990s, especially to the eastern and southern United States (fieldnotes on LASA panel, September 8, 2001; Perez-Monterosas 2001).

8. Pseudonym.

9. Exactly how the company could act on this threat is unclear, since in so doing they would have to admit they committed a crime—hiring and retaining undocumented immigrant workers—although they could perhaps avoid this with an anonymous tip to the INS, a not uncommon reporting tactic.

10. One provision specifies that if INS representatives arrive at a plant seeking specific workers, management will not just turn them over quickly (as was typical until now), but rather must allow a union shop steward to meet with the INS agents first, whose main purpose will be to see that they have a proper arrest warrant, and if they do not, then refuse to turn over the worker. The second provision is that the company will recognize the work history (for seniority and benefits) of workers who change their names in the event of any sort of immigration amnesty, after which many could use their real names (Martinez interview, September 13, 2002).

REFERENCES

Barbalet, J. M. 1988. *Citizenship*. Milton Keynes, U.K.: Open University Press.

Baubock, Rainer. 1994. *Transnational Citizenship: Membership and Rights in International Migration*. Brookfield, Vt.: Edward Elgar.

Borland, Katherine. 2001. *Creating Community: Hispanic Migration to Rural Delaware*. Wilmington, Del.: Delaware Heritage Commission.

Brubaker, William Rogers, ed. 1989. *Immigration and the Politics of Citizenship in Europe and North America*. Lanham, Md.: University Press of America.

Business Economic and Community Outreach Network (BEACON). 2002. *Economic Forecast 2002: A National and Local Overview*. Salisbury University. Unpublished Paper. Available at: http://pmg.salisbury.edu (accessed October 28, 2004).

Eschbach, Karl, Jacqueline Hagan, Nestor Rodriguez. 2001. "Migrant Deaths at the U.S.-Mexico Border: Research Findings and Ethical and Human Rights Themes." *LASA Forum* 32(2): 7–10.

Eschbach, Karl, Jacqueline Hagan, Nestor Rodriguez, Rubén Hernández-León, and Stanley Bailey. 1999. "Death at the Border." *International Migration Review* 33(2): 430–54.

Feagin, Joe R., and Hernán Vera. 2001. *Liberation Sociology*. Boulder, Colo.: Westview Press.

Goodwin-Gil, Guy S. 1998. "Migration, International Law and Human Rights." In *Managing Migration: Time for a New International Regime?*, edited by Bimal Ghosh. New York: Oxford University Press.

Hernández-Truyol, Berta Esperanza. 1997. "Reconciling Rights in Collision: An International Human Rights Strategy." In *Immigrants Out! The New Nativism and the Anti-Immigrant Impulse in the United States*, edited by Juan F. Perea. New York: New York University Press.

Heyman, Josiah McC. 1995. "Putting Power in the Anthropology of Bureaucracy: The Immigration and Naturalization Service at the Mexico-United States Border." *Current Anthropology* 36(2): 261–87.

Horowitz, Roger, and Mark J. Miller. 1999. *Immigrants in the Delmarva Poultry Processing Industry: The Changing Face of Georgetown, Delaware, and Environs*. JSRI Occasional Paper #37. East Lansing: Julian Samora Research Institute, Michigan State University.

International Migration Review. 1991. Special issue on the "New International Convention on the Protection of the Rights of all Migrant Workers and their Families." *International Migration Review* 25(4): entire issue.

Jacobson, David. 1996. *Rights Across Borders: Immigration and the Decline of Citizenship*. Baltimore: Johns Hopkins University Press.

Jonas, Suzanne, ed. 1996. Special issue on "Immigration: A Civil Rights Issue for the Americas in the 21st Century." *Social Justice* 23(3): entire issue.

Jopke, Christian. 1998. *Challenge to the Nation-State: Immigration in Western Europe and the United States*. New York: Oxford University Press.

Marshall, Thomas H. 1950. *Citizenship and Social Class and Other Essays.* Cambridge, U.K.: Cambridge University Press.

Nickel, James W. 1983. "Human Rights and the Rights of Aliens." In *The Border that Joins,* edited by Peter G. Brown and Henry Shue. Totowa, N.J.: Rowman and Littlefield.

Perez-Monterosas, Mario. 2001. *"Tejiendo los caminos, se construyen los destinos": redes migratorias de Veracruz a los Estados Unidos.* Paper presented at the international congress of the Latin American Studies Association (September 8, 2001).

Sassen, Saskia. 1998. *Globalization and Its Discontents: Essays on the New Mobility of People and Money.* New York: New Press.

Shuck, Peter H. 1998. *Citizens, Strangers, and In-Betweens: Essays on Immigration and Citizenship.* Boulder, Colo.: Westview Press.

Sjoberg, Gideon. 1996. "The Human Rights Challenge to Communitarianism: Formal Organizations and Race and Ethnicity." In *Macro Socio-Economics,* edited by David Sciulli. Armonk, N.Y.: M.E. Sharpe.

Sjoberg, Gideon, Elizabeth A. Gill, and Norma Williams. 2001. "A Sociology of Human Rights." *Social Problems* 48(1): 11–47.

Soysal, Yasemin Nuhoglu. 1994. *Limits of Citizenship: Migrants and Postnational Membership in Europe.* Chicago: University of Chicago Press.

Stull, Donald D., Michael J. Broadway, and David Griffith, eds. 1995. *Anyway You Cut It: Meat Processing and Small Town America.* Lawrence: University of Kansas Press.

Turner, Bryan S. 1990 "Outline of a Theory of Citizenship." *Sociology* 24(2): 189–217.

———. 1993. "Outline of a Theory of Human Rights." In *Citizenship and Social Theory,* edited by Bryan Turner. London: Sage Publications.

———. 2001. "The Erosion of Citizenship." *British Journal of Sociology* 52(2): 189–209.

———. 2002. "States, Citizenship, and Human Rights." *Journal of Human Rights* 1(1): 135–38.

U.S. Census Bureau. 2002a. *Census of Population and Housing 1990.* Washington: U.S. Census Bureau. Available at: http://factfinder.census.gov (accessed October 28, 2004).

———. 2002b. *Census of Population and Housing 2000.* Washington: U.S. Census Bureau. Available at: http://factfinder.census.gov (accessed October 28, 2004).

Van Gunsteren, Herman. 1978. "Notes on a Theory of Citizenship." In *Democracy, Consensus and Social Contract,* edited by Pierre Birnbaum, Jack Lively, and Geraint Parry. London: Sage Publications.

———. 1998. *A Theory of Citizenship: Organizing Plurality in Contemporary Democracies.* Boulder, Colo.: Westview Press.

Weiner, Myron. 1995. *The Global Migration Crisis: Challenge to States and to Human Rights.* New York: Harper Collins.

PART III

INTERGROUP RELATIONS: CONFLICT AND ACCOMMODATION BETWEEN NEWCOMERS AND ESTABLISHED RESIDENTS

CHAPTER 8

⋈

THE SOCIOPOLITICAL DYNAMICS OF MEXICAN IMMIGRATION IN LEXINGTON, KENTUCKY, 1997 TO 2002: AN AMBIVALENT COMMUNITY RESPONDS

BRIAN L. RICH AND MARTA MIRANDA

Lexington, Kentucky, the metropolitan center of the Bluegrass Region—famous as "the Horse Capital of the World"—and a major tobacco-producing area of the United States, is currently in the process of receiving a major influx of Hispanic-Latino[1] immigrants, about 90 percent of them from Mexico. This flow began in the early 1990s in response to labor needs in the region. Despite the presence of over 10,000 Hispanic workers by 1997—most of them undocumented—the greater Lexington community was still virtually ignorant of their economic importance and social needs. This changed in 1998 when the Lexington-Fayette Urban County Government (hereafter LFUCG)—forced primarily by the political pressure and advocacy of the Lexington Hispanic Association–Asociación de Hispanos Unidos (hereafter AHU)—attempted to identify the needs of its rapidly growing Latino population. The fact that the Latino population in this area has increased as much as 500 percent between 1990 and 2000 meant that major changes in the social fabric of the community were inevitably coming.

The process and dynamics of this Hispanic-Latino migration and settlement in the area throughout the 1990s and into the new century can be characterized as a quiet and benign, yet unsettled and troubled, accommodation on the part of established residents. The Lexington community response to its Latino newcomers is an ambivalent mixture of paternalistic concern and xenophobia. In this chapter we describe the development of this ambivalent community response to the new Mexi-

can immigrant community and present an analytic model for understanding it.

Because the settling out of Mexican and other Hispanic immigrants
into the Lexington–Fayette County area is a very recent phenomenon,
this analysis is by definition tentative, as the situation is still dynamic
and subject to change. There are interesting and contradictory dynamics at work in this case that are both promising of ongoing constructive
interactions between established residents and the new immigrants, as
well as foreboding and troubling issues that threaten to perpetuate
some very serious social problems for Latinos in Lexington. Furthermore, the larger interethnic relations among resident whites and African Americans and Hispanic immigrants are still quite undefined, as the
long-established white-black relationship has been somewhat displaced
and disrupted; new, multicultural tensions have emerged as a topic of
concern in the community, especially between African Americans and
Latino newcomers.

The interethnic experience created by the new Mexican immigrant
presence in Lexington has shifted during this period from one of invisibility and neglect by established residents—both white and black—to
a grudging recognition and slow, but positive, steps toward accommodating this immigrant community's needs. However, some recent interethnic experiences, exacerbated since the events of September 11, 2001,
show that these steps toward accommodation may be fragile and short-
lived. Furthermore, the political weakness of the Hispanic community
is a central problem undermining the progress made so far. Thus the
ambivalent reception Latino immigrants have received from both whites
and blacks can be understood as both a typical case of negative, racialized, and xenophobic community response to new immigrants, as well
as a novel case of paternalistic, benign, or cooperative reception, potentially promising multicultural accommodation.

Scholars have long addressed the issues of Latino immigrant social
integration and the community response of settled residents to this immigration (for example, Acuña 1972; McWilliams 1935/1978; Portes
and Bach 1985; Portes and Truelove 1987; Tienda 1989); however, the
novel character of the receiving contexts discussed in this volume present new opportunities to examine the dynamics of reception and integration and to evaluate extant theories of intergroup relations under
these novel conditions. While we do not directly engage the theoretical
literature, our analysis suggests that any localization of these dynamics
must be cognizant of both the internationalized context of reception
and integration, as well as the specific local variables bearing on these

dynamics (see Massey, Durand, and Malone 2002; Portes and Rumbaut 1996; Bach 1993; Cornelius and Bustamante 1989).

Our purpose is to describe the contours of this recent immigrant influx and settlement and to analyze how Lexington's community and institutional response has unfolded. We argue that the recent history of this area shows that the accommodation of Latino immigrants has depended on four key factors: the perceived need for their labor by prominent employer groups; perceptions by poor whites and blacks of competition in low-wage labor markets; the level of funding support for immigrant accommodation in schools, social services, and the greater community by government, nonprofit, and corporate sources; and the ability of the Hispanic community to develop further organizational and political infrastructure to represent and advocate for itself well. These factors account for the ambivalent mixture of paternalism and xenophobia currently crisscrossing the community response here.

DATA AND METHODS

We draw on a variety of both empirical and experiential data. Our sources include census data, survey data from four local, nonrandom, convenience samples of Hispanic immigrants (totaling nearly a thousand respondents), initial results from four focus groups with Latinos in the community, human service providers' data on trends in provision of services to Hispanics, newspaper and other locally produced articles and documents related to the Mexican immigration here, and our own ethnographic, political, and personal experiences.[2]

We use various methods to analyze and understand this information. The quantitative data is used to describe and analyze particular demographic and social features of the Hispanic and Mexican newcomers to the area. The qualitative data is used to describe and analyze the history, politics, and social dynamics involved that emerged from the authors' joint experiences as participant observers, social activists, administrator of social service programs, and focus group researcher on problems in the Hispanic community. Also, we draw on an archive of all local, and some regional and national, news coverage of the growing Latino community in central Kentucky over the period.

For baseline data on the Mexican and Latino population of the area and its rapid increase, figures from the 1990 and 2000 censuses were consulted. For more detailed information on the composition and demographics of this group, we draw on four nonrandom, convenience surveys of local Hispanic residents.

In 1998, a local community-based organization founded in 1997, the Asociación de Hispanos Unidos (AHU), carried out a survey of 428 Hispanics as an initial attempt to assess the social service needs of the growing and, in the minds of the association, greatly neglected, Latino population. The data collection was carried out by distributing surveys to Latino residents throughout the urban area. The survey asked about occupations, earnings and benefits, education, language, housing, and access to social services.

In 1999, the local Kentucky Migrant Network Coalition, a network of social service agencies which meet monthly and maintain an intensive email listserve to communicate and coordinate services to migrant workers, collected survey data from Hispanic participants at its annual Hispanic health fair. Including 178 persons, this data is used here for comparisons with other surveys, mainly regarding age, marital status, and occupations. This data was collected within the highest density Latino residential area of Lexington (Cardinal Valley) and therefore may reflect a higher proportion of settled families, as it asked questions about respondents' children and older relatives, as well as garnering information about the economically active adults who attended the health fair.

In the spring of 2000, a local Hispanic minister and student at the Lexington Theological Seminary, Job Cobos, carried out a survey of 386 Hispanic churchgoers in five local churches, including the Catholic, Assemblies of God, Baptist, Pentecostal, and a Christian Church (Disciples of Christ) and Methodist joint Hispanic congregation. Of those returning these surveys, 329 indicated Mexican origin and the findings used here are based only on those data. This survey was carried out by Cobos himself, a native of Mexico, with the assistance at the Catholic Church of Abdón Ibarra, the city government's Immigrant Services coordinator. The survey asked for basic demographic, occupation, wage, remittances to Mexico, housing, language, and other information of local interest (Cobos 2000).

In the winter of 2001, Ibarra published the results of a study he carried out in the largest Hispanic neighborhood in Lexington, Cardinal Valley, where he was the coordinator of the city's Latino social service center (Ibarra 2001). Ibarra, a descendent of Mexican immigrants and a native of Texas, drew on his ready cultural and linguistic ease with Mexicans here and interviewed 129 families about various quality of life issues, including housing, employment, documentation, and social service needs (Michelle Ku, "Survey Highlights Latinos' Plight: Study

Looks at 129 Cardinal Valley Hispanic Families," *Lexington Herald-Leader*, March 11, 2001, pp. B1, B3).

Although all these surveys are based on nonrandom, convenience samples, the sample sizes and relative consistency between them give us fair confidence in their validity. Nonetheless, until we have better data, we must be cautious about assuming the reliability and representativeness of these numbers.

The qualitative data we use derives mainly from our direct participant observation and ethnographic experience. The types of information that we have derived from our direct participation in this case fall into three categories: political, administrative, and sociological. In terms of the political information we use here, both authors were involved in the leadership of AHU during this period. The central aims of the organization are the development of a positive community response to the social needs of Latino newcomers and to provide help and advocacy for their human needs and rights. These goals implied that we needed to engage leaders in governmental, corporate, and nonprofit organizations to educate and advocate on behalf of the Hispanic community.

Further qualitative knowledge of this history was gained through Miranda's responsibilities as an administrator of the "Hispanic Initiative Network" (hereafter HIN)—a small, collaborative program involving governmental, corporate, and nonprofit organizations to provide a set of bilingual and bicultural social service workers to assist local Hispanics. This program was the result of AHU's political work. As a bilingual, bicultural authority figure in this project, professionally trained in social work, Marta Miranda gained in-depth insight into the micro politics of this project, as well as the social problems faced by Latino newcomers.

Finally, the sociological data, over and above the participant observation and ethnographic field notes developed, include preliminary results from four focus groups with Hispanic-only respondents, organized and run by Brian Rich (2000; 2001a; 2001b; forthcoming).[3] The primary goal of these focus groups was to ask Latinos from various segments of the newcomer community what they thought were the most salient problems faced by Hispanics in the area.

HISTORY AND SOCIAL COMPOSITION OF THE MEXICAN MIGRATION TO LEXINGTON

An unequal power relationship between Mexican immigrants and U.S. elites has always characterized the migrant experience (Acuña 1972;

McWilliams 1935/1978; Cornelius 1989a; 1989b; Vernez 1994; Portes and Rumbaut 1996; Camarota 2001). The case under discussion here, while part of this larger history, marks perhaps a new and brighter chapter. What we are witnessing in the development of new destinations of Mexican migration is nothing less than a test of, and a challenge to, the possibility of realizing a pacific normalization of multicultural relations in areas previously characterized by settled interethnic group relations based on white, privileged-class domination (see Perrucci and Wysong 1999). While this process is still burgeoning, the contours of the formation of multicultural interethnic group relations are beginning to take shape throughout many parts of the United States (see Bach 1993). Therefore, much can be learned from careful observation and analysis of the formative period of these relations; initial social dynamics typically have long-lasting effects on the structure of intergroup relations.

While a great body of research already details the long history and politics of Mexican migration (see Acuña 1972; Portes and Bach 1985; Carrasco 1997; Suarez-Orozco 1998; Martínez 2001; Massey, Durand, and Malone 2002), we know very little about the current dynamics and potential changes at work in Mexican-U.S. migration in the post-IRCA, post-NAFTA era. It would seem that we are on the threshold of seeing either a continuation of the subordination of Mexican immigrants to the lowest rungs of the North American social order or the possibility of working out new, more egalitarian relations between our nations, multiple ethnic groups, and classes in the greater political economy. We situate this case study within such a larger question.

In Kentucky, and the southeastern region in general, the appearance of a significant number of Mexican immigrants presents a new chapter in this long history. Long being a north-south border state, Kentucky has an interesting history of being "on the edge" of southern culture, while still maintaining an openness to northern and western U.S. influences, especially since the Great Depression and World War II. A rural and mostly agricultural and mining state, Kentucky experienced very little domestic in-migration until the beginnings of the 1970s, when high tech and light industrialization brought some new, mostly educated, mostly white immigrants.

In the aftermath of the Civil Rights Movements of the 1950s and 1960s, Lexington, like other southern cities, had seen some demographic decline in its black population, mainly through emigration to urban areas in bordering states to the north and east. The Central Kentucky Bluegrass region, of which Lexington is the center, settled into a new race relations regime between blacks and whites that was based upon a mixture of an old cultural relationship of white elite paternalism and superiority with some economic, social, and political concessions to blacks, such as improved voting rights, integration of public accommodations and schools, and some state antipoverty programs. Like many other parts of the "Old South," this fairly settled pattern of white paternalism and black appeasement or benign neglect in the post–Civil Rights Era frames this discussion. The economic basis for this interethnic relationship between whites and blacks is crucial to understanding the changing character of race relations today in the face of a growing and now visible Mexican immigrant population. What we see unfolding now is a new and uncertain set of interethnic and multicultural group relationships that are destabilizing past ones.

The economic pillars of Central Kentucky have long been horse breeding and tobacco farming, along with more recent, if relatively minor, developments in both light and heavy industries. When both the horse and tobacco industries began to feel the pinch of labor shortages in the late 1980s and early 1990s, the development of a Mexican migrant labor stream began.[4] By the mid 1990s, close observers and leaders in the tobacco farming and thoroughbred horse breeding industries were well aware of the need for new sources of labor.[5] Employers made public and legal, as well as covert and illegal, attempts to procure and stabilize a Mexican stream of this needed labor.[6] U.S. census data, which we know greatly underestimates the real size of this population,[7] shows that the Hispanic population in Fayette County[8] grew 235 percent between 1990 and 2000, from 2,556 to 8,561, while the county population grew only 16 percent from 225,366 to 260,512 during the same period (U.S. Bureau of the Census 2002a; 2002b).

Twin facts teamed up to increase rapidly the recruitment and employment of Mexican workers in Central Kentucky from the early 1990s to the present: tobacco farmers have been facing a severe economic squeeze due to the gradual yet certain withdrawal of federal price supports and labor shortages (Hamilton 1990); and migrant Mexican labor—a small amount recruited under the Federal H-2A temporary worker program,[9] but most often undocumented—was easily attractable and flexible for seasonal harvest work in tobacco and on the horse farms (Kentucky Legislative Research Commission 2002). The fact that the majority of these workers arrived without documentation made them a cheap and exploitable workforce, given they have no officially autho-

rized standing in the United States and therefore cannot protect themselves legally (Valarie Honeycutt, "Hispanic Workers Being Abused,
Panel Told," *Lexington Herald-Leader*, October 1, 1998, p. B1).[10]

As is very often the case in such new opportunities for migrant labor,
the source of Mexican workers initially consisted of young male sojourners, itinerant laborers that seek out and explore new labor opportunities. This sojourning (or "target worker") labor supply is often part
of conscious Mexican familial strategies to maximize household income
or to reach a family economic project goal in the sending country (Cornelius 1992; Massey and Espinosa 1997), often via remittances from
migrant work by young fathers and older, unmarried sons (López 1998).
However, the seemingly rapid change in the demographic profile of the
Mexican-origin population of this region suggests that a new type of
migration is forming, perhaps because of the legalization of sizable
numbers of Mexican immigrants through the amnesty provisions of the
1986 Immigration and Reform Control Act (see Cornelius 1992; Hernández-León and Zúñiga 2000; Massey, Durand, and Malone 2002).

As we show, the labor market insertion of Mexican immigrants indicates that we are already past the initial, transient, seasonal migratory
phase of Mexican settlement in our area. By now, it appears that Latinos have already become "structurally embedded" in the urban labor
market (see Cornelius 1998). That is to say, the urbanized settling out
of this migrant stream has occurred as the result of a structural need
for their labor within the local economy, mostly in low-wage service
jobs (especially in the hospitality industries—hotels and restaurants),
but also significantly in construction and factory work. Furthermore,
the social composition of the immigrant community has already become
characterized by a substantial proportion of women and children, indicating some degree of commitment to permanent residence here. Therefore, the larger institutional response to this immigration (government
services, corporate, and nonprofit social service policies) is now being
forced to change in new ways to accommodate Latino newcomers. We
now describe how the demographic and social contours of the Hispanic
immigrants reflect this transition from a migratory, transient agricultural labor force into a more urbanized, settled community.

Demographic Characteristics of the
Latino Population in Lexington

Who are the new Mexican-Latino immigrants to the Lexington area?
In what follows we briefly describe some of the demographic and social

characteristics of this population, including age, gender, family structure, and marital status.

Age Structure   "The majority of Hispanic adults residing in Fayette
County are young adults between the ages of 21 and 40" (Asociación
de Hispanos Unidos 1998, 6). Table 8.1, combining the Cobos and MNC
data, supports AHU's finding and extends it by incorporating some
children in their samples.

The MNC data show larger proportions of children and older adults
because those surveys asked one adult to give the ages of children and
other relatives accompanying them to the health fair where this data
was collected. The Cobos (2000) survey did not ask any direct question
about number of respondents' children. Ibarra's survey of 129 families
found 33 percent of them had children; these forty-two families with
children reported an average of three (Ibarra 2001, 7). In sum, these
data demonstrate that somewhere between 80 and 90 percent of the
Latino community in Lexington is younger than forty years old and
many have children, as we show in more detail later.

Gender Composition, Family Structure and Marital Status   Of the
secondary survey data available, only the Cobos and AHU data asked
for the gender of the respondent. Of the 329 Mexican origin subjects
that replied in the Cobos (2000) study, only 246 (or 75 percent) answered the question, with 57 percent responding male and 43 percent
responding female. For an immigrant community this young, one might
expect a larger percentage of males. Indeed, the AHU data collected

TABLE 8.1   Age Distribution of Hispanics in Fayette County,
Kentucky, 1998 to 2000

Age	Frequency	Valid Percentage	Cumulative Percentage
One to ten	36	7.4	7.4
Eleven to twenty	74	15.2	22.6
Twenty-one to thirty	200	41.2	63.8
Thirty-one to forty	92	18.9	82.7
Forty-one to fifty	47	9.7	92.4
Fifty-one to ninety-nine	37	7.6	100.0
Total	486	100.0	

Source: MNC data (Kentucky Migrant Network Coalition 1999); Cobos data (Cobos 2000).

only two years earlier, found that 71 percent of the respondents were male. Given that the Cobos data was collected through churches how- ever, women's greater religiosity relative to men may be a factor inflat- ing their numbers and skewing the gender composition; alternatively, the AHU data could be a reflection of the more public nature of the sampling strategy. Combined, these samples could indicate a rapid femi- nization of the Latino population in recent years. In any case, data pre- sented later demonstrate how Hispanic family structure in the area has become quite complex, indicating that the male sojourner period of ini- tial migrant exploration of the area is now past.

These data in table 8.2 show that a clear majority of Mexican immi- grants (about 75 percent across the samples) are living with family and relatives, many of them with children. Only about a quarter of the im- migrants surveyed in these samples reported living without relatives, although Ibarra reported that almost half (48 percent) stated they were "here alone." Ibarra's study also found that of the forty-two of the 129 households surveyed with children (33 percent), 60 percent of those children were six years and younger, and that 85 percent of these were

TABLE 8.2   Family Composition of Hispanics in Fayette County, Kentucky, 1998 to 2000

Do you have children?[a]		
Yes	96	55.8
No	76	44.2
Total	172	100
How many living with you?[a]		
Zero	76	45.2
One	23	13.7
Two or more	69	41.1
Total	168	100
Household members living with you[b]		
Children	98	35.8
Siblings	91	33.2
Parents	13	4.7
Other relatives	6	2.2
Others	66	24.1
Total	274	100%

Source: [a]MNC data (Kentucky Migrant Network Coalition 1999); [b]Cobos data (Cobos 2000).

U.S. citizens, having been born here (Abdón Ibarra, "Legal or Illegal Immigrants Add to City's Economy," *Lexington Herald-Leader*, April 9, 2000, pp. D1, D3). Among these data, we find that anywhere from 36 to 62 percent of respondents indicate having children with them. Furthermore, the MNC and Cobos data show that a large majority of Hispanics (about 66 percent) is or has been married. It would appear that the reliability of these data on household structure and number of children is not great, as the variance between samples is high. Nonetheless these data and community observation confirm that Latino immigrants are settling as families here, possibly on a permanent basis.

We can infer from this data on age structure, gender composition, family structure, and marital status—as well as from the accounts of social service workers within the Hispanic community—that the Mexican immigrant population here is no longer predominantly comprised of young single men. Furthermore, in a few short years (approximately 1995 to 2002) we have gone from a mostly male sojourner migrant population to a much more heterogeneous immigrant community composed of a growing proportion of women, extended and multigenerational kin, and children.

The causes of this change have much to do with the changing labor market participation of Mexican immigrants. Because work in the tobacco fields especially and agricultural work in the area is often temporary and seasonal, many found a growing demand for more permanent work in the urban low-wage service job market. As can be seen in table 8.3, over the years under study here, Lexington has had very low unemployment rates compared with both Kentucky and national figures.

Establishments throughout the city, especially in the restaurant industry, have for years been dotted with signs indicating "help wanted" along with various explicit recruitment strategies, such as signing bo-

TABLE 8.3   Unemployment Rates (in Percentages)

Year	United States	Kentucky	Fayette County
1997	4.9	5.4	2.5
1998	4.5	4.6	2.0
1999	4.2	4.5	2.0
2000	4.0	4.1	1.8
2001	4.8	5.5	3.0

Source: Kentucky Department for Employment Services (2002a, 2002b, 2002c, 2002d, 2002e).

nuses and entry-level wages well above the minimum wage posted publicly. The shortage of entry-level labor has been especially acute here, due mainly to a lack of young cohorts of native workers and the extremely high demand for services of all types.[11] A study commissioned by the Kentucky State Legislature supports this point: "Employers interviewed said they hire noncitizen workers because there are not enough applicants among U.S. citizens to fill their work demands at the wages they offer. With a supply of workers not readily available, they have turned to recruiting and hiring immigrants and refugees. Some employers noted that it was a matter of "survival" for their companies" (Kentucky Legislative Research Commission 2002, 31–2).

Finding more stable, permanent work leads often to bringing other kin, including wives and children. These data also show that many have begun to bear children here and thus have perhaps already begun to settle more permanently. Data from the Cobos survey found that while there is still a substantial proportion of the Mexican-origin immigrant community (36 percent) that intends to stay for relatively short periods of time (that is, less than two years), 64 percent reported intending to stay anywhere from three to ten or more years. In response to the question "are you thinking of returning to your country?" fully 40 percent responded negatively or that they didn't know. We see these responses as a strong indicator that many immigrants are now settling permanently here. Furthermore, as others have emphasized, the fortification and increased enforcement of the U.S.-Mexico border have increased the risk of not being able to return to the United States, having the ironic effect of encouraging rather than discouraging permanent settlement in the United States, regardless of immigration status (Massey, Durand, and Malone 2002). Mexican family and community strategies have thus shifted with regard to whom and for how long migrants should go to the United States in search of work, leading to the immigration of more women, children, and extended kin, including older family members.

This rapid change in the demographic composition of the Hispanic population in Lexington, while very recent, has enormous implications for every facet of the interethnic relationships that we discuss further later. Examining current dynamics in the way that Latino workers are being integrated into the local labor market will allow us to help explain the larger complex pattern of both resistance and accommodation found in the interethnic relations between Latinos, whites, and African Americans in Central Kentucky.

Labor Market Incorporation

Data on the incorporation of Latinos into the local occupational structure reveal that a significant proportion of this population is now working in urban jobs, as opposed to being solely concentrated in work in
agriculture or the horse industry. Given that labor shortages in these
rural industries were the true magnet for the beginnings of Mexican
migration to this area, the shift to urbanized employment raises the
issue of how the new Hispanic immigrants have affected interethnic
relations in the city. Here, through a brief examination of the contours
of Latino employment in Lexington, we discuss how the incorporation
of Hispanics into the local labor market is related to interethnic relations and the community response to, and politics of accommodation of,
the new immigrant influx.

Table 8.4 summarizes all the survey data available on the occupational distribution of Hispanics in Fayette County. Before examining
these data, we should first point out that the survey data we have at
hand most likely over-samples working-class Hispanics. While there is
a small layer of professional and entrepreneurial Latinos in Lexington,

TABLE 8.4   Hispanic Occupational Structure in Fayette County
(in Percentages)

Category	AHU 1998	MNC 1999	Cobos 2000	Weighted Averages
Agriculture or horse	38.7	26.0	39.4	37.0
Construction	7.2	19.6	7.8	9.3
Restaurant or hotel	13.8	6.5	14.7	13.0
Domestic	9.1	7.3	12.8	10.2
Professional or managerial	0.3	0.1	2.8	1.2
Other services	1.0	4.4	5.0	3.0
Factory	11.5	32.6	17.0	16.8
All others	11.7	2.9	.5	6.2
No answer	6.7	NA	NA	NA
Total (percentage)	100.0	99.4	100.0	96.7
Total N	428	138	329	895

Sources: AHU data (Asociación de Hispanos Unidos 1998); MNC data (Kentucky Migrant Network Coalition 1999); Cobos data (Cobos 2000).
Note: NA = not applicable.

the odds that they are represented in these surveys in any proportion to their true numbers is low, given the venues and methods used for data collection.[12] (It is important to note that most of the Hispanics in the middle class here are non-Mexican Hispanics, most of South American origin.) Despite this, the occupational distribution presented demonstrates the concentration of Hispanics in a few key sectors of the labor market. While there are some important variations in the occupational distribution of Latinos depending on the samples reported, overall there is fairly good consistency between them, lending greater robustness and validity to the weighted averages shown in the last column of the table.

The first thing to note in this table is that a strong majority of Hispanic workers (60 percent or more) are now working in urban jobs. The MNC data probably over samples these workers, as that survey was administered in an urban Latino residential area, showing that almost 75 percent of Hispanics are working in urban jobs. Furthermore, that sample shows that over half of the sample (58 percent) is concentrated in only two urban job categories, construction and factory work. The data from this MNC sample are perhaps the strongest indicator that the process of Hispanic incorporation in the labor market here has gone beyond the initial migration-magnet of work in agriculture and the horse industry and has developed into more urban and permanent work. Even when we look at the weighted averages across the samples, we see that fully half of the Latino workforce is now employed in urban jobs.

This is an important signal with respect to the longer term accommodation and community response to the new Latino immigrant community. Furthermore, many of the Mexican workers in the horse industry are in stable and permanent work—as opposed to those who work seasonally in the tobacco fields, especially during the late summer harvest, or other agricultural jobs. Women's settlement and incorporation into urban labor markets emphasizes this trend towards potential permanent settlement.

Not surprisingly, the gender distribution of Hispanic workers reveals that the urbanization of Latino labor has been accompanied by greater numbers of women. Taking only urban labor markets into consideration (excluding agricultural and horse-related occupations), we find that women comprise 41 percent of all Mexican-origin workers employed in the city, paralleling the gender composition of this group. Furthermore, 93 percent of Mexican-origin women are employed in urban jobs (Cobos 2000).

Given the Latino movement into the urban labor market, alongside a permanent incorporation of workers in stable horse industry jobs, it appears very likely that the bulk of these workers would now prefer to settle permanently.

THE AMBIVALENT COMMUNITY RESPONSE: XENOPHOBIA AND PATERNALISM

The foregoing analysis of the labor market incorporation of Hispanics demonstrates that their labor power in this region of Kentucky is structurally embedded in the economic life of Lexington (that is, Mexican workers are essential to the continued functioning and growth of the local and regional economy). Therefore, the dependence of powerful economic actors in the region—be they owners of horse farms, the agricultural bureau, manufacturers, or corporations employing substantial numbers of low-wage service workers—necessarily means that these actors have a vested interest in continuing to have access to this labor supply, legally or otherwise. Hence, these sectors of the community have, by definition, a paternalistic relationship to these workers, that is, they want to protect and "take care" of them insofar as such care is necessary to provide for their disposability as a useful and necessary workforce. This paternalism only becomes salient or visible when the nature of this relationship is questioned or when the relationship itself appears to be failing, for example, when the level of the social problems of Hispanics as human beings surpass their smooth functioning as mere suppliers of labor power. Both of these conditions have been now met in the Lexington area. In what follows we go beyond the paternalism of powerful economic actors to examine how the reactions of other ethnic groups in the working class, the level of funding support for immigrant accommodation, and Hispanic representation have combined with the need of employers to give shape to the ambivalent community response we see here.

INTERETHNIC RELATIONS IN THE LEXINGTON COMMUNITY

The initial incorporation of Mexican immigrant labor in the horse industry and on tobacco farms had little, if any, impact on the community response of native white or black workers. Until the mid-1990s, significant and visible numbers of Hispanics in the Lexington urban area were practically nil, given that the vast majority of them were employed in rural areas as seasonal agricultural workers or on the horse farms. The urbanization of Latino workers into construction, factory, hotel and restaurant, and domestic-type jobs in the late 1990s is therefore crucial to explaining how the institutional and community response has developed. It was this urbanization—combined with an overall rapid growth in numbers—that brought Latinos visibility in the community, in neighborhoods, and in the urban political scene. This also created the beginnings of some negative and xenophobic ethnoracial reactions from both white working-class residents and segments of the black community.

To analyze how Hispanic urbanization and growing visibility have affected the community's response, we first examine how Latino labor market incorporation relates to other ethno-racial groups in the labor market; subsequently, we use this analysis to illuminate intergroup dynamics at the level of the larger community.

Mexican and other Latino workers in Fayette County are quite poor, consistently earning below poverty-level wages. The Cobos data show that Mexican-origin workers who reported their income averaged only $983 a month; furthermore, 59 percent of the Mexican-origin sample reported that they were regularly remitting earnings back to family members in Mexico. This subsample reported remitting an average of $358 a month, further depressing their available resources here. The AHU data showed that 58 percent reported making between $101 and $250 per week, or somewhere between $400 and $1,000 per month, while another 31 percent reported making between $251 and $500 per week or $1,000 to $2,000 per month. In both samples, over 95 percent of the respondents reported earning less than $2,000 per month and about 90 percent reported earning less than $1,500 per month (Cobos 2000; Asociación de Hispanos Unidos 1998).

When beginning to compare distinct ethnic segments of the working class in Lexington, these data reflect the class situation of the average Latino immigrant here. The typical Hispanic worker in the Lexington area is making about $6 an hour and sending $2.50 of that back to Mexico; most of these workers have no insurance, no job security, no legal recourse in case of work discrimination or exploitation, little chance of accessing social services available to U.S. citizens, and no chance of someday recapturing their contributions to the Social Security system. Mexican immigrants in Kentucky form the newest and poorest segment of the working class.

As a new ethnic group working overwhelmingly in low-paid labor markets, Latinos have begun to threaten working-class blacks at the bottom of the ethnoracial and occupational hierarchy. This is a very new phenomenon in this area of the country; however, the development of tensions in Lexington between blacks and Hispanics, we believe, has little so far to do with direct black-brown competition for jobs. A recent state-sponsored report on immigration supports this view: "Employers commented generally that the unemployment rate has been so low for the past few years that in their opinion hiring immigrants...has not taken jobs from U.S. citizens" (Kentucky Legislative Research Commission 2002, 32).

That there is tension between blacks and Latinos has been manifest both directly in public and indirectly through the community grapevine. These tensions have been publicly voiced by negative, racialized comments in a number of community forums on this issue[13] and manifested in targeted criminal activity. A series of twenty-two armed assaults and robberies of Hispanics by blacks occurred in a span of six weeks in the fall of 1999; this was later discovered by police to be an organized campaign, Tom Lasseter explained in back-to-back local newpaper articles.[14] In the first few months of 2002, another rash of such interethnic assaults appeared to be recurring. Indirect evidence of the tensions between blacks and Hispanics is provided by anecdotal evidence from contacts throughout the black community as well as by local African American newspaper columnist Merlene Davis, well known for her close ties to the wider black community here:

> I have noticed an undying racism in the black community toward Hispanics, mostly Mexicans. A couple of years ago when I first heard disparaging words, racist words, used by blacks against Hispanics, I thought it would go away once the newness of having another minority in town faded.... That hasn't happened. ("Be Kind, Considerate to Hispanic Neighbors," *Lexington Herald-Leader*, August 28, 2000)

It is our belief that these tensions are due more to a sense of symbolic challenge posed by Latinos to the feelings of oppression and disadvantage felt by working class African Americans, in addition to the language and cultural barriers that make many English-speaking residents uncomfortable with the new Hispanic presence here. Black leaders in the community have occasionally expressed some concern that Latinos may be "taking away" jobs from poor blacks, but the urban occupational niches that Latinos have entered (especially restaurant and domestic work) along with the generalized labor shortage lend little credence to this concern (Ibarra 2000). There has so far been little evidence of Latino job competition with blacks in these niches, as job growth in these occupations and the generalized shortage of labor in low-wage markets have meant very low unemployment. Nonetheless, here as in many aspects of social life, perception may be more important than reality; the appearance and rapid growth of Latinos within the urban scene may be threatening blacks with the concern that their own economic marginalization may be worsened by poorer Latinos that are willing to work for low wages and endure or ignore the American stigma associated with such work. There is also some sense that Hispanic self-help and ethnic solidarity amongst workers contrasts with the social disorganization and fragmentation often noted in Lexington's poorer African American neighborhoods, adding shame to misfortune.

This was evidenced in one exchange amongst Hispanic community leaders in one of Rich's focus groups. In discussing the discrimination that Latinos face in Lexington, "Jorge"[15]—a Hispanic leader working in social services—noted that he saw racism amongst blacks, that there were "blacks dogging Hispanics . . . one black man . . . said that Mexicans stick together and that 'they have something over on blacks that way' . . . that this doesn't exist in the black community. . . . [Hispanic] assimilation is hurt by this lack of intermixing. . . . But . . . Hispanic connection is an asset to them." Immediately following this statement, "María"—a social worker well known in the immigrant community—responded: "Anyone willing to dog the Hispanic community should look at themselves, go into the community and see how Hispanics value family, stick together."

Other focus group participants—especially those in the two workers' groups, one of just Hispanic men and the other Hispanic women—stated often that they felt more prejudice from blacks than from whites. Here is one example from "Dolores," an unemployed factory worker who lost her job to a work-related injury:

> I've been able to see it more, uh, on the part of black people, I don't know why . . . they, sometimes they've treated me badly too . . . but nevertheless I have an affection towards them because of . . . uh, the situation they lived in, in the past, right . . . that they were slaves and all that, for me those stories are very . . . very painful, but nevertheless they also, you can see that they sometimes treat us Hispanics badly too, because I've gotten more . . . eh, bad treatment at the hands of . . . black people, than Americans.

In sum, while there has been some tension and evidence of negative feelings between blacks and Hispanics in Lexington that have surfaced in various ways, the cause of this tension seems to be due more to noneconomic factors (symbolic territory, cultural racism) than to competition in the labor market. The situation with working-class whites is similar in this regard.

White working-class reaction to the influx of Latinos into the urban scene has been characterized by a rather benign neglect and lack of concern. However, in reaction to a 1998 proposal to establish a city government community center to provide social services to Hispanics in the Cardinal Valley neighborhood, a petition was circulated by white working-class residents of the neighborhood to oppose this action. When the petition was to be presented to the city council for consideration, the organizer of the petition did not appear, the issue was dropped, and the center was established. In response to the petition movement, several segments of the community came out vocally and expressed extensive opposition to such a petition (Cheryl Truman, "Overcoming Differences: Influx of Hispanic Residents Changes Face of Community," *Lexington Herald-Leader*, June 16, 1999, p. 3). Letters to the editor in support of the petition and residents' comments mentioned complaints about the social and cultural behavior of Hispanics of which they disapproved (for example, litter, public hygiene, drinking outdoors, and noisiness). Nonetheless, there has been little, if any, organized voice of whites complaining about the incursion of Latinos into "their" economic realm in the labor market; rather, what we have seen is more of a racialized sentiment about their linguistic and sociocultural "foreignness." This seems to be a widespread response to the Hispanic Diaspora in the southeast region; the Mexican migration has been received in a cultural vacuum where the Spanish language and Latino cultures are unfamiliar (see Yeoman 2000).

An example of this unfolded in early 2000, when Fred Nessler—a Kentucky state legislator from a rural county in Western Kentucky—proposed a resolution to urge the federal government to enforce immigration laws in Kentucky. In the process, Nessler made blatant and public racist comments about how undocumented Mexican immigrants "bring quite a bit of disease with them" and that they were taking a big bite out of food banks for low-income families, as John Cheeves reported ("Legislator Slams Illegal Immigrants," *Lexington Herald-Leader*, March 14, 2000, pp. A1, A7). In reaction to this, many voices were raised in opposition to his statements, including those of other politicians, employers of Hispanics, community representatives of various stripes, and the local newspaper in an editorial entitled "Demeaning Moment—Nessler's Resolution an Insult to Hispanic Workers" (*Lexington Herald-Leader*, March 15, 2000, p. A8).

As a final example of how the white and black Lexington community has reacted to racism against Latinos in the area, when it was rumored that the Ku Klux Klan was planning to stage a rally at the Fayette County Courthouse in downtown Lexington, a community meeting was called by the National Conference for Community and Justice and others to organize against it. Even though the rumor about the imminent Klan rally was found to be baseless, the meeting was attended by hundreds of residents and contingency plans were made to be prepared to respond in the future to any such xenophobic actions and racist manifestations. In general, the Lexington community has been fairly receptive and protective of its Hispanic newcomers; until only quite recently, the Latino immigrant community was so invisible that no response at all was the norm. Most Lexingtonians have been blissfully unaware that the Hispanic community was even present, not to mention growing rapidly, and soon to become an important demographic and sociopolitical force in the future of the Central Kentucky Bluegrass Region.

FUNDING MEXICAN IMMIGRANT ACCOMMODATION: THE HISPANIC INITIATIVE NETWORK (HIN)

While a xenophobic tension now characterizes the white and black working-class response to Mexican immigrants, a more positive, if paternalistic response has come from major employers of Hispanics, local government agencies, and various human service providers. In this section we illustrate how the issue of funding for services needed by immigrants is a key factor in shaping the nature of the community response. Specifically, the extent and form of funding support for immigrant accommodation here in Lexington reflects both the recognition of the importance of Latino immigrants' needs and the assumption that a paternalistic response is the most effective way of meeting those needs. To illustrate this point, we draw on the single most salient and public example of institutional community response to the immigrant community's needs: the Hispanic Initiative Network (HIN).

This initiative was the largest single outcome of the city government's response to the advocacy of AHU for recognition of the Hispanic community's needs, as well as to other pro-immigrant groups, such as the Kentucky Migrant Network Coalition (Figueras 1998). The HIN resulted as an indirect result of the advocacy that led to the formation of the Hispanic Labor Task Force. In July 1998 LFUCG Mayor Pam Miller, responding to continuous political pressure from AHU, created the Lexington Hispanic Labor Task Force to study the growing human needs of the Hispanic community. This political response was the first acknowledgment that Latino workers were present and contributing to the economic and cultural fabric of Fayette County. The task force consisted of twenty-four members representing city government, social service agencies, and employers, and identified key members of the community who had particular interest and information regarding the Hispanic population. Among this latter group was included Ben Figueras, the president and founder of AHU and the primary voice condemning the invisibility and neglect of Hispanic immigrants at that time. The task force was split into various subcommittees charged to explore specific issues of concern to Hispanic newcomers.

The task force met and worked from July 1998 until February 1999. They identified seventeen areas of prioritized concerns, organizing these into three groups: identification of financial and service aid support, technical assistance for service delivery, and support for further recognition and facilitation of collaborative efforts to find solutions for Hispanic community problems (Maurer 1999).[16]

These first priority recommendations resulted in the LFUCG hiring, in January 2000, of Mr. Abdón Ibarra to be a liaison between city government, service agencies, and the Hispanic community (Marquita Smith, "Ex-migrant is New Official," *Lexington Herald-Leader*, February 10, 2000, pp. B1, B3). The creation of this position, titled Immigrant Services Coordinator, and the hiring of a highly qualified, bilingual, and bicultural person to fill it, was one of the most positive actions towards better accommodation of the Mexican immigrant community here. Along with this action, the LFUCG pooled some money with the United Way and the Thoroughbred Association to provide a three year grant to create the HIN.

In the fall of 1999, a request for proposals was issued by these three funders (a coalition of government, nonprofit, and private sector entities) to create a single community coalition of service providers to develop a network to deliver services to Spanish-speaking newcomers to Fayette County (Valarie Honeycutt and Geoff Mulvihill, "Combine Forces to Help Hispanics, United Way Urges," *Lexington Herald-Leader*, April 23, 1999, pp. B1, B4). As a result of this request for one community proposal, a political split developed between an AHU-led coalition of providers and a splinter group led by Catholic Social Services (Marquita Smith, "Alliances Formed to Assist Hispanics—Two Groups with Different Intentions Vie for Grant," *Lexington Herald-Leader*, November 11, 1999, pp. B1, B5).

The competition for the limited resources (only $150,000 per year for three years) became fierce, creating conflict and illuminating the issues of institutional racism evidenced by the assumptions made by the funders and established agencies that AHU was not capable of managing the funds on their own and therefore needed to form partnership with an established fiduciary agent or just remain an advocacy organization which would receive no funding at all. This created divisiveness within AHU; its board of directors was split on whether to collaborate for a small piece of the funding or simply to refuse to be part of the project altogether, given that some felt that the grant itself was only the result of its own advocacy and was intended for the Latino community. Those in AHU who disagreed with the marginal majority vote to engage in the collaborative effort, experienced the decision to become part of the grant as a betrayal of the work of the past advocacy of AHU and as a cooptation by paternalistic, white-led social service agencies[17] (Marquita Smith, "Hispanic Assoc. Leader Steps Down: Figueras Wants New Leaders to Emerge," *Lexington Herald-Leader*, March 23, 2000, p. B3; "Hispanic Group Elects Three to Leadership Posts," *Lexington Herald-Leader*, April 7, 2000, pp. B1, B6).

Others within AHU believed that being part of establishing a legitimate relationship with established service providers would give the association a track record for future funding and visibility away from the margins of the community. After painful internal dialogue and a difficult mediation process, the HIN was formed (Anonymous, "Partnership to Aid Hispanic Community," *Lexington Herald-Leader*, May 3, 2000, p. B3). The formation of HIN was seen as "putting Band-Aids on heart attacks" (Miranda, quoted in Johnson 2001, 45). AHU knew that the needs of Hispanics for services, advocacy, and empowerment were far greater than could be met by providing case management services, English as a Second Language classes, employment referrals, case management, and volunteer services—the resulting staff responsibilities created by the grant. Nonetheless, the HIN was born with firm, if scant and paternalistic, financing and support from important institutions in the community. Here the precedent was set for a new and positive response to the rapid influx of Latino immigrants.

In July 2000, the HIN began providing services to Hispanic residents in the Lexington community; it met the three-year goals of the grant in the very first year. This success gave evidence of the tremendous need for services to Hispanics in the Lexington area and the capacity of AHU to be part of the established service providers in Fayette County. Using HIN as a vehicle, AHU has had a seat at the table with both social service partners and it has developed a successful track record.

HIN has also identified major blocks to providing services, including language and institutional barriers in the health care area. For example, local health departments, hospitals, and private practitioners continually demand that Hispanic patients provide their own translation. HIN continues to provide bilingual translators when possible, while at the same time educating these health care providers that they have a legal responsibility to provide translation if they receive federal funding or payments. Cultural misunderstandings are widespread regarding Hispanic family structure, child rearing practices, and the role of extended family and kinship ties. Whites often assess Latino poverty, poor education, and group norms as dysfunctional when compared with traditional middle-class Anglo practices. Another serious barrier to services is the justified mistrust of established service documents, interviews and questionnaires; the bureaucracy which is necessary for functioning in the United States not only creates difficulty and fear for undocumented Hispanic workers and their families, but also frustration and misunderstanding by service providers (Michelle Ku, "Community Action Studies Hispanic Aid: Task Force Focuses on the Makeup of Council's Staff," *Lexington Herald-Leader*, October 5, 2000, pp. B1, B4).

In sum, the HIN represents a success, albeit limited, in responding positively to the Hispanic immigrant community. As a result of a combination of the well-intentioned, if paternalistic, concern on the part of employers, city government, and nonprofit social service sectors, HIN has begun to provide an institutionalized infrastructure on which to build a long-term facilitation of the social needs of the immigrant community. Its ability to communicate and address the social needs and the positive economic contributions of the Latino community is also a bulwark against the xenophobic attitudes and tendencies amongst other sectors of the community.

The evidence accumulated in the first year and a half of the HIN shows decisively that the needs for, and barriers to, social service provision far outstrip the HIN's ability to deal with both. Insofar as this is the case, the HIN can be viewed as an appeasement to the social needs of the immigrant community, a token gesture of care, intended to assuage the sufferings of Latinos here, but not necessarily, or perhaps even possibly, a tool for their own self-sufficiency. In that sense, the HIN can also be viewed as a damper on the fuller, more robust realization of the political potential of Hispanics to represent themselves more forcefully, with better results.

CONCLUSIONS

In the short space of a decade, from approximately 1991 through 2001, Lexington, Kentucky, has witnessed a large influx of Latino, predominantly Mexican-origin, immigrants. The size of this immigrant community may soon surpass the size of the native black population in the Lexington urban area, if it hasn't already. This influx was originally attracted to work in the rural, late-summer tobacco harvest and new openings in the horse industry—migrant, transient, seasonal; over this period the influx has shifted its orientation dramatically. It is now attracted also by urban work opportunities in construction, manufacturing, and service industries. Originally composed primarily of young, sojourning Mexican men working as target earners and returning to Mexico, it is now increasingly composed of young women also, many of them mothers of children born here in the United States, as well as in Mexico. Policy developments in recent years that have made crossing the U.S.-Mexico border more dangerous and less worth the risks involved, have had the effect of making permanent or semi-permanent settlement here more likely. Furthermore, to make the character of this migration perhaps critically distinct from its origins in agriculture, the increasing urbanization and full-time, year-round nature of their work in labor markets that are absolutely dependent on them, means that Latino newcomers are here to stay in the longer term. Therefore, the dynamic character of the community's response to date is critical to assess in terms of what it portends for the future.

Our analysis demonstrates that the character of the greater Lexington community's response to the Latin influx of the past decade has been a movement from no response at all (invisibility) to a contradictory, or at least tense, mixture of xenophobia and paternalism. In summary, we have argued that major employers' dependence on Mexican labor power in key occupational markets leads to a paternalistic orientation on their part that mixes social protection and ethnic-class subordination, while supporting Hispanics' basic ability to live and work here. This is an important and potentially powerful source of social and political support. Meanwhile, white and black working-class response to Latinos is more problematic. It is formulated with little historical intercultural experience of tolerance or understanding. It occurs in a social environment for the black working class where their subordination makes the appearance of another ethnic minority threatening economically and culturally, if only via symbolic perception, as opposed to a material reality of resource competition with Latinos. From the white working-class, we have not seen much response, although observations in public spaces and historical relations between whites and nonwhites in the region suggest that there is a substantial reservoir of xenophobic suspicion towards Hispanics from this sector as well.

In our discussion of the institutional response of local government and the nonprofit human service community through the example of the creation of the Hispanic Initiative Network (HIN), we argued that in conjunction with the financial support of the horse industry, these sectors have responded positively by attempting to accommodate the Latino population's social service needs. However, the extent to which and the manner in which this positive response has come leads us to conclude that these sectors have been paternalizing the Hispanic community through this process. This paternalism, we believe, has had the effect of undermining, rather than empowering, the self-sufficiency of the Latino immigrant community. The level of funding of the HIN and other attempts to address the needs of immigrants has been far too limited, and the way that these attempts have been made have often been discriminatory towards, or at the least, ignorant of and insensitive to the culturally specific aspects of the immigrant community that are most important for its successful integration into the community.

Finally, the development of political and social self-representation of Latinos in Lexington also reflects both xenophobic and paternalistic responses from residents. To the extent that elements within the growing Hispanic community have been able to mobilize, organize, and articulate the most pressing needs of immigrants, positive responses have occurred. However, to the extent that white and black residents ignore, presume, or assume the integration needs of immigrants, they marginalize and institutionally exclude political representatives of the Hispanic community. The internal marginalization and disjuncture of some Latino leaders from their own community has been mainly the result of class and nationalistic differences. As the internal conditions ripen for the development of Mexican-origin leadership to emerge and develop, the social and political response of the greater community will have to shift to accommodate and share further resources with the Hispanic newcomers (Risa Brim, "Local Hispanics Look for Leaders," *Lexington Herald-Leader*, December 24, 2001, p. C1; Rich 1999). Unless this happens, long-standing and serious social problems within the Latino community (for example, lack of legal status, access to health care and schooling, social alienation, alcoholism, crime, and domestic violence) are likely to lead to public disruption and greater publicity, producing either further xenophobic responses for expulsion or greater measures to ensure these problems are faithfully and effectively addressed.

What we see to date is an attempt by the larger community to accommodate the needs of the Hispanic community only insofar as that accommodation does not significantly disrupt established intergroup relations of domination; specifically class and interethnic control by white elites. Concessions of resources or attention given by the privileged class in Lexington appear to be attempts to incorporate the Mexican-Latino immigrant community through a perpetuation of subordination. Alleviating the worst evidences of immigrant suffering and social deprivation could be seen as leading to the worst outcome of paternalism, that is, a relation that actually promotes the acceptance of the ongoing group subordination in economic, social, political, and cultural life. Until there is recognition of, and attempts to reconfigure, the structural relations of unequal access to social resources (money, power, and status), multicultural relations will continue to be characterized in the Bluegrass region by white privileged-class domination of all other groups alongside tense and competitive ethnic relations between poor white, black, and Latino subordinate classes.

How the configuration of these factors will develop in the years ahead—the business sector's need for Latino workers, interethnic relations, funding support for further accommodation, and the development of Hispanic political infrastructure—should determine whether Central Kentucky will continue in its ambivalence towards new Mexican immigrants. A more welcoming response might develop;[18] but so might a movement towards further xenophobia and social exclusion.[19] In any case, it would appear that with or without documents, the Latino population here is large, still growing, and settling in for the longer term. It can no longer be invisible nor neglected.

This research was partially funded by a grant from the American Sociological Association's Sydney S. Spivak Program in Applied Social Research and Social Policy, as well as three grants from Transylvania University: two summer grants from the David and Betty Jones Fund for Faculty Development and a sabbatical grant from the Kenan Fund for Faculty and Student Enrichment. The authors would like to thank Adela DeLeón, Ben Figueras, Josie Ghosal, Linda Hutchison, Leslie Moyers, Martha Ojeda, Laura Rice, Laura

Roberts, Josh Santana, Margaret Upchurch, Todd Van Denburg, and Mary Webb for research assistance and/or moral support. Special thanks to Reverend Job Cobos for sharing the data from his Hispanic church survey and to the Kentucky Migrant Network Coalition for sharing the data from their Hispanic Health Fair survey.

NOTES

1. We use the terms Latino and Hispanic interchangeably to describe persons closely affiliated with or descended from Spanish-speaking persons, regions, or countries, as this is still the current practice in our community. We narrow the group identity to Mexican when data can be identified that specify their nationality. At this time, we estimate that approximately 90 percent of Hispanics in our area are Mexicans, and, of those, a large majority (60 percent to 80 percent) seems to be undocumented. Abdón Ibarra's study (2001), the only one that asked about documentation, found that 85 percent of his sample of 129 households was here without documents. That figure seems too high for the general Hispanic population; his sample is all working class and Mexican and thus excludes Hispanics from the middle class and other nationalities whose documentation rate is much higher.

2. Both authors have been actively involved in this story in various capacities: both have been board members, leading officers, and co-chairs of "AHU"—la Asociacíon de Hispanos Unidos–The Lexington Hispanic Association—a community-based organization attempting to serve and represent the interests of Latinos in our area. Miranda has also been integrally involved in the politics, administration, and provision of human services to Hispanics. Rich has also been conducting research on Latino community problems through secondary survey data analysis, focus groups, and content analysis of newspaper articles, as well as ethnographic and participant observation in the Hispanic community.

3. The selection of participants for these focus groups was developed from the theoretical sampling frame posed by the Hispanic community. Each of the four focus groups were comprised of members of distinct social groups within the Latino community: community leaders (including representatives from political, educational, and religious organizations); professionals and employers; male workers, with little to no English proficiency; and female workers, with little to no English proficiency. The first two focus groups were conducted in August of 1999 and the second two in August of 2000. Each of the four sessions were conducted with four to eight Hispanic residents and lasted between one and a half to two hours. Four questions formed the basis of every group and were asked and discussed in the following order: what, in your opinion, is the most important problem faced by the Hispanic community in Lexington? Then a

sheet listing sixteen "issues of concern" was presented to the participants and the following question was asked: Are there any problems on this sheet that you believe are as important as those we have so far discussed? Given the problems we have discussed, please prioritize what you think are the first through third most important for the community; and what question could we ask of the community to help learn more about this problem?

4. The causes of this labor shortage are most notably a demographic decline in young and willing native workers (both black and white) for the tobacco harvests, along with aging tobacco farmer cohorts. In the horse industry, these demographic trends were also at work, along with a growing demand for skilled horse workers, coupled with a growing shortage of same (Hamilton 1990; Kentucky Legislative Research Commission 2002).

5. A recent report by the research arm of the Kentucky State Legislature on immigration to the state highlights the essential role of Hispanics in the horse breeding industry: "Immigrant laborers have become an integral part of the thoroughbred industry workforce. An official of the Kentucky Thoroughbred Association estimated that immigrants currently make up 80 to 90 percent of thoroughbred farm workers. He said they are mostly Hispanic, and that 85 to 90 percent are men. . . . He estimated that 75 to 80 percent of the farms in these areas hire immigrants and that there are approximately 460 to 500 farms with an average of thirteen employees per farm. If these estimates are accurate, there may be over 5,000 immigrants working on the thoroughbred farms. This does not include tobacco farms." (Kentucky Legislative Research Commission 2002, 36).

6. See Brenda Rios, "Helping Hands Ease Transition to Kentucky," *Lexington Herald-Leader*, 1996, available at www.kentuckyconnect.com/herald-leader/news (accessed May 27, 1999); and "Tobacco Growers Embrace Migrants as Vital to Harvest," *Lexington Herald-Leader*, 1996, available at www.kentuckyconnect.com/heraldleader/news (accessed May 27, 1999).

7. More accurate estimates of the Latino population in Fayette County are very difficult to ascertain (Geoff Mulvihill, "Census Takers Face Difficult Task Counting Students: Growing Hispanic Population Also Poses Challenge for Enumerators," *Lexington Herald-Leader*, April 1, 2000, p. C7). However, at the time of this writing, Hispanic leaders and service workers in the community estimate the population to be anywhere from twenty-five thousand to thirty-five thousand, three to five times the latest census count.

8. Lexington is the county seat of Fayette County, which is now almost entirely urbanized.

9. "The most recent estimates indicate that 467 Kentucky farmers were approved to bring in almost 3,000 H2A workers in FY 2001, which established Kentucky as the fourth largest state in terms of importing H2A workers. In interviews with tobacco farmers who are now involved with

the H2A Program, several issues were raised. Each interviewee noted that in the early 1990s it became more difficult to find domestic help to harvest the tobacco crop. An improving economy further exacerbated the situation. In essence, farmers suggested that the H2A workers help them fill jobs that domestic workers simply do not want in such robust economic times" (Kentucky Legislative Research Commission 2002, 49).

10. In the focus group research on community problems conducted with Hispanic newcomers to our area, the problem of lack of documentation was continually tied to nearly every other problem Mexicans and other Latinos face (Rich, forthcoming).

11. Lexington has relatively large and very wealthy upper and upper middle classes, which has also had the related effect of producing one of the highest restaurant per capita ratios in the nation, contributing to this pressure for service workers in the food industry.

12. The AHU survey was distributed widely in areas of Hispanic worker concentration, including restaurants, stores that cater to Latinos, places where they would await day employment, and areas of working-class Hispanic residential concentration (for example, Cardinal Valley). The MNC data was collected at a Migrant Health Fair in the Cardinal Valley neighborhood. The Cobos data was predominantly collected at the Catholic Church, although a substantial proportion was collected at Protestant churches that may have higher proportions of better-off Latino residents. In sum, these venues in general are not places where middle-class Latinos in Lexington were likely to become respondents to these types of convenience-sample surveys.

13. Rich moderated two back-to-back sessions on "Black-Brown Relations" at the 2001 Kentucky Migrant Network Coalition's annual meeting in Lexington, Kentucky. These were wide ranging discussions involving mostly social service providers to the Hispanic community and various professional representatives of the black community. Most comments emphasized the commonality of interests that blacks and Hispanics have in the community (mainly class and minority status), while decrying the extent of negative interethnic relations.

14. See Tom Lasseter, "Police Get Break in Robberies: Shooting of Two Men Sheds Light on String of Stickups of Hispanics," *Lexington Herald-Leader*, October 1, 1999; and "Lives Tainted by Fear: Hispanic Laborers in Fayette County Have Been the Targets of a Series of Robberies and They're Scared," *Lexington Herald-Leader*, October 2, 1999.

15. All names used in quoting focus group participants are pseudonyms.

16. The Hispanic Labor Task Force resulted in the identification of many issues and led to many positive changes in the overall response of the LFUCG to the Latino community. However, space limitations force us to focus mainly on the nature of the HIN component of this response.

17. The details of this process are an interesting case of both institutional

racism and paternalism at work. While a bit tangential to our argument, we should point out that through this grant competition AHU representatives were convinced that the funders were already decided against the AHU-led proposal, despite the fact that AHU had marshaled a far wider and larger community coalition of service providers and had a more culturally and socially appropriate model of service delivery. AHU's suspicion turned out to be true; they were denied the grant, although a merger of the two groups' proposals was mandated through professional mediation. AHU got only a small portion of the grant and that only after fierce negotiation to ensure it had some control over the project.

18.   See Bob Babbage, "Migrants' Needs Require Creative Local Response," *Lexington Herald-Leader*, March 7, 1999; Juleyka Lantigua, "Immigrants Shouldn't Be Made to Feel Like Second-Class Citizens," *Lexington Herald-Leader*, February 7, 2002; Ben Figueras and Marta Roller, "Hispanics Deserve Better than Distrust and Bad Treatment," *Lexington Herald-Leader*, January 20, 2002; and Figueras and Roller 2002.

19.   See Stephen A. Calvert, "Illegals Not Trustworthy," letter to the editor, *Lexington Herald-Leader*, February 6, 2002; Nicole Morgan, "Alone and in Need: Isolation May Be Putting Lexington Latinos at Risk," *Lexington Herald-Leader*, December 5, 2001; Michelle Malkin, "Ailing Illegal Aliens a Burden to Americans," *Lexington Herald-Leader*, January 4, 2002.

REFERENCES

Acuña, Rodolfo. 1972. *Occupied America: The Chicano's Struggle Toward Liberation.* San Francisco: Canfield Press.

Asociación de Hispanos Unidos. 1998. *Hispanic Community Survey Results.* Unpublished summary report. Lexington, Kentucky.

Bach, Robert L. 1993. *Changing Relations: Newcomers and Established Residents in U.S. Communities:* A Report to the Ford Foundation by the National Board of the Changing Relations Project. New York: Ford Foundation.

Camarota, Steven A. 2001. *Immigration from Mexico: Assessing the Impact on the United States.* Washington, D.C.: Center for Immigration Studies.

Carrasco, Gilbert P. 1997. "Latinos in the United States: Invitation and Exile." In *Immigrants Out! The New Nativism and the Anti-Immigrant Impulse in the United States,* edited by Juan F. Perea. New York: New York University Press.

Cobos, Job. 2000. "Mano Abierto: Project in the Practice of Ministry." Unpublished paper and survey data. Lexington Theological Seminary, Lexington, Kentucky.

Cornelius, Wayne A. 1989a. "Mexican Migration to the United States: An Introduction." In *Mexican Migration to the United States: Origins, Consequences, and Policy Options,* edited by Wayne A. Cornelius and Jorge A. Bustamante. San Diego: Center for U.S.-Mexican Studies, University of California, San Diego.

———. 1989b. "The U.S. Demand for Mexican Labor." In *Mexican Migration to the United States: Origins, Consequences, and Policy Options*, edited by Wayne A. Cornelius and Jorge A. Bustamante. San Diego: Center for U.S.-Mexican Studies, University of California, San Diego.

———. 1992. "From Sojourners to Settlers: The Changing Profile of Mexican Immigration to the United States." In *U.S.-Mexico Relations: Labor Market Interdependence*, edited by Jorge A. Bustamante, Clark W. Reynolds, and Raúl Hinojosa-Ojeda. Stanford, Calif.: Stanford University Press.

———. 1998. "The Structural Embeddedness of Demand for Mexican Immigrant Labor: New Evidence from California." In *Crossings: Mexican Immigration in Interdisciplinary Perspectives*, edited by Marcelo Suarez-Orozco. Cambridge, Mass.: Harvard University Press and the D. Rockefeller Center for Latin American Studies.

Cornelius, Wayne A., and Jorge A. Bustamante, eds. 1989. *Mexican Migration to the United States: Origins, Consequences, and Policy Options*. Volume 3 of Dimensions of United States—Mexican Relations. San Diego: Center for U.S.-Mexican Studies, University of California.

Figueras, Ben 1998. Asociación de Hispanos Unidos Proposal to Mayor Pam Miller. Unpublished manuscript. Lexington, Ky.

Figueras, Ben, and Marta Roller. 2002. "No Todos Somos Creados Iguales en Kentucky [Not All of Us Are Created Equal in Kentucky]." *La Voz de Kentucky* (February): 6.

Hamilton, Hal. 1990. "Organizing Rural Tobacco Farmers: Central Kentucky in Global Context." In *Communities in Economic Crisis: Appalachia and the South*, edited by John Gaventa, Barbara Ellen Smith, and Alex Willingham. Philadelphia, Penn.: Temple University Press.

Hernández-León, Rubén and Víctor Zúñiga. 2000. "'Making Carpet by the Mile': The Emergence of a Mexican Immigrant Community in an Industrial Region of the U.S. Historic South." *Social Science Quarterly* 81(1): 49–66.

Ibarra, Abdón. 2001. *Survey 2000: A Snapshot of Latino Families Living in the Bluegrass*. Lexington-Fayette: Lexington-Fayette Urban County Government, Office of Immigrant Services, Department of Social Services.

Johnson, Yielbonzie C. 2001. "Asociación de Hispanos Unidos: An Unfolding of Relational Power." In *Organizations of the People: The Charles Stewart Mott Foundation 1999–2000 Intermediary Support Program for Emerging Organizations*, edited by Gary Delgado. Oakland, Calif.: Applied Research Center.

Kentucky Department for Employment Services. 2002a. *Kentucky Labor Force Estimates: Annual Averages 2001*. Available at: http://www.kycwd.org/des/lmi/labor/clf/annual01.htm.

———. 2002b. *Kentucky Labor Force Estimates: Annual Averages 2000*. Available at: http://www.kycwd.org/des/lmi/labor/clf/annual00.htm.

———. 2002c. *Kentucky Labor Force Estimates: Annual Averages 1999*. Available at: http://www.kycwd.org/des/lmi/labor/clf/annual99.htm.

———. 2002d. *Kentucky Labor Force Estimates: Annual Averages 1998*. Available at: http://www.kycwd.org/des/lmi/labor/clf/annual98.htm.

————. 2002e. *Kentucky Labor Force Estimates: Annual Averages 1997.* Available at: http://www.kycwd.org/des/lmi/labor/clf/annual97.htm.

Kentucky Legislative Research Commission. 2002. *Immigration in Kentucky: A Preliminary Description.* Research Report No. 305. Frankfort: Kentucky State Government.

Kentucky Migrant Network Coalition (MNC). 1999. *Hispanic Health Fair Survey Data—1999.* Lexington, Ky.

López, Gerald P. 1998. "How Much Responsibility Does the U.S. Bear for Undocumented Mexican Migration?" In *The Latino/a Condition: A Critical Reader,* edited by Richard Delgado and Jean Stefancic. New York: New York University Press.

Martínez, Oscar J. 2001. *Mexican-Origin People in the United States: A Topical History.* Tucson: University of Arizona Press.

Massey, Douglas S., Jorge Durand, and Nolan J. Malone. 2002. *Beyond Smoke and Mirrors: Mexican Immigration in an Era of Economic Integration.* New York: Russell Sage Foundation.

Massey, Douglas S., and Kristin E. Espinosa. 1997. "What's Driving Mexico-U.S. Migration? A Theoretical, Empirical, and Policy Analysis." *American Journal of Sociology* 102(4): 939–99.

Maurer, Richard C. 1999. Lexington Hispanic Labor Task Force: Report and Recommendations. Unpublished paper. Lexington, Ky.

McWilliams, Carey. 1935/1978. *Factories in the Field.* Santa Barbara, Calif.: Peregrine Smith.

Perrucci, Robert, and Earl Wysong. 1999. *The New Class Society.* Lanham, Md.: Rowman & Littlefield.

Portes, Alejandro, and Robert L. Bach. 1985. *Latin Journey: Cuban and Mexican Immigrants in the United States.* Berkeley: University of California Press.

Portes, Alejandro, and Rubén Rumbaut. 1996. *Immigrant America: A Portrait.* 2nd ed. Berkeley: University of California Press.

Portes, Alejandro, and Cynthia Truelove. 1987. "Making Sense of Diversity: Recent Research on Hispanic Minorities in the United States." *Annual Review of Sociology* 13: 359–85.

Rich, Brian L. 1999. "Making Multiculturalism More Difficult: Globalization, Inequality, and Ethnoracial Antagonism," Paper presented at the Annual Meetings of the North Central Sociological Association, Troy, Michigan. (April 1999).

————. 2000. "'The Biggest Problem is Fear': Conceptualizing Immigrant Community Problems with Latinos in Kentucky," Paper presented at the Annual Meetings of the American Sociological Association, Washington, D.C. (August 2000).

————. 2001a. "What are the Real Problems Hispanic Newcomers Face? Evidence from Focus Groups and Political Activism in Central Kentucky," Paper presented at the Annual Meetings of the Pacific Sociological Association, San Francisco (March 2001).

————. 2001b. "'Does Anyone Really Care about Us?' The Impossible Hispanic Community in Lexington." Public lecture to the Lexington Network, Lexington, Kentucky (April 2001).

————. Forthcoming. "'The Most Important Problem is Fear': Results from Focus Groups with Hispanic Newcomers on Community Issues in Lexington, Kentucky."

Suarez-Orozco, Marcelo M., ed. 1998. *Crossings: Mexican Immigration in Interdisciplinary Perspectives.* Cambridge, Mass.: Harvard University Press and the D. Rockefeller Center for Latin American Studies.

Tienda, Marta. 1989. "Looking to the 1990s: Mexican Immigration in Sociological Perspective." In *Mexican Migration to the United States: Origins, Consequences, and Policy Options,* edited by Wayne A. Cornelius and Jorge A. Bustamante. San Diego: Center for U.S.-Mexican Studies, University of California, San Diego.

U.S. Bureau of the Census. 2002a. *General Population and Housing Characteristics: 1990. Geographic Area: Fayette County, Kentucky.* Available at: http://factfinder. census.gov/servlet/QTTable?_ts=32645234168 (accessed February 24, 2002).

————. 2002b. *Profile of General Demographic Characteristics: 2000. Geographic Area: Fayette County, Kentucky.* Available at: http://factfinder.census.gov/bf/ _lang=en_vt_name=DEC_2000_SF1_U_DP1_geo_id=05000US21067.html (accessed February 24, 2002).

Vernez, Georges. 1994. "Undocumented Immigration: An Irritant or Significant Problem in U.S.-Mexico Relations?" Rand Labor and Population Reprint Series #94-18. Santa Monica, Calif.: Rand.

Yeoman, Barry. 2000. "Hispanic Diaspora." *Mother Jones* (July/August): 34–41.

CHAPTER 9

⋈

RACIALIZATION AND MEXICANS
IN NEW YORK CITY

ROBERT COURTNEY SMITH

Writing in the 1930s, W. E. B. DuBois (1935/1977, 700) observed that poor southern whites got a "public, psychological wage" by being white that enabled them to feel superior to blacks despite the many commonalities in their material living conditions. Historian David Roediger (1991, 12) and others use DuBois's insight to analyze how the "Irish became white." When Irish immigrants started coming to the United States in significant numbers in the 1830s, they had much in common with African Americans. They both did America's dirty work, had both been victimized by systematic racism, and often lived side by side in the poorest parts of town. Roediger answers the question of how the Irish came to not only disassociate from blacks but to embrace an anti-black racism by analyzing their racialized mobilization by the Catholic Church and the Democratic Party. What the Irish had learned, in essence, was that to be full members of American society, one had not simply to be "not black" but also in some instances "anti-black"[1] (Roediger 1991; Ignatiev 1995; Jacobson 1998). This dynamic of incorporation has lived on through generations in the "immigrant analogy" which asks the question, "why descendants of black slaves in the United States are in such worse shape on average than the descendants of white immigrants, if both faced discrimination?" The formulation of the question mistakenly equates the historical experiences of blacks and immigrants, and leads to the facile answer that blacks have failed due to their own lack of effort and moral shortcomings, while immigrants have prospered because of their hard work ethnic and moral virtue. "My grandparents suffered when they came here," goes the refrain, "but we prospered. Why can't blacks and their descendants do the same?"

This refrain takes this form for descendants of earlier white, European immigrants, but recurs for recent nonwhite immigrants, such as the second generation Caribbeans studied by Mary Waters (1994; 1999), who also try to distance themselves from native minorities. Mexicans in New York are just one of the new immigrant groups that must negotiate their way through New York's and America's system of social and racial hierarchies, but they deserve special attention for several reasons. First, they are a growing population on the East Coast, especially in and around New York City, but also up and down the eastern seaboard, in places such as Athens, Georgia; Kennett Square, Pennsylvania; and New Brunswick, New Jersey. The U.S. Census Bureau enumerated more than two hundred and sixty thousand Mexicans in New York State in 2000, and more than one hundred and eighty thousand in New York City, which means that, allowing for the undercount, there are probably about four hundred and fifty thousand to five hundred thousand Mexicans in the state and three hundred thousand in the city alone. Census experts predict, reporter Ricardo Alonso-Zaldivar pointed out in the *Los Angeles Times*, that within ten years Mexicans will be the largest minority on the east coast ("Big Apple Takes on a Flavor of Mexico," February 19, 1999, p. P22). In many places, especially those with relatively small minority populations and few Latinos, such as some towns in the Hudson Valley and Delmarva Peninsula, they already are. Mexicans in New York are mainly from the Mixteca region in southern Mexico, which includes large parts of the states of Puebla, Oaxaca, and Guerrero—tierra caliente. It is a poor, hot, agricultural region that has sent migrants to New York since the 1940s, but from which migration has exploded since the late 1980s. The second largest source of migrants is Mexico City and the state of Mexico, which includes larger numbers of more urban migrants.

Second, Mexicans do not fit "naturally" into any one spot in New York's and the East Coast's social and racial hierarchies. That is, most of our conceptions of race are based in America's "original sin" of slavery, with blackness historically signaling a group is unfit and whiteness that it is fit for full membership in society. But this categorization is complicated in New York City—and increasingly in other places too—by two things. Blacks share the most stigmatized position at the bottom of the hierarchy with a Latino group, Puerto Ricans, and there are also stronger degrees of white ethnicity and racialization due in part to the presence of white immigrants such as Greeks, Russians, and Italians. Many Puerto Ricans possess phenotypes that most Americans would consider "black" and experience consonant levels of racial segregation and discrimination; but they also speak Spanish and are Latinos. Hence, many Mexican parents and their New York–born children wonder whether their futures will look more like the hard lives they associate with Puerto Ricans and blacks or more like the upwardly mobile lives they associate with white ethnic immigrants? Will Mexicans in New York become a marginalized, racialized minority or an incorporated ethnic group?

The contingency of such ambiguous locations in New York's racial and ethnic hierarchies offers an analytical opportunity to study the process of racialization as it happens. Rather than the retrospective analysis of the system that racialization produced, this chapter analyzes processes of racialization where the outcomes are both variable and still in play for many. These processes can be observed in urban social spaces (schools, parks, neighborhoods) that Mexicans occupy with other ethnic groups, especially blacks and other Latinos. These social spaces are sometimes emergent and constituted ephemerally in a location, as when groups of Mexicans informally occupy a park on a Sunday for their basketball league or rent a club for a dance. Their occupation of that space makes it "Mexican" for that time. This will sometimes occasion ethnic antagonism from other groups, thus situating Mexicans in a particular stance to racial hierarchies. More often, there is ethnic accommodation. But even with apparent accommodation, Mexicans sometimes attribute particular cultural meanings to their gathering, taking a positive meaning from the event and explicitly juxtaposing it to other groups' potential for such events. Such practices create a racialized meaning even in the absence of racial or ethnic confrontation, and show us racialization at work. Racialization and ethnicitization are two sides of same coin. The first refers to the process of being pushed into and adopting a social location similar to stigmatized or oppositional groups, with similar constraints on life chances. The second refers to being allowed into and pursuing social locations approximating those of higher status groups, with correspondingly greater life chances and the presumption of moral worth.

Finally, the conditions of incorporation of Mexicans in New York are yielding both significant upward mobility in work and education, but also stymied prospects for a large segment of the U.S.-born and new immigrant population. About one-fifth of the second generation boys and one-third of the girls are upwardly mobile in terms of occupation and education, but the large majority of both are either showing little progress or, for a smaller number, are slipping backward (Smith 2001b; 2005). These numbers are roughly consistent with the results of large scale studies using the Census in California (see Myers and Cranford 1998). In highly racialized contexts of reception such as New York, such a pattern of limited mobility often leads to pressures to oppositionally reject American institutions like school, as part of what Alejandro Portes and Rubén Rumbaut (2001) call a "rainbow underclass" (see also Zhou 1999). Such outcomes are not inevitable, and we can and should do things to change them, but we must first recognize them and take their measure.

A BRIEF HISTORY OF MEXICAN MIGRATION TO NEW YORK[2]

"We opened the road," said Don Pedro, sitting at his kitchen table in a town I call Ticuani in 1992 and looking back at the fifty years of Mexican migration from the Mixteca to New York City that started when he and his brother Fermin crossed the U.S.-Mexico border on July 6, 1943. Indeed, most Mexican migration to New York can be traced to a historical accident. Don Pedro and his brother and cousin had been unsuccessful in bribing their way into a bracero contract, that is, a contract in the government to government labor program that recruited Mexicans to work in U.S. agriculture between 1942 and 1964 (brazo means arm.). Getting a bracero contract would probably have brought Don Pedro and his relatives to the U.S. southwest, and the history of Mexican migration in New York would have been quite different. Instead, Don Pedro and his brother hitched a ride with a New Yorker named Montesinos who vacationed in Mexico City every summer. Montesinos brought them to New York and put them up in a hotel for two days until they found work. Work was easy to get. "There was a war on, so they were happy to have us working," said Don Pedro. He worked in restaurants, factories, and later as a mechanic. In the nearly sixty years since that first migration, the Mixteca region from which Don Pedro comes has been the origin of approximately two-thirds of New York's Mexican population (Valdes de Montaño and Smith 1994; Smith 1995).

Don Pedro was not the first Mexican labor migrant to come to New York. In fact, up through the 1920s migrants from the Mexican state of Yucatan came to New York in small numbers and established a social club at the 23rd Street YMCA. This migration died off for two reasons. According to Alejandro Nivon, who came to New York in the 1940s as a small child and knew many of these Yucatecos, large-scale migration became impracticable once the hemp trade from the Yucatan peninsula dried up in the early part of the twentieth century, during World War

I, when prices became too expensive and shipping too dangerous. The Yucatan was accessible to most of Mexico only by boat at the time. Without the cheap transportation of the hemp boats, leaving what was often called the "neighboring republic of the Yucatan" was very difficult. Second, a significant part of this early migration was from the upper classes and due to political divisions in the Yucatan. These immigrants quickly intermarried, often with Irish immigrants (Nivon 2002) and did not continue to organize themselves mainly as Mexicans.

Migration from the Mixteca and now other regions reflects larger trends. We can separate the migration from Mexico to New York into four phases, all of which implicate different processes pushing and pulling at each end of the migration route. The first two phases involve mainly migration from the Mixteca region, a cultural and ecological zone that includes the contiguous parts of three states, southern Puebla, northern Oaxaca, and eastern Guerrero. In 1992, the Mixteca accounted for two-thirds of Mexican migrants to New York, with 47 percent from Puebla alone (Valdes de Montaño and Smith 1994; Smith 1995).

The first phase of migration from the mid-1940s to the mid-1960s involved small numbers of individuals from a few families and towns in southern Puebla who had relatives in New York. In the second phase, from the mid-1960s to mid-1980s, this tightly networked dynamic was maintained. Increasing numbers of people, however, including the first appreciable number of women, began to come to the United States to seek their fortunes. The attraction of this country in those days would have been obvious: much higher wages than in Puebla, and modern conveniences that most people could not even imagine. Indeed, most of the Mixteca did not get electricity until the mid-1960s, and this improvement was resisted by caciques (political bosses) who did not want outside influences, such as radio and electric lights, intruding upon their control over their local populations (Pare 1975). Flight from political violence also features prominently in the histories of many of the pioneer migrants from Puebla, including Don Pedro, who was living in Mexico City to escape his hometown's political violence when he met Montesinos.

The third stage of migration runs lasted from the late 1980s to the mid-1990s and can be characterized as an explosion. Three factors combined to create it. First, by the late 1980s, Mexico had been in the grips of a profound economic crisis for nearly a decade, and conditions in many places were still dire. Indeed, poor states were especially hard hit, and Puebla experienced a net contraction of its economy between 1981 and 1985 (Cornelius 1986). Within Puebla, the Mixteca was one of the worst-off regions—in fact, one of the most marginalized areas in the country. Even worse, the "lost decade" of the 1980s stretched through the 1990s and into the new century for most Mixtecos and many Poblanos. Severe material conditions, and the loss of faith in a Mexican future, combined to create very serious push pressures in the Mixteca. These push pressures were matched by a second factor: the demand side in the United States, with Mexicans becoming identified in New York during the 1980s as a highly available and compliant labor force (Smith 1995; Kim 1999). Also, New York's Mexican population had reached a critical mass by the mid-1980s, such that the costs of migration for many people from the Mixteca region had been lowered a great deal by the presence of relatives and friends (see Massey et al. 1987).

The key factor in catalyzing the explosion of migration in the late 1980s and early 1990s was the Amnesty program of the 1986 Immigration Reform and Control Act, or IRCA. The Amnesty provision enabled immigrants to apply for temporary, then permanent, residency if they had been continuously in the United States since 1981, or if they had worked in agriculture for ninety days during the past year. Mexicans surprised many by accounting for the second highest number of amnesty applications in New York City, with about nine thousand, behind Dominicans' roughly twelve thousand (see Kraly and Miyares 2001). The Amnesty program profoundly changed the nature of Mexicans' relationship to their hometowns. Migrants who had been caught in a holding pattern for years or even decades suddenly found that they could return home when they wanted. More important, they now had a legal right to reunite their families in the United States. Between the late 1980s and the mid-1990s, tens of thousands of wives and children left the Mixteca region and moved to New York to be with their families. The suddenness of this impact is reflected in an anecdote told by one school official in Puebla. On being investigated because his school reported only half as many students in 1993 as it did in 1992, he told officials that the explanation was simple: they had all gone to New York to be with their parents. Similar stories repeated themselves throughout the Mixteca (Smith 1995). One corollary was the 232-percent increase in the Mexican birthrate in New York in the mid-1990s.

The last phase of migration, which began in the late 1990s, involves changes in the larger process of migration to the United States. The story has several parts. First, by now, many towns in the Mixteca region have reached an "asymptotic stability" (Smith 1995; see Massey, Goldring, and Durand 1994; Durand, Massey, and Parrado 1999) in which most people there who want to leave have already done so, and those who remain behind are unlikely to migrate soon in large numbers (Massey, Goldring, and Durand 1994; Massey and Espinosa 1997). At the same time, on the United States' end, the number of settled Mexican migrants, both legal and undocumented, who plan to remain permanently in New York has increased. Hence a first part of the story is that the internal process of migration from the Mixteca has reached a kind of consolidated stability, in which new migrants will continue to leave the Mixteca but the number will decrease from its former highs.

A second part of the story is that the process of migrating to and settling in the United States has changed (Cornelius 1994; Durand, Massey, and Parrado 1999). Migrants crossing illegally are now less likely to engage in circular migration, in which the family stays at home and the migrant returns. An important factor in producing this change has been the tightened enforcement at the U.S.-Mexico border, which has had the ironic but predictable effect of causing increased settlement among migrants. The logic of family reunification fostered by IRCA has also reinforced this trend, even among the undocumented (see Durand, Massey, and Parrado 1999). In effect, what Leigh Binford (1998) calls "accelerated migration," now is the pattern, in which new migrant towns pass through the stages of migration—from solo migrant to family reunification in the United States—much more quickly than before or even skip stages and just go straight to settlement. Accelerated migration also includes a great increase in the medium-term to semi-permanent migration of adolescents without their parents, as a by-product of the acceleration and subsequent disorganization of the migration process.

A third part of the story is that migration has returned to an earlier, pre–Bracero Program pattern of wider dispersal in the United States. The Bracero Program funneled nearly five million Mexicans to work mainly in southwestern agriculture between 1942 and 1964, and this geographical pattern still largely persists. But in the 1990s, migration to varied U.S. destinations—including the northeast and southeast—boomed. Corresponding with this increase in destinations is the increase in the variety of Mexican origins. During the 1990s, New York became an important site for migration from a variety of nontraditional origins, including the states of Tlaxcala, Tabasco, Morelos, and, perhaps most important, from Mexico City and several huge slums in the state of Mexico, such as Ciudad Nezahualcóyotl, or Neza as migrants call it. According to the Mexican Consulate (2003), some 11 percent of immigrants seeking its services are from Mexico City, a number that has remained roughly constant over the last decade. In that time, migration from Neza has become so common that migrants now say that they live in "Neza York" (Vecino 1999). This change toward more urban origin and younger migrants is likely to have important implications for the future of Mexicans in New York. One result of this was the emergence of a new category of teen migrant, whose experience of the United States and racialization is different in some ways from that of first-generation adult migrants and their second- or 1.5-generation born or raised children.

These changes in New York reflect a fundamental shift in larger Mexico-U.S. migration patterns, with greater tendencies towards family settlement in the United States (Durand, Massey, and Parrado 1999; Cornelius 1994). During the 1990s, new areas in Puebla and surrounding states, inside and outside the Mixteca region, began to send migrants. Moreover, increasing numbers of children and, more particularly here, adolescents were coming to New York, some to be reunited with their families, and some a la aventura (in search of adventure) (Hernández-León 1999).

DATA AND ANALYSIS

My research with Mexicans in New York over the last fifteen years has yielded a complex picture of responses to the need to define oneself within racialized hierarchies.[3] This chapter draws on data from two main projects. One is an ongoing ethnographic project analyzing transnational life between New York and Ticuani, which forms the basis of my forthcoming book. A second major project, an outgrowth of the first, is an ethnographic and interview study of second and 1.5 generation Mexican immigrant schooling and school to work transition, which will form the basis of a second book. The data here draw on about one hundred and twenty life history interviews, as well as ethnographic research with a subset of this sample, in school, at home and in the community, in New York and in Mexico. This chapter analyzes how engagement with racialization varies by four elements: migratory generation (first, 1.5, or second generation); stage of the life cycle one is in (pre-teens, teens, adults); intra- or intergenerational social mobility; and the relational articulation between the perception of others and perception of self in regards to racialization.

The immigrant first generation has usually responded by embracing the immigrant analogy, though in different ways in different contexts. Often, statements expressing the immigrant analogy are framed in the classic formula. "Not all Puerto Ricans (or fill in another group) are like that—I have friends who are Puerto Rican who are good people—but many of them are like this." Such formulations are not simply the following of the contemporary American custom of always creating an individual exception when making any ethnic or racial group generalization. Rather, they reflect the two sides of the experience these migrants have had. One the one hand, first generation Mexican immigrants have had very positive experiences with other Spanish-speaking groups in New York. Mexicans often feel indebted, to Puerto Ricans in particular but also to other Latinos, who helped them when they first came to New York, when the Mexican community was much smaller. Some have married non-Mexican Latinos, especially Puerto Ricans, or have family members who have done so. In other cases, Mexican immigrants benefited from the extended family networks or informal social customs of Puerto Ricans. For example, several families I know had older Puerto Rican women neighbors who lived in the same building that babysat their children while both parents worked. Usually, these relationships developed into intimate ones that militated against an overly racialized perception of Puerto Ricans. On the other hand, the immigrant analogy has helped to frame much of the experience of the first generation, both in terms of rhetoric in schools and in public places, at work, and within their own community. The first generation in particular sees dramatic differences between the current social reality of Puerto Ricans in New York City—whom they see as too settled, and "Americanized" and their own imagined futures. This tendency is compounded by the high incidence of overlap in Mexican and Puerto Rican settlement areas. Mexicans have settled in six or seven mainly Spanish-speaking areas of the city, and many of these—such as El Barrio in Manhattan or Sunset Park in Brooklyn—are publicly identified as Puerto Rican neighborhoods. They look at Puerto Rican social distress in the city and fear they are looking into their own futures, and hence look for ways to construe their own social challenges as leading down another path. The immigrant analogy is a handy way to do this— they will prosper via their hard work, despite facing the same kinds of challenges, made even worse by not having the citizenship the Puerto Ricans had.

The second generation's engagement is more complex for a variety of reasons, including the fact that they have grown up more immersed in New York's racial hierarchies and in its public schools, parks, and other social spaces. They are likely both to have Puerto Rican friends and to identify to a certain extent with the position of blacks and Puerto

Ricans, especially to the extent that they see these groups as similarly oppressed by society. This tendency to identify with blacks and Puerto Ricans as oppressed minorities (which would comport with Portes and Rumbaut's category of a "rainbow underclass") competes with the tendency to also adopt the immigrant analogy position of their parents, in which being Mexican is being better. This is especially so for those who are upwardly mobile and more involved in transnational life, including a transnationalized adolescence.

The first generation's experience in the labor market engages racialization through what one can call "doubly bounded solidarity."[4] While many Korean, Greek, Italian, or "native" white American employers explicitly or implicitly and favorably compare Mexican immigrants to native-born blacks and Puerto Ricans (hence treating them as part of the out-group), they also see them as immigrants like themselves, or like their immigrant predecessors in the case of the native born. This leads to an emphasis on the similarities of the Mexican immigrant employees by their employers and difference from native minorities. For example, I have heard more than one employer identify with his employees. One Greek restaurant owner extolled the virtues of Mexican employees in the same breath as talking about how unreliable and unpleasant blacks were as employees (even while telling me earlier that he had never hired a black employee, but had just seen them working in other places). With tears in his eyes, he told me about working twelve-hour days like his Mexican workers, saying, when I came to this country "I was a good Mexican." Their willingness to work hard makes them different from native minorities, he said, and detailed how Mexicans moved up step by step from being busboys, to dishwashers, to cooks. Native whites are also sometimes but less often included in these unfavorable comparisons (see Smith 1996).

The second generation's experience in the labor market is more diverse. A growing minority of the second generation are upwardly mobile, through paths in which their engagement with racialization is less charged than for their parents or for less upwardly mobile second generation youth. For example, many second-generation youth work while in college in decently paid part-time jobs in work study, or more interestingly, in the private sector in companies like the GAP, Starbucks, Borders Books, and others. These jobs exhibit what Victoria Malkin (2000) incisively described as a "Benetton" context—one in which their ethnicity is cool and chic, not racialized and stigmatized. This is an especially important pathway for mobility for young men who can take advantage of it, because of their tendency toward the immigrant economy (factories or restaurants) or other sector of the economy with limited prospects. It is young women who have the highest rates of upward mobility according to the census—17 percent for women versus 9 percent for men in the professional and technical sector in 1990. Part of their upward mobility comes from their entry into the "pink" collar economy, working in jobs such as medical or legal secretary, travel agent, or other service sector jobs. Such jobs are highly prized, and these women are understood to be successful in their careers because they make good money, have paid vacation and health insurance, and work in an office, doing "clean" work.

Yet the majority of men and women are not upwardly mobile, and many are getting stuck in the same kinds of jobs as their parents. Many parents in the second generation study sample I have talked to have dragged their children with them during the summers to have them work in the factories beside them, to dissuade them from working young and dropping out of school. While the kids dislike the factory work, many end up following their parents into it. Some even describe what good jobs their immigrant parents had been able to get. In one case I know, a young man who dropped out of college and now works for a very low wage in the kitchen of a large institution spoke of his father's job as a cook at a fancy restaurant with envy. He said that his father could not help him get a job there for several reasons, including that they only wanted to hire immigrants, not the U.S.-born. For the upwardly mobile segment of the second generation, then, their Mexican-ness is more likely to assume an ethnic meaning in the labor market, but for those who are stuck or downwardly mobile such Mexican-ness risks a racialized meaning.

Racialization processes also take place in the house and community, though in different forms. For example, while some parents express no preferences regarding who their children date, many do not want their children to date blacks and in some cases Puerto Ricans, even while they themselves have black and Puerto Rican friends, or have Mexican relatives who have married Puerto Ricans. Many parents speak of how Puerto Ricans helped them when they came to New York many years earlier, when there were fewer Spanish speakers, but lament what they see as the Puerto Rican population's miserable social conditions. In particular, Mexican immigrants and their U.S.-born children I have worked with point to what they see as the tendency of Puerto Rican young men to engage in crime, especially against Mexicans, and Puerto Rican young women to get pregnant, and many Puerto Ricans to depend on government assistance, as evidence of the Americanization that robs them of their culture and leaves them vulnerable to the urban vices that Mexicans can resist. Listen to the words of unrelated first and second generation Mexicans in separate interviews:

Immigrant mother comparing Mexican women and Puerto Rican women:

> I had one Puerto Rican friend who has had five husbands in her lifetime. Tell me, what are you giving to your family? And us, my aunt she says, "You can be screwed in life, but there you are, see?" Because you have to think about your kids . . . with my countrymen, almost never is there a divorce.

Second-generation Mexican youth talking about Puerto Rican youth:

> In a Mexican family, you move out with your boyfriend, he's your husband, 'cause you sleep with him. . . . We've had girls getting pregnant, you know . . . but it's not taken so lightly. . . . I see Puerto Rican girls and it's just like they get pregnant, pregnancy after pregnancy. They either get an abortion or just get on welfare. . . . When I was smaller, we had meat on the table but maybe once or twice [a week] but we never went on welfare. It's a matter of pride. Puerto Ricans have gotten a lot Americanized . . . and we still have strong values from over there, you know, religion like I said, and I don't know, like, you know they run around at an early age.

In both cases, the Americanization of Puerto Ricans is seen as a cause of their failure, but Mexicans are seen to be insulated by their culture from such erosions of values. The story line here finds some apparent empirical support in, for example, the higher female-headed household and welfare usage rates of Puerto Ricans compared to Mexicans. But by interpreting these differences using the lens of the immigrant analogy—by attributing these differences to culture, writ large—this analysis elides the role of citizenship in producing these differences, and disallows consideration of how conditions of reception are already acting on Mexicans too. For many immigrants, longer term residency and intergenerational presence in the United States negatively affects them and their descendants, in ways ranging from increased levels of heart disease to increased rates of public assistance usage.[5]

Yet some in the first and a larger number in the second generation do not buy into the immigrant analogy. Witness what a second-generation woman who has noted the tendency of Mexicans to assert that they are better than blacks and Puerto Ricans, but disagrees with it, has to say.

> RS: ... tell me more about that, 'cause I hear that lots of times, like we're not like blacks, we're not, like, Puerto Ricans.
> INF: They don't wanna be like them. But I believe they are, because they I believe they do the same things. Why do they have to have a gang? Supposedly that's only blacks and Puerto Ricans, so if that's blacks and Puerto Ricans, why do they have a gang? Supposedly that's only blacks and Puerto Ricans. You know, and why do they have to go around drinking "forties," what they call 'em, the big bottles of beer? Mexicans? Puerto Ricans and blacks do it, but why do they have to look down on Puerto Ricans and blacks and not on Mexicans? I guess it's just their way of thinking, 'cause I think everybody's the same.

This woman has identified a problem in the collective self-image of much of the Mexican community in New York. If that self-image is premised on a juxtaposition with blacks and Puerto Ricans, it is being challenged by rising indicators of social distress resulting from the settlement and incorporation of Mexicans into New York. These include increasing numbers of upwardly mobile second-generation youth, but also increasing numbers of youth, born in Mexico and in the United States, who leave school or join gangs, or become pregnant. The formation of such gangs grows out of the migration process itself and the often hostile reception that Mexican youth get here. Concretely, many second-generation youth see that their lives are very similar to the blacks and Puerto Ricans with whom they share neighborhoods and parks, and go to school. Many see limited employment options, little payback from school, and feel that the larger society and its institutions think they will fail.

As mentioned, a significant cause of the surge in the Mexican population during the 1990s was family reunification made possible by the "amnesty" provision of the 1986 Immigration Reform and Control Act (IRCA). To most people's surprise, Mexicans were the second largest group that applied for amnesty, with about nine thousand to Dominicans' eleven thousand applicants in New York City. By the mid-1990s many of these immigrants were permanent residents and were bringing up their families, with or without visas; friends and other relatives also followed. During the mid-1990s, therefore, there was a huge increase in the Mexican youth population that resulted in the sudden public presence of Mexican youth in schools, parks, and neighborhoods where they had been fewer, and had been mainly people who worked very long hours and were not much seen. As Mexican youth report the story, other local youth—especially but not exclusively blacks and Puerto Ricans—responded by preying on Mexicans, insulting, beating, and robbing them. Mexicans formed gangs and crews to defend themselves.

This process too engages with racialization. One of the first Mexican gangs in the city (which formed in the mid-1980s and no longer exists) called itself ODR (Organization to Defend the Race), where the race was defined as the "Raza Hispana" and included Mexicans, Central and South Americans, and Puerto Ricans born on the island. The purpose was to defend themselves against Puerto Ricans and blacks born in New York, whom they saw as their primary antagonists. This definition of Raza Hispana and its mission resonates very deeply with the racialization inherent in the immigrant analogy. It is also an understandable response to hostile group dynamics, which have been repeated for most new ethnic groups in New York (Schneider 2000; Vigil 1988; Horowitz 1983). For example, Mexican adult and teen immigrants told me during the 1990s that Puerto Rican and black youth would wait for them on payday to rob them. In his book *In Search of Respect*, the anthropologist Philippe Bourgois (1995) documents that some of his informants adopted exactly this strategy with Mexicans in the same neighborhoods at this time. One of the original members of ODR told me that they had formed the gang to defend against the attacks of:

> Drugged out people, Boricuas (Puerto Ricans) and blacks that if you don't give them money they hit you. They abused you, passing by and shouting, "Mexico!_____ [leaves words unsaid]." This is something that no one can tolerate. And only together could we do something about all this stuff. That they respect us.

He went on to say that at one point he and his friends interrupted a group actually trying to take the clothes off a young Mexican, and they stopped it. His comment on why these other groups failed and Mexicans would succeed was that "one needs morals. Morals, culture, and you need this call from your people . . . an example to advance." His framing of the issue strongly resonates with the immigrant analogy. He lists "drugged out people, Boricuas and blacks" in the same category of groups that abused Mexicans, and went on to say that these groups lacked the morals and culture that Mexicans had, which would help them to succeed in the same dangerous urban environments in which these other groups fail. These words reflect a racialized view of the social world, and places Mexicans in a morally superior position to these other groups.

The growth in Mexican youth during the 1990s has produced varied "ethnicitization" and racialization patterns in schooling. Two are more frequent, and three less so. A first frequent pattern is an increase in the number of upwardly mobile youth who use their Mexican ethnicity to differentiate themselves from other minorities in their schools and neighborhoods, whom they see as not serious about school. "Being Mexican helps us do better" is how this group understands itself. This group is also most inclined towards regular transnational activity, in some cases participating in what I have described as a "transnationalized adolescence" (Smith 2002a; 2005). The regular return back to their parents' home village has provided a site for them to redefine the meaning of their Mexican-ness away from the many negative meanings it can acquire in New York. Instead of signifying being powerless and being victimized, or dropping out of school and getting bad jobs, it comes to be associated with having a place to show one's academic success, to participate in "authentic" Mexican customs, and a set of adolescent rituals in which they have full ownership of the processes and the physical space in which these take place in their parents' home towns. This sense of ownership contrasts sharply from what their experience is in most places in New York, where their Mexican-ness often means being a preyed upon, dispersed minority.

A second frequent pattern is that youth are dropping out of school at alarming rates and some boys (and a few girls) are joining gangs. More girls are also getting pregnant. Some of these youth see themselves as a racialized minority youth, such as blacks or Puerto Ricans, as segmented assimilation would predict. Others seem not to identify with native minorities, but rather see themselves as retaining and defending what is Mexican and thus different from native minorities. Rather than seeing themselves as being part of a rainbow underclass, these youth would see themselves as racialized Mexicans. This is especially true of "teen migrants" who constitute a growing and increasingly important segment of the youth population.

A third pattern can be illustrated with three less frequent but very interesting groups, which could be called "cosmopolitans" and "black Mexicans" and "nerds"; sometimes, elements of each category were seen in the same person, at the same or at different times. In my second-generation sample, these three groups were disproportionately successful, an outcome that is also related to Mexicans' engagement with racialization because each avoids the "racialized Mexican-ness" that is causally related to the increasing dropout rate just discussed.

Cosmopolitans see their Mexican-ness as one but not their only important identity and tend to do well in school and at work. Girls are more likely to be cosmopolitans than boys, and this identity is easier to sustain in academically better high schools in New York (see Smith 2002b; 2005).

"Black Mexicans" dissociate themselves from Mexican-ness in public places and identify instead, in most cases, with upwardly mobile blacks. (That the sample showed very few doing this with whites reflects, I think, the fact that most of the schools we were in did not have many white students.) This group sees successful black students as role models whose success they wish to emulate. Several of the students in this group strategically chose to change their primary in-school peer group, because they feared that if they continued to hang around with other Mexicans they would be pressured to cut school frequently and eventually drop out. For other students, there was a less conscious but still notable shift in their friendships and identification over time, which coincided with their articulating their academic goals more concretely.

The final group, the nerds, stayed away from public places where their Mexican-ness could end up imposing on them the burden of "representing" Mexicans in some conflict or of cutting school to prove they were cool with other Mexicans. Hence, they often would either eat lunch quickly and leave the lunchroom or skip it altogether and go to the library instead. They also went directly home after school, in part to avoid the negative pressures they felt that their Mexican-ness was imposing on them, either as a potential victim of another group, or by being pressed into some kind of gang or ethnic conflict.

In the case of the nerds and the cosmopolitans, Mexican American youth try to neutralize the meaning of their Mexican-ness to prevent it from assuming a negative racialized meaning. Black Mexicans, however, have attempted to adopt a positively racialized identity—of educationally successful blacks who have developed, in Kathryn Neckerman, Prudence Carter, and Jennifer Lee's (1999) words, a "minority culture of mobility." In both cases, these youth are attempting to avoid the negative and racialized meanings that Mexican-ness is often coming to have in New York.

The results of these engagements with racialization have sometimes been ironic. For example, many Mexican youth, especially boys, now fear being "stepped up" to—stopped by others to verify if they are in a rival gang—by Mexican gangs more than they fear confrontation with blacks or Puerto Ricans. Most Mexican gang confrontations actually involve conflicts with other Mexicans, not Puerto Ricans or blacks. Some Mexican parents I have come to know purposefully put their children into high schools where there are few other Mexicans in an attempt to avoid the entanglements they fear will come. Some Mexican youth we have interviewed report that they are not stepped up to because they "look Dominican" or "look Ecuadorian," and hence are let pass uninspected. All these social realities point to processes of racialization among Mexicans.

IMPLICATIONS AND CONCLUSIONS

This analysis raises interesting issues regarding the intergroup relations between Mexicans and other groups. In the data reviewed earlier, relations with Puerto Ricans and other Latino groups vary according to generation (first, 1.5, second), to age (pre-teen, teen, adult), to inter- and intragenerational mobility and to the perception of the relationship between Mexicans and other groups to New York's racial hierarchies. In general, the first generation seems to have embraced the immigrant analogy more strongly than the second generation, though this statement requires qualification. The first generation often has very positive experiences of other groups, such as Puerto Ricans, but desperately wants a better future for their own children than what they perceive has been the fate of Puerto Ricans. But the second and 1.5 generations also have intragenerational differences by educational and work trajectories. Those who are more successful in school and work have an easier time sustaining the image of the immigrant analogy, and positing cultural and other essential differences between Mexicans and other groups as causal in the predicted differentials of their futures. These students tend to have parents who are more successful as well, making these findings quite similar to Mary Waters's (1994; 1999) findings with Caribbean second-generation youth. Many of those who are less successful feel that the United States gives, in one youth's words, a "serious beat down" to all minority groups, including Mexicans.

Finally, two other groups complicate the relationship. Teen migrants in particular are likely to embrace a "racialized Mexican-ness" that is both downwardly mobile and rejecting of any identification with other minorities. This is an interesting variation on Waters's (1994; 1999) work, where immigrant-identified youth tended to do better than American-identified. In the Mexican case in New York, the American-identified youth—who feel America offers a "beat down" to all minorities, including Mexicans—do in fact do badly, but so do the racialized Mexicans, who see themselves as being better than native minorities because they are Mexicans, but engage in the same kinds of oppositional stances, for example, on schooling, usually associated with these stigmatized groups. Finally, the black Mexicans, Cosmopolitans, and Nerds have all worked out a different relationship with Mexican-ness and New York's racial hierarchies, in which they attempt to disengage with it through avoiding public spaces where ethnicity or identity might structure their social world (nerds), by adopting an ethnic, pluralist vision (cosmopolitans), or by inverting the whole order on its head and following the good students (lack Mexicans).

This analysis raises an important question, not often framed this way: what does America do to its immigrants? According to the census, Mexicans as a group went from having one of the highest per capita incomes of all Latinos in New York in 1980 to having one of the lowest in 1990. Mexicans also had the largest percentage of sixteen- to nineteen-year-olds not in school and not graduated—47 percent in 1990, versus 22 percent for Dominicans and Puerto Ricans and 18 percent for blacks and 8 percent for whites. Part of the reason for these high indicators of social distress was the huge surge in youth migration during the 1990s—younger people earn less, and teen migrants often do not enter school. But they also reflect what is happening in New York. The news in the 2000 census will, I suspect, show continued progress for many but alarming difficulties for more. There seems to be a larger process by which America both rewards some immigrants but also "beats down" its immigrants over the course of a generation or two. The cost of Americanization for many is too high.

Part of the answer to where Mexicans will ultimately "fit in" in New York's social, political, and racial hierarchies will be answered via macro-level definitions of ethnicity, such as those that occur in politics and in labor markets. As the third largest Latino group in the City, whose potential for growth is much larger than those of Puerto Ricans and Dominicans, Mexicans in New York are beginning to draw the attention of political and community leaders. How their Mexican-ness will be defined in politics is an interesting question. Will there emerge a pan-Latino movement in New York politics? Will differences between politically less powerful immigrant Latinos and politically more powerful U.S. citizen Puerto Ricans make collaboration difficult? Will cultural splits emerge between Caribbean (Puerto Rican and Dominican) and Mesoamerican (Mexican, South, and Central American) Latinos? How will they relate to blacks, whites, and Asians? While there is much reason to believe that Mexicans are becoming a positive political force in the City, there is also reason for concern.[6] One important implication of this research is that a particular segment of the second-generation population, and especially teen migrants, are experiencing their Mexican-ness in a racialized as opposed to an ethnicized form. The implications for the possibility of an oppositional subculture framed using "Mexicanidad" along the lines supposed by segmented assimilation theory are disturbing.

It is also interesting that the comments I have heard usually compare Mexicans to Puerto Ricans and blacks or other minorities, and not with whites. Part of the reason for this is that the life worlds of most Mexicans and Mexican Americans, especially youth, do not include too many whites. Many of the people we have interviewed for our projects report not knowing many whites, except for teachers or employers, and that most of their classmates, workmates, or people they see in the parks or in their neighborhoods, are black and Latino. The tendency to compare Mexicans to these groups and not to whites seems consistent whether the interviewer was white or Mexican American. In interviews done in Westchester County (an affluent one just north of the City), there was a greater likelihood that whites would be included in these juxtapositions.

In thinking about how these issues will play out in New York, comparisons with California might offer insight. Processes of ethnicity and race occur differently in different contexts despite the fact that the same national origin group is involved. In California, there has already been a racialization and stigmatization of Chicanos, despite the fact that there has been significant upward mobility in the population there as well, especially among women, but also disproportionate stagnation and downward mobility among later than earlier generations (Myers and Cranford 1998). New York has a different set of racial and social hierarchies, and the meaning of Mexican-ness is still in play here. At present, most natives in New York see Mexicans (to the extent they see them at all) through the proud eyes of inheritors of a City of Immigrants. Mexicans are seen as hard workers whose children will continue in this vein and prosper. This is certainly the view of the "liberal establishment" in City government, both Republicans and Democrats. And Mexicans as a group do not see themselves as victimized minorities, at least not yet or not mostly. I call U.S.-born people of Mexican descent in New York "Mexican Americans" or "Mexicans" because this is the language they use. They also use Hispanic, and not Latino, when they use a larger category. They see "Chicano" as a politicized category, often with negative connotations of urban and gang life, that refers mainly to those who live in California. While I personally think there are more meanings to "Chicano" (including very positive, political ones), it is analytically worth noting how the meaning of Mexican-ness is different so far in New York than in California.

Other developments in the possible meanings of Mexican-ness in New York—compared to California are—in order (see Smith 2001b; 2002b). First, transnational, governmental, religious, and community structures are different in the case of New York and California. For example, Poblanos in New York as a group have settled during a period when transnational activity by community groups and by the federal and state governments in Mexico has been especially high. New York also offers a myriad of ways for ethnic groups to be formally recognized by the mechanisms of government and civic groups. Its has large numbers of CBOs that engage groups positively on the basis of their ethnic identity, and New York politics has a more positive sum notion of how ethnicity works in politics than California seems to have had for much of its history (though New York has its own share of shameful stories, too; see Smith, Cordero-Guzman, and Grosfoguel 2001; Cordero-Guzman and Navarro 2000). Together, these activities should steer the segments of the population involved in them toward ethnic as opposed to racial "Mexicanidad."

Yet another current of mobilization in New York involves religious nationalism coupled with international and local class rhetoric, through for example, Asociación Tepeyac. This movement emphasizes identification with Mexico and the Virgin of Guadalupe, while also speaking in the class-based idioms that would lead it to associate Mexican-ness with other oppressed racialized minorities. These are differences from California, where the formation of a Chicano identity in all its various meanings happened largely in the absence of Mexican government involvement or in opposition to an exclusive white power structure (Mollenkopf 1999). These comments are meant as analytical speculations rather than definitive statements.

A final process that merits discussion is that of the exportation of a particular, Hollywood version of "Mexicanidad" from California to New York, which I will discuss via one example. During the mid-1990s, one of the catalysts for the growth of Mexican gangs in New York City was the release of two movies, *Blood In, Blood Out* and *American Me*. What resonated with the Mexicans, including gang members, with whom I have spoken about *American Me*, is that Santanna (played by James Edward Olmos, who also directed the film) demands and gets respect from the black and white gangs in the prison. This resonated deeply with the humiliation that Mexicans felt and their desire to get the respect of other groups, to be one as equals among them. The point with respect to the comparison with California is that I know of the social dynamics—including youth adopting the same gang names and language—in a variety of settings on the East Coast, from rural settings in Pennsylvania to suburban settings in New Jersey to inner city settings in New York. *American Me* has served in many ways as a template for what it means to be Mexican, a manual of how to be "authentically" Mexican for youth in settings where their Mexican-ness had negative meanings, including victimization by others. As such, it means that a certain vision of Mexican-ness has been exported from California to other parts of the country. While of course such images and narratives would not have so much influence if they did not resonate with lived experience, their power as mass popular culture in depicting what it means to be Mexican in this way can also be viewed as an assimilative pressure by which the larger society is saying that this is how "real" Mexican young men act. Especially in areas of new settlement on the east coast, where what being Mexican means is still being negotiated, where ethnic relations may be conflictive, such images become more powerful and dangerous by their offering alternatives to negative images and social realities. There is a lot of work to be done to make sure these are not the only images and social realities on offer to these youth.

NOTES

1. A shorter, earlier version of this chapter was published as Smith (2001a). My thanks to NACLA editor Fred Rosen and the editors of this book for graciously agreeing to this arrangement. My work and this article have been deeply influenced by David Roediger's work (see especially Roediger 1991, chs. 1 and 7). See also Joel Ignatiev (1995) and Matthew Jacobson (1998).

2. This section is taken in large part from a similar section published in Nancy Foner (2001). My gratitude to her for her permission to do so.

3. This work is developed further in my other studies, cited in the bibliography. Research assistance from 1998 to 2000 done by Sara Guerrero Rippberger, Sandra Lara, Agustin Vecino, Carolina Perez, Griscelda Perez, Linda Rodriguez, and Lisa Peterson is gratefully acknowledged.

4. "Doubly bounded solidarity" is my adaptation of the concept of bounded solidarity as developed by Alejandro Portes and his colleagues. I developed the idea in a paper in 1994 that was never published. The concept of "segmented assimilation" which Portes and his colleagues developed is also relevant here, though as I analyze elsewhere, it requires some modification

to take better account of the racialization process. (See Portes's chapters in Portes 1995; Zhou 1999.)
5. See, for example, the work of Rubén Rumbaut (1997) of University of California, Irvine.
6. See my article in Nancy Foner's book, cited earlier (Smith 2001b).

REFERENCES

Binford, Leigh. 1998. "Accelerated Migration from Puebla to New York." Paper presented at Conference on Mexican Migration at Barnard College and the New School. New York (October 14–16).
Bourgois, Philippe. 1995. *In Search of Respect: Selling Crack in El Barrio.* New York: Cambridge University Press.
Cornelius, Wayne A. 1986. *De la Madrid: The Crisis Continues.* La Jolla, Calif.: Center for U.S. Mexico Studies.
———. 1994. "Los Migrantes de la Crisis: The Changing Profile of Mexican Migration to the United States." In *Social Responses to Mexico's Economic Crisis of the1980s,* edited by Mercedes Gonzalez de la Rocha and Agustin Escobar Lapati. La Jolla, Calif.: Center for U.S. Mexican Studies.
Cordero-Guzman, Hector, and Jose Navarro. 2000. "What Do Immigrant Groups, Organizations and Service Providers Say About the Impacts of Recent Changes in Immigration and Welfare Laws?" *Migration World* 28(4): 20–28.
DuBois, W. E. B. 1935/1977. *Black Reconstruction in the United States, 1860–1880.* New York: Atheneum.
Durand, Jorge, Douglas S. Massey, and Emilio A. Parrado. 1999. "The New Era of Mexican Migration to the United States." *The Journal of American History* 86(2): 518–36.
Foner, Nancy, ed. 2001. *New Immigrants in New York.* New York: Columbia University Press.
Hernández-León, Rubén. 1999. "'A la Aventura!' Jovenes, Pandillas y Migracion en la Conexion Monterrey-Houston." In *Fronteras Fragmentadas,* edited by Gail Mummert. Zamora, Michoacan, Mexico: El Colegio de Michoacan.
Horowitz, Ruth. 1983. *Honor and the American Dream: Culture and Identity in a Chicano Community.* New Brunswick, N.J.: Rutgers University Press.
Ignatiev, Joel. 1995. *How the Irish Became White.* New York: Routledge.
Jacobson, Matthew. 1998. *Whiteness of a Different Color: European Immigrants and the Alchemy of Race.* Cambridge, Mass.: Harvard University Press.
Kim, Dae Young. 1999. "Beyond Co-ethnic Solidarity: Mexican and Ecuadorean Employment in Korean-owned Businesses in New York City." *Ethnic and Racial Studies* 22(3): 481–99.
Kraly, Ellen Percy, and Ines Miyares. 2001. "Immigration to New York: Policy, Population, and Patterns." In *New Immigrants to New York,* edited by Nancy Foner. New York: Columbia University Press.

Malkin, Victoria. 2000. Personal communication with author (April 10).

Massey, Douglas, Rafael Alarcon, Jorge Durand, and Humberto Gonzalez. 1987. *Return to Aztlan: The Social Process of International Migration from Western Mexico.* Berkeley: University of California Press.

Massey, Douglas, and Kristin Espinosa. 1997. "What's Driving Mexico-U.S. Migration? A Theoretical, Empirical, and Policy Analysis." *American Journal of Sociology* 102(4): 939–99.

Massey, Douglas, Luin Goldring, and Jorge Durand. 1994. "Continuities in Transnational Migration: An Analysis of Nineteen Mexican Communities." *American Journal of Sociology* 99(6): 1492–1533.

Mexican Consulate. 2003. *Statistics on the Presumption of Nationality Document.* Data from Mexican Consulate, New York.

Mollenkopf, John. 1999. "Urban Political Conflicts and Alliances: New York and Los Angeles Compared." In *Handbook of Immigration: The American Experience*, edited by Charles Hirschman, Philip Kasinitz, and Josh DeWind. New York: Russell Sage Foundation.

Myers, Dowell, and Cynthia Cranford. 1998. "Temporal Differences in the Occupational Mobility of Immigrant and Native-born Latina Workers." *American Sociological Review* 63(1): 68–93.

Neckerman, Kathryn, Prudence Carter, and Jennifer Lee. 1999. "Segmented Assimilation and Minority Cultures of Mobility." *Ethnic and Racial Studies* 22(6): 945–65.

Nivon, Alejandro. 2002. Personal communication with author (June 10).

Pare, Luisa. 1975. "Caciquismo y Estructura de Poder en la Sierra Norte de Puebla." In *Caciquismo y Poder Politico en el Mexico Rural*, edited by Roger Bartra. Mexico, DF: Instituto de Investigaciones Sociales, UNAM.

Portes, Alejandro, ed. 1995. *The Economic Sociology of Immigration: Essays on Networks, Ethnicity, and Entrepreneurship.* New York: Russell Sage Foundation.

Portes, Alejandro, and Rubén Rumbaut. 2001. *Legacies.* Berkeley: University of California Press.

Roediger, David. 1991. *The Wages of Whiteness.* New York: Verso.

Rumbaut, Rubén. 1997. "Assimilation and Its Discontents: Between Rhetoric and Reality." *International Migration Review* 31(4): 923–60.

Schneider, Eric. 2000. *Vampires, Dragons and Egyptian Kings: Youth Gangs in Postwar New York.* Princeton, N.J.: Princeton University Press.

Smith, Robert. 1995. "'Los Ausentes Siempre Presentes': The Imagining, Making and Politics of Community Between Ticuani, Puebla, Mexico, and New York City." Ph.D. diss., Columbia University.

———. 1996. "Mexicans in New York City: Membership and Incorporation of New Immigrant Group." In *Latinos in New York*, edited by Sherri L. Baver and Gabe Haslip Viera. Notre Dame: University of Notre Dame Press.

———. 2000. "How Durable and New Is Transnational Life? Historical Retrieval Through Local Comparisons." *Diaspora* 9(2): 203–34.

———. 2001a. "Mexican-ness in New York: New Immigrants Seek Place in Old Racial Order." *North American Congress on Latin America* 35(2, September/October): 14–17.

———. 2001b. "Mexicans: Social, Educational, Economic and Political Problems and Prospects in New York." In *New Immigrants in New York*, edited by Nancy Foner. New York: Columbia University Press.

———. 2002a. "Globalization, Adolescence, and the Transnationalization of Mexican Gangs in New York." Unpublished manuscript. Barnard College, New York.

———. 2002b. "Gender, Race and Schools in Educational and Work Outcomes of Second Generation Mexican Americans in New York." In *Latinos in the 21st Century*, edited by Marcelo Suarez-Orozco and Mariela Paez. Berkeley: University of California Press.

———. 2005. *Mexican New York: Transnational Worlds of New Immigrants.* Berkeley: University of California Press.

Smith, Robert C., Hector Cordero-Guzman, and Ramon Grosfoguel. 2001. "Introduction: New Analytical Perspectives on Migration, Race and Transnationalization." In *Migration, Race and Transnationalization in a Changing New York*, edited by Hector Cordero-Guzman, Robert Smith, and Ramon Grosfoguel. Philadelphia: Temple University Press.

Valdes de Montaño, Luz Maria, and Robert Smith. 1994. "Mexicans in New York: Final Report to the Tinker Foundation." Tinker Foundation, New York.

Vecino, Agustin. 1999. "Crews and Gangs—Fieldnotes for NSF project" for Robert Smith.

Vigil, James Diego. 1988. *Barrio Gangs: Street Life and Identity in Southern California.* Austin: University of Texas Press.

Waters, Mary C. 1994. "Ethnic and Racial Identities of Second Generation Black Immigrants in New York City." *International Migration Review* 28(4): 795–820.

———. 1999. *Black Identities: West Indian Immigrant Dreams and American Realities.* Cambridge and New York: Harvard University Press and Russell Sage Foundation.

Zhou, Min. 1999. "Segmented Assimilation: Issues, Controversies, and Recent Research on the New Second Generation." In *Handbook of International Migration: The American Experience*, edited by Charles Hirshman, Josh DeWind, and Philip Kasinitz. New York: Russell Sage Foundation.

CHAPTER 10

✕

APPALACHIA MEETS AZTLÁN: MEXICAN IMMIGRATION AND INTERGROUP RELATIONS IN DALTON, GEORGIA

RUBÉN HERNÁNDEZ-LEÓN AND VÍCTOR ZÚÑIGA

During the late twentieth century, Mexican immigration exploded in regions and localities of the United States with no prior history of Latino settlement. In no other region was this phenomenon more conspicuous than the South, where between 1990 and 2000 the Latino population nearly tripled. The arrival of thousands of Mexican and other Latin American newcomers has transformed the linguistic, cultural, and ethnic landscape of the South and begun to redefine the dynamics of local public and private institutions—from workplaces to banks to public schools.

This chapter explores the impact of Mexican immigration on the discourses, representations, and dynamics of interethnic relations in Dalton, Georgia, a small and economically thriving city of the southern Appalachia region. We describe these dynamics comprehensively, using two fundamental sociological principles. First, that interethnic relations have their own local and regional history and that—as William I. Thomas and Florian Znaniecki recognized nearly a century ago—women and men use that history to face and make sense of new situations. As they do so, they repeat patterns and establish new ones. Thus, the approach to intergroup relations adopted in this essay is both historical and interactionist: individuals construe new meaningful social relations based on their personal experiences and on those of their forebears. Second, that interethnic interactions do not develop separately from class relations. We seek to convey the idea that the ethnic makeup of this locality and the region is intimately tied to social class and class structure, which have played a central role in the broader spectrum of social relations.

We thus have three goals: to describe the various phases of inter-group relations vis-à-vis immigration analytically, to examine the discourses and debates that immigration has generated as it has changed the local ethnic landscape, and to explain the subversion of previous arrangements as well as the emergence of new patterns of intergroup interaction. In sum, how has immigration destabilized and transformed the existing intra- and interethnic landscape in Dalton, Georgia?

Deep in the southern Appalachia region, Dalton, Georgia, is internationally known as the largest manufacturing hub of wall-to-wall carpet in the world. The city is the seat of Whitfield County and the economic center of a five-county region in northwest Georgia, where carpet production and its auxiliary industries are clustered. Thus Dalton and its hinterland house carpet manufacturing companies of Fortune 500 stature, with billions of dollars in annual sales, as well as subsidiary firms providing specialized services to the big producers. This industrial landscape remains in place despite recent waves of business consolidation, where a few large manufacturers are in control of the market. By the late 1990s, 80 percent of the carpet produced in the country was manufactured here (Carpet and Rug Institute 2002; Patton 1999).

Although the mass production of carpets only began in earnest in the South during the 1950s and 1960s—prompting scholars to call it a New South industry (Patton 1999)—industrialization per se was not new to Dalton. During the last two decades of the nineteenth century local cotton merchants established textile mills in the city, relying on a labor force mostly of impoverished rural whites from the surrounding Appalachia region. The exclusion of blacks from mill jobs, the absence of European immigrants, and the continuous resistance of rural whites to the factory regime, created endemic labor shortages and high worker turnover for the textile industry. Local entrepreneurs sought to address this problem by developing a system of corporate paternalism, which included inexpensive housing in mill villages, savings, life insurance, and funeral plans for laborers and their families, company-sponsored recreational activities, health and schooling services, and, most important, higher wages. This system sought to create a stable labor force by fostering a close identification between workers and corporate interests, yet inaugurated a tradition of business involvement and control of the community's social and political affairs. By bringing millhands together, these policies unintentionally contributed to the formation of the few unions that have ever existed in the region (Flamming 1992; McDonald and Clelland 1984; Patton 1999).

Historians of southern industrialization attribute the development of carpet manufacturing in Dalton to the production of tufted bedspreads. Initiated as a craft industry by middle-class women around the turn of the nineteenth century, tufted-bedspread creation developed through a putout system in which merchants commissioned work to rural and blue-collar households in the town's vicinity. During the period between the two world wars, bedspread production turned into an increasingly centralized and mechanized operation and one of Dalton's most important economic activities. At this point the tufting technique was only used to produce bedspreads, bathrobes, curtains, and rugs. By the 1940s, technological innovations, such as the broadloom tufting machine, allowed for the production of wall-to-wall carpets. It is worth noting that Dalton entrepreneurs benefited from the city's proximity to Chattanooga, Tennessee, and its concentration of machinists, whose expertise and technological experimentation set the stage for the next phase of the industry (Flamming 1992; Patton 1999; Engstrom 1998).

The 1950s and 1960s were a critical period for carpet manufacturing. Several developments signaled the new era. Textile and carpet capitals moved from the Northeast to southern states, which had lower wages and a largely union-free environment. The tufting method and new materials, such as nylon, displaced the old woven technique based on wool. By 1968, tufted carpets and rugs accounted for 91 percent of the industry's output (Patton 1999, 198). Dalton turned into the hub of the new industry as local manufacturers of various sizes entered the trade, followed by companies providing such subsidiary services as dyeing, drying, and backing application for carpets. In the sociopolitical arena, carpet entrepreneurs became the heart of an urban regime also composed of local politicians, merchants, professionals, and boosters of different types. Organized in the Tufted Textile Manufacturers Association, they successfully fended off unionization efforts and articulated a social consensus binding white workers with their white employers. This pact included plentiful job opportunities, higher wages (particularly for unskilled workers), modern management practices, and a culture of "good corporate citizenship," which revived aspects of the old corporate paternalism of the textile mills, such as scholarship programs and funding for recreational facilities (Patton 1999; Engstrom 1998; Flamming 1992).

The slower growth of the 1970s did not challenge either the social contract or Dalton's role as the "Carpet Capital of the World." In fact, production continued to increase at an unprecedented pace, based on the postwar construction boom and on the evolution of carpet from luxury item into a household "necessity." According to figures provided by Randall L. Patton (1999) and the Carpet and Rug Institute (2002), carpet shipments went from 395 million square yards in 1968 to 1.9 billion square yards in 1999. The growth of carpet manufacturing and its transformation into a mass production industry is best illustrated with the case of Shaw Industries. By the end of the 1990s, this corporation generated more than $4 billion in revenues and employed more than 30,000—making the company the largest carpet producer in the world (Patton 1999, 2000; Engstrom 1998). The dominance of carpet production in the local economy can be gauged from the fact that 42 percent of the county's total occupied workforce was in 1990 employed in a single industry, the manufacturing of nondurable goods (U.S. Census Bureau 1999).

Although largely a white town throughout the twentieth century, Dalton has never been homogeneous. Racial fault lines run deep in the region. Following the canon of Jim Crow segregation, black Daltonians were politically, socially, and educationally disenfranchised. African Americans were excluded from employment in the textile mills and relegated to cleaning and domestic service jobs. This exclusion was central to the white intragroup consensus sustaining the nascent industrial order during the late nineteenth and early twentieth centuries. Thus, despite class differences, "[T]he one societal norm which poor whites and wealthy whites readily agreed was that blacks should be subordinate to all whites, economic status notwithstanding" (Flamming 1992, 66). The Crown Mill, the textile factory that initiated Dalton's industrial revolution, never hired a black in its more than eight decades of operation (Flamming 1992, xxx). African American interviewees in Dalton recalled how an army of white women would leave the spread houses in the late afternoons, covered with lint and hence looking like "ghosts." "Colored" people were conspicuously absent from the scene. Marginalized from the local manufacturing boom, blacks left the city and the region for northern destinations. Their share of the county's population declined dramatically from 15 percent in 1890 to 6.6 percent in 1930. Today, African Americans make up only 3.8 percent of Whitfield's residents (see table 10.1).

This intraethnic consensus, which excluded blacks from the mills, was intimately connected to yet another of Dalton's fault lines—social class. The rise of an industrial order in this city during the late nineteenth century entailed the formation of two social classes: an urban bourgeoisie, composed of mill owners, managers, merchants, and boosters, and a rural yet increasingly urbanized working class, made up of impoverished whites from the surrounding upcountry. The growing divide of wealth and status separating these two classes was bridged by

TABLE 10.1   Main Ethnoracial Groups in Whitfield County, Georgia

Census Year	Total Population	Blacks (Percentage)	Whites (Percentage)	Latinos (Percentage)
1890	12,916	1,930 (15)	10,984 (85)	—
1900	14,509	1,824 (12.6)	12,683 (87.4)	—
1910	15,934	1,719 (10.7)	14,214 (89.2)	—
1920	16,897	1,345 (8)	15,552 (92)	—
1930	20,808	1,371 (6.6)	19,424 (93.3)	—
1940	26,105	1,463 (5.6)	24,617 (94.3)	—
1950	34,432	1,423 (4.1)	33,006 (95.8)	—
1960	42,109	1,904 (4.5)	40,192 (95.4)	—
1970	55,108	2,133 (3.8)	52,898 (96)	—
1980	65,789	2,518 (3.8)	62,722 (95.3)	526 (.8)
1990	72,462	2,901 (4)	66,745 (92.1)	2,321 (3.2)
2000	83,525	3,214 (3.8)	60,338 (72.2)	18,419 (22.1)

Sources: University of Virginia Geospatial and Statistical Data Center 1998; U.S. Department of Commerce, Bureau of the Census n.d., 1973, 1982.

the privilege of race. In Dalton's textile mills this meant that factory jobs were for whites only (Flamming 1992). Still, the rich and poor chasm would have long-term consequences, one of them being the patterning of social class in urban space. The proverbial railroad tracks divide the city between an affluent East Side and a low-income and working-class West Side, which now concentrates minorities and immigrants as well. The latter section also houses many of the carpet mills. Although Dalton boasts one of the best public education systems in the state of Georgia, the schools and their various socioeconomic and attainment indicators reflect the inequalities between the East and West sides (Hamman 1999). This social and spatial class-based polarization was firmly ingrained in the imagination of several white Daltonians we interviewed, who argued that for a long time "there wasn't much of a middle class" in town. It is worth noting that this urban landscape cannot be fully grasped without acknowledging the decision of Dalton's homegrown bourgeoisie to live in Dalton rather than nearby Chattanooga or Atlanta. In a mostly post-industrial United States, Dalton resembles more an old Fordist city, where corporate headquarters and production facilities are in the same place and where workers and managers face together, although not evenly, the consequences of social change (Hamman 1999; Zúñiga et al. 2002).

This context sets the stage for the sudden and massive arrival of Mexican and other Latino immigrants to Dalton from the late 1980s to the present. Although Mexican migration to the city and the surrounding region began in the early 1970s, the newcomer community remained small and stable, growing slowly over the following decade. The 1986 Immigration Reform and Control Act (IRCA) marked a watershed in Mexico-U.S. migration history and signaled the initiation of mass Latino inflows to Dalton and many other nontraditional destinations across the country. IRCA's programs allowed for the legalization of 2.3 million previously undocumented Mexicans, flooding the immigrant labor markets of the Southwest and Illinois. Faced with a downward pressure on wages but with residency papers in hand, newcomers moved to localities with lower concentrations of co-ethnics but still in need of immigrant labor. In the same way, oversupplied farm labor markets and the availability of legal documentation prompted those working in agriculture to "settle out" of the stream (Durand, Massey, and Parrado 1999; Hernández-León and Zúñiga 2000). On the other hand, labor-intensive industries, such as poultry and meatpacking, and their formal and informal recruitment also played a role in the establishment of atypical destinations, mainly in the Midwest and eastern seaboard. In fact, one of Dalton's early cohorts of Mexican immigrants was actually recruited to work in a local poultry plant. Moreover, IRCA's employment sanctions legislation fostered a renewed usage of recruiters, many of them former farmhands, as employers sought to avoid legal responsibility for hiring undocumented workers (Durand 1998; Krissman 2000).

A comparison of 1990 and 2000 census data for Whitfield County illustrates the momentous growth of the Latino population. Where in 1990 Latinos made up 3.2 percent of the county's residents, by 2000 they constituted 22.1 percent of the local population—a growth of nearly 600 percent (see table 10.1). Reflecting this increase and a pattern of high concentration in the city itself, the proportion of Latinos in Dalton expanded from 6.5 percent in 1990 to 40.2 percent in 2000. School enrollment data confirms this phenomenal growth. While during the 1989 to 1990 academic year Latino pupils were less than 4 percent of the enrollment of Dalton Public Schools, by the 2000 to 2001 school year they had become the majority, with more than 51 percent of the student body (see table 10.2). Although categories such as Latino or Hispanic attest only indirectly to the spur in the presence of Mexican immigrants in Dalton, a survey of Hispanic parents whose children were attending the city's public schools in the 1997 to 1998 academic year confirmed that 90 percent in fact had been born in Mexico. The large

TABLE 10.2   Race–Ethnic Distribution in Dalton Public Schools (DPS): Four Main Groups

Year	Hispanic		Asian		Black		White		DPS Totals N
	N	Percentage	N	Percentage	N	Percentage	N	Percentage	
2000–2001	2,707	51.5	142	2.7	480	9.1	1,852	35.2	5,260
1999–2000	2,280	45.44	108	2.15	511	10.18	2,041	40.67	5,018
1998–1999	1,992	41.5	89	1.85	507	10.57	2,136	44.55	4,794
1997–1998	1,688	36.73	81	1.76	528	11.49	2,244	48.83	4,596
1996–1997	1,512	33.04	83	1.81	514	11.23	2,420	52.88	4,576
1995–1996	1,178	26.77	77	1.75	523	11.88	2,580	58.63	4,400
1994–1995	902	21.26	77	1.81	557	13.13	2,674	63.03	4,242
1993–1994	591	14.94	57	1.44	534	13.50	2,739	69.25	3,955
1992–1993	380	9.86	62	1.60	529	13.72	2,865	74.35	3,853
1991–1992	296	7.60	54	1.39	545	14.01	2,972	76.40	3,890
1990–1991	220	5.71	59	1.53	518	13.45	3,042	78.99	3,851
1989–1990	151	3.89	42	1.08	527	13.60	3,131	80.78	3,876

Source: Georgia Department of Education (various years).

proportion of Latino children in public schools suggests that this immigrant flow differed from the pattern of the single male sojourner. Indeed, many of the new arrivals were moving to Dalton together with offspring and spouse or making this city a site for family reunification. Attracted by an urban industry—carpets—offering all year round employment, significant numbers of newcomers have settled and have bought homes. According to the Dalton survey, nearly 80 percent of the parents expressed their intent to settle in the city over the next three years, while 20 percent had already purchased a house. Reflecting the size of the immigrant settlement but also the social capital of its members, Mexicans and other Latinos have established more than seventy small businesses catering to the needs of the ethnic community (Hernández-León and Zúñiga 2000; Zúñiga and Hernández-León 2001).

Mexican immigration to Dalton is producing a dramatic transformation of this city and its surrounding region (Zúñiga et al. 2002). These transformations include, first, a redefinition of the social and cultural symbols associated with this community as the Spanish language, Catholicism, soccer leagues, and Mexican cuisine and music are conspicuously present in public and private spaces. Second, the dislocation of class relations, with Mexican and other Latino immigrants and their children becoming part of the local middle class and thousands of new arrivals changing the face of the working class. Third, the redefinition of the role of institutions, including schools, banks, workplaces, churches, and associations, which find themselves mediating the incorporation of newcomers into Dalton and have had to introduce Spanish into their daily operations. However, no other institution has been as affected as the public schools, which are now in the midst of discussions about bilingualism, multiculturalism, parallel curricula, and cross-cultural exchange—issues for the most part absent from the local educational policy debate only a few years ago. Fourth, an emerging redefinition of local politics, in response to the demographic transformation and potential role of Latinos as a swing vote in regional and state elections. In Dalton, Republicans and Democrats have started to court young Mexican Americans and middle-class Latinos. On the other hand, immigrants themselves have begun to organize and to run for public office, albeit unsuccessfully, in the city's school board. Finally, mass Mexican immigration of the last ten years has destabilized the existing landscape of inter- and intraethnic relations. The main goal of this chapter is to show how the new Latino presence is subverting both the biracial order typical of the South and the intra-white consensus constructed around the industrialization of this locality.

After discussing our theoretical framework and the methods used for data collection, we analyze the evolution of inter- and intraethnic relations vis-à-vis immigration, dividing them in three different periods: a first period, from the early 1970s, when the first Mexican immigrants settled in Dalton, to 1987, the year IRCA began to be implemented; a second phase, beginning in the late 1980s through the late 1990s, when thousands of newcomers arrived in this city and the county; and a third, ongoing period, which suggests various types of interethnic accommodation but also raises questions about intergroup competition and conflict. As we discuss these three phases, we look at public and private discourses of interethnic relations and immigration, perceptions and representations of self and other groups, and the actual interactions of members of the three main ethnic groups in Dalton, whites, Latinos and blacks.

FRAMEWORK

Mass migration from Latin America and Asia into the urban United States over the past thirty years has sparked interest in intergroup relations beyond the black and white paradigm. But while immigration induced diversity has been a fact of life in metropolitan areas like New York City, Los Angeles, San Francisco, Chicago, and Houston, this has not been the case of the U.S. historic South. The rise of this region as a new destination for Mexican migration during the 1990s presents a unique opportunity to study the destabilization of existing patterns of interethnic relations—largely based in terms of black and white polarity—as well as the formation of yet to be defined positions and structures of inter- and intragroup interaction. This does not mean that immigration erases the history and context of interethnic relations or that immigrants arrive with no preconceived notions of themselves and other groups. Clearly, history and experience make up the apparatus used to approach and articulate interactions between long-term residents and newcomers. Yet, as it has happened with other immigrants in localized areas of the South—most notably the Chinese in the Mississippi Delta (Loewen 1988)—Mexicans do not easily fit in the racialized social order of this region. We claim that as they negotiate their place in this order—initially as outsiders—immigrants as well as their hosts may reproduce old patterns but also create new ones.

This juncture, in which intergroup relations are going through a process of transformation from a biracial structure to a multi-ethnic order, offers both opportunities and challenges. This transitional stage requires a great deal of attention to processes of interaction and group position formation rather than a commitment to a particular theory of interethnic relations. As we argue in the following section, this demands an inductive approach as well as the formulation of multiple preliminary hypotheses to guide research. Although at some point of the process the interethnic landscape will be one in which social actors formulate a clear sense of group position (Blumer 1958), as scholars we are still witnessing the moments of initial intergroup contact.

With this background in mind, we take stock of theoretical issues and developments in the field of interethnic relations, which we use to frame our study. Several recent theoretical and analytical developments have come to define this field as researchers assess the effect of post-1965 immigration on the ethnoracial structure in the United States. First, investigators have recognized that no single theory can account for all dimensions of interethnic relations and that a theoretical synthesis is necessary and possible. In this spirit, recent studies have combined group position, self-interest, prejudice and stratification belief models to explain intra- and intergroup interaction (Bobo and Hughes 1996; Morawska 2001). Second, that in the contemporary context of high immigration, such models should be used not only to study relations between dominant and subordinate groups—traditionally the white majority and black minority—but also to analyze interactions between minority groups, most notably between Asian, Latin American, and Caribbean immigrants, and African Americans (Bobo and Hughes 1996; Johnson Jr., Farrell, and Guinn 1997).

Third, researchers have recognized that any comprehensive framework should address the objective conditions that allow for specific patterns of intergroup relations as well as the perceptions and discourses that the groups under study produce about each other and about themselves (Morawska 2001). Such objective conditions include elements as varied as the class background of immigrants and established residents, the characteristics of the housing and labor market, and the demographic weight and composition of local groups. Perceptual elements refer to prejudice, notions of exclusive or shared rights and entitlements, and nativistic, neutral, or welcoming responses to immigration, to name a few. Fourth, besides understanding national contexts and policies, scholars have found it increasingly relevant to study local and regional settings in order to observe how larger trends are reshaped in specific locales, with their own histories, demographic traits, and intergroup dynamics (Hagan and Rodríguez 1992; Morawska 2001). Thus, Elijah Anderson and Douglas Massey argue that "a full understanding of intergroup relations . . . requires an understanding of how general social processes are filtered through local contexts and structures to determine specific outcomes" (2001, 8).

We complement the discussion of these issues and developments with three critical observations. Studies in the field of interethnic relations have persistently focused on conflict, competition, and tension between groups and substantially less attention has been paid to cases and circumstances that lead to accommodation, collaboration, or simply the absence of heightened conflict (Johnson Jr., Farrell, and Guinn 1997; Morawska 2001; Rodríguez 1999). Even though we consider the study of conflict and tension of foremost relevance, we also see as a drawback the lack of interest on more peaceful forms of intergroup coexistence. It should be noted here that accommodation and even collaboration do not imply the absence of prejudice, inequality, and subtle competition and tension. Yet we contend that by ignoring the junctures and mechanisms through which ethnic groups find accommodation and inclusion, researchers might be missing a significant and less flashy part of the story. Accommodation may stem from self-interest of both dominant and subordinated groups yet signal intragroup cleavages.

A second, yet related criticism has to do with the emphasis on dramatic events as a focal point or prism to understand intergroup relations. A now classic example is the case of the Los Angeles riots in 1992. The riots have been studied as the moment when ongoing conflicts between Asian and Latin American immigrants and African Americans boiled over (Johnson Jr., Farrell, and Guinn 1997). Similar though not as sensational events have taken place in Dalton in recent years: a wave of anti-immigrant letters to the editor of the local newspapers, public protests against newcomers, the establishment of an office of the Immigration and Naturalization Service in town, and INS raids of carpet plants. Yet again, even though we recognize that such critical events can be useful for uncovering antagonistic dynamics, we also want to redirect attention to the significance of "excavating the cultural and social interactions that occur in the structures of everyday life" (Higham 1999, 387) in order to achieve a comprehensive view of interethnic relations. Thus the observations we have conducted in a wide variety of social spaces in Dalton have led us to ponder about the small yet recurrent acts of interaction that take place daily and suggest tension and separation as well as engagement and coexistence.

A final critical point is that ethnic and racial groups are not homogeneous. Although this may seem an obvious point, much of the literature on interethnic relations conveniently forgets about intragroup differences and cleavages. We contend that in the case of Dalton, neither immigrants nor black and white native residents form homogeneous groupings. In fact, we argue that the emerging interethnic landscape in northwest Georgia cannot be fully grasped without understanding the class cleavages that exist, particularly amongst whites. To be sure, immigration did not create such fractures—they are a long-standing feature of the social structure in the South—yet the arrival of thousands of newcomers to this region has added new dimensions to them. Thus, if we were to treat whites as a monolithic group, we would be taken aback by the seemingly contradictory discourses that whites produce about Mexican immigrants. Although such discourses and perceptions are indeed contradictory, they can be fully explained by taking into account within-group differences, including those based on such social markers as class and gender. A similar statement can be made about immigrants. Despite the fact that newcomers are highly homogeneous in terms of their national origin, differences based on legal status, class, gender, regional roots within Mexico, and experience in the United States slowly become more relevant in the intragroup dynamics of the immigrant population (see Hernández-León and Zúñiga 2003).

METHODS AND SOURCES OF DATA

The observations and data used stem from nearly five years of field research in the city of Dalton and Whitfield County as part of a multifocal study of Mexican immigrants and their experiences of incorporation in a nontraditional destination. Yet our presence in this town of southern Appalachia has been distinctively marked by a role not only as observers but also as participants in the processes of transformation resulting from mass Mexican immigration. In December of 1996, after several months of telephone consultations, a group of Dalton public school officials and civic leaders visited Universidad de Monterrey (Monterrey, Mexico)—where both of us were faculty members—to explain their basic dilemma. In a matter of a few years, the city's schools had become flooded with Spanish-speaking children, an obvious challenge to their mostly English monolingual teachers. Contacting a Mexican university was clearly an unusual step, one that can be explained by at least two factors: first, the lack of responsiveness to these leaders' calls for assistance from state institutions, such as Georgia's Department of Education and local universities, and second, their access to the joint venture ties between the largest carpet manufacturer in Dalton and industrialists in Monterrey, who in turn had links with the university's president (see Hamann 1999, 2002).

This meeting and a reciprocal visit by University of Monterrey's faculty and officials in January of 1997 culminated with an agreement between this institution and the school districts of Dalton and Whitfield to develop and provide various educational services. This uncommon binational initiative—known as the Georgia Project—included four different initiatives: a bilingual teacher program to bring graduates from the university to Dalton, the design of a bilingual education curriculum, a Latino adult education and leadership initiative, and a summer institute for local Georgia teachers to learn Spanish and Mexican history and culture in Monterrey, Mexico. Active involvement in the negotiation, design, and implementation of these programs and in the local debates which they sparked, turned us into both observers and participants of the profound changes that immigration has been producing in northwest Georgia and of the complex process of institutional response to this phenomenon. At the same time, the carpet industry's initial yet indirect sponsorship of the Georgia Project, which provided its programs with political legitimacy and support, gave us unprecedented access to actors and research sites. This sponsorship neither hindered our research activities nor prevented the initiatives of the project from meeting resistance and clashing with school officials and the middle management of the carpet industry itself.

This intervention as Mexican scholars in Dalton—working under the banner of a Mexican higher education institution—generated its own set of contributions and consequences: provided institutional legitimacy to otherwise highly contentious positions and debates (that is, the defense of the use of Spanish in public schools); contributed schools and other entities with cultural knowledge as they responded to the challenges of immigration; and performed the roles of interlocutory dialogue and mediation between diverse members of the Latino community and local authorities and business leaders, helping to establish direct channels of communication between these actors and fostering the creation of a Latino immigrant organization (Zúñiga et al. 2002). Furthermore, our research and institutional activities in favor of the social and political enfranchisement of Latinos in Dalton also lent prestige and status to the immigrant community, frequently rendered invisible because of racial, class, and linguistic barriers and prejudices.

To investigate newcomers and long-term residents in Dalton we have followed the methodological principles of community studies. Our research has thus been persistently committed not only to a multifocal approach but also to the exploratory and inductive strategies that characterize such studies. This openness was also mandated by the newness of Mexican immigration in this state and the region. In consonance with an inductive perspective, we have considered diverse and complementary hypotheses while taking note of the different and often contradictory accounts of an array of social actors. We have striven to offer an inclusive account of the multiple and changing narratives in play, including those that allude to community consensus, disagreement, legitimization and reinterpretation of old and new forms of interethnic relations. Yet we also recognize that as sociologists we do not have a panoptic eye. As Mexican sociologists, in particular, we have been able to access and collect the various versions of inter- and intragroup interaction produced by immigrants. However, as outsiders, we have been less successful in gaining entry into the world of working-class African Americans and low-income whites, particularly those with rural backgrounds. On the other hand, our role as leading staff of the Georgia Project provided us with local legitimacy and access to the most disparate social actors.

During the past five years, we have adopted multiple strategies of data collection, including unobtrusive and participant observation, in-depth life history and thematic interviewing, focus group, and survey research. In accordance with our multifocal interest, we have gathered data in a broad variety of settings. We have spent hundreds of hours of unobtrusive and participant observation in neighborhoods, weddings and dances, households, restaurants, shopping centers, community meetings, schools, churches, soccer fields, and factories. In these locales, we have conducted dozens of unstructured interviews and informal conversations with carpet and poultry workers, youths, women, entrepreneurs, teachers, and school officials, religious and political leaders, managers and supervisors, service providers, corporate executives, and journalists. Many of the questions we asked were geared toward understanding both the old regime and the emerging configuration of intergroup relations.

Besides amassing this wealth of qualitative material, we have collected survey data with the purpose of constructing a quantitative profile of the Mexican and Latino immigrant population in Dalton. In late 1997, we implemented a self-administered survey of Hispanic parents with children enrolled in the Dalton public school system. Fathers and mothers answered questions about their migratory and labor histories, household composition, current economic and housing conditions, individual human capital, social capital resources, and leisure and cultural preferences. Although the resulting nonrandom sample of about 850 adult men and women was not representative of the overall Latino immigrant settlement—again, the sampling frame was made only of those Hispanics whose children were students of Dalton's public schools—the quantitative picture we were able to draw matched the findings of our previous ethnographic research (Hernández-León and Zúñiga 2000).

In the fall of 2001 we conducted a series of individual and group interviews with Mexican immigrants and black and white Daltonians, dealing with issues of conflict, tension, and accommodation between newcomers and long-term residents. These interviews also included questions addressing patterns of interracial relations during the segregation and desegregation eras, which we specifically posed to black and white respondents. Seeking to go beyond the traditional interview format, we presented these individuals with our hypotheses about intergroup relations in Dalton, discussed with them our preliminary findings and, at times, confronted them with their own ethnic and racial prejudices and stereotypes. We also recorded our observations in the town's historic black neighborhoods.

These different methodological stances and opportunities have allowed us to blend traditional and less conventional strategies for data collection, to combine observation and participation, and to become local actors while remaining outsiders. We continue to navigate the social worlds of Dalton and northwest Georgia as foreigners, who constantly resort to the assistance and expertise of old and new Daltonians.

How Did Mexicans Make It to Dalton, Georgia? 1970 through 1987

The first Mexican newcomers arrived in northwest Georgia in the post–civil rights era. Although the Ku Klux Klan had originated in neighboring Murray County (Flamming 1992) and elderly interviewees recalled memories of a local lynching in the 1930s, race relations were not particularly heated in Dalton. As in the rest of the South, segregation and Jim Crow had indeed set the norms for intergroup interactions. Yet partly because of the historically small numbers of African Americans, the city and its county were not sites for any momentous battles during the Civil Rights movement. Between Reconstruction and the Civil Rights era, the most significant social and political debates in Dalton and its region had been about social class and unions, namely, the matters that divided the white and urban upper classes from a white semi-rural industrial proletariat (Flamming 1992; Patton 1999). A member of the local elite who grew up in Dalton during the 1920s and 1930s provided a snapshot of these class cleavages:

> there was an obvious class distinction ... it was there obviously in the schools ... you could look at a particular girl and you could tell whether this was a daughter of a mill worker or a daughter of a grocery store owner ... particularly the hair: unless the hair was naturally curled, none of the mill girls had curly hair.

Whites did disagree amongst themselves during the 1950s and 1960s about the end of segregation and upcoming integration with blacks, yet it seems that in Dalton a much more enduring and acrimonious debate had been the one around unionization. It is worth noting that some of the old cotton textile mills were unionized but that by the 1950s their influence was clearly in decline (Flamming 1992). The new carpet industrialists fought bitterly against union organizing drives in their plants, although a trade union was actually established in a carpet mill in nearby Calhoun in 1962 (Patton 1999). There are no unions in Dalton today, a fact proudly touted by local boosters (Dalton and Whitfield Chamber of Commerce 2002).

The first Mexican immigrants began to arrive in Dalton in the early to mid-1970s through two unconnected recruitment schemes. One group was recruited in Dallas in 1973 to work in the construction of a water dam just north of Dalton. Facing several weeks of inactivity due to rain and having heard of the carpet plants in that city, several workers decided to leave the reservoir project and try their luck in the mills. Although several of these workers were later on deported to Mexico, they found their way back to Dalton. They had in fact recognized the advantages of working in the carpet mills as opposed to agriculture and construction, characterized by itinerancy, low wages, and constant exposure to the weather. Describing Dalton, these pioneer immigrants would tell their friends and kin in Texas and Mexico: allá se trabaja adentro (up there you work indoors). A few families left ranches and fields in Texas and moved to this city, responding to this call. A second group of thirty male and female laborers was recruited in El Paso, Texas, to work in Dalton's poultry plant in 1974. They were housed in local hotels, spending their days between the dormitory and the plant. Without an ethnic community and entertainment options at hand, the overwhelming majority of these workers left Dalton after a few months.

The original Mexican settlement resulted then from a small group of individuals and families who stayed after this initial phase of recruitment. Although some of them provided the contacts for a few more families to move to Dalton, the immigrant community remained quite small for the rest of the 1970s and most of the 1980s. The pioneers of this original wave, composed of a few households whose members knew and greeted each other by name, describe the Mexican settlement in almost idyllic terms. The arrival of a new Mexican family in town was celebrated as an uncommon event. Newcomers to Dalton during this period recount their surprise with the absence of a sizable ethnic enclave and the cultural commodities and spaces associated with it: "[en ese entonces] no había chiles en la tiendas" (at that time, you couldn't find chili peppers in the stores) and "no Catholic church either." Dalton and Georgia were clearly in the periphery of Mexican migration to the United States—a frontier of sorts in which the sighting of a can of hot peppers or a Mexican national were rare. The group of pioneers who decided to settle in this frontier in the mid-1970s played the role of trailblazers, opening the way to ensuing waves of immigrants (Hernández-León and Zúñiga 2000). Their children were the first Latinos to attend the city's public schools and some of them intermarried with local Anglo women. Although some of the children of the pioneers reported instances of harassment and discrimination—being called mojados (wetbacks) and being prevented from dating fellow youths by Anglo parents—their small numbers made them largely inconspicuous.

Despite these cases, from the standpoint of established residents—both black and white—Mexicans were basically an invisible segment of the population. Such invisibility is clear in the statement of a long-time local political leader, former congressman, and state senator, who candidly said: "I didn't even know there were Mexicans in Dalton!" Still, a few important changes occurred during this period. A Mexican entrepreneur opened the first Mexican restaurant in town in 1982. During this decade, more immigrants began to arrive in this city, many of them settling out of the eastern seaboard migratory flow, and the Atlanta dioceses started sending a priest who would give mass twice a month in Dalton.

REDEFINING INTERETHNIC RELATIONS: VISIBILITY, TENSION, AND SEPARATE COEXISTENCE (1987 THROUGH 1997)

Things began to change dramatically in the late 1980s. After the passage and implementation of IRCA, hundreds of Mexican immigrants and other Latinos moved to Dalton—leaving behind traditional urban destinations like Los Angeles and Chicago and farm worker camps in Florida and other states. As expected, men arrived first but women and children quickly followed, moving directly from Mexico and also from California, Illinois, and Texas (Hernández-León and Zúñiga 2000). Three features of the new inflow contributed to make Mexicans a visible presence in Dalton: their growing numbers, the rapidity of such growth and the demographic composition of the flow—with many families in its midst. Newcomers brought with them human, monetary, and social capital accumulated through prior sojourning experiences in the United States, a fact that facilitated settlement and has accelerated incorporation (Hernández-León and Zúñiga 2003). As they started to concentrate in defined neighborhoods and established grocery stores, restaurants, meat markets, bakeries, and other businesses catering to the needs of co-ethnics, immigrants left an indelible mark on the urban landscape. No longer invisible, Mexicans were gradually making two additional yet central contributions to this changing locality: the use of Spanish in an increasing number of social spaces and the growing profile of Catholicism (Zúñiga et al. 2002). By the end of the period in question, the Catholic Church was embarking on a major project to build a new five-hundred-seat facility.

The rapid settlement of hundreds of immigrants took everyone by surprise, including the members of the pioneer Mexican wave of the 1970s. They saw their small community change not only numerically but also in composition. Many of the new arrivals were coming from the inner cities of Chicago and Los Angeles and not from the villages and towns of north-central and western Mexico. Providing an exhaustive account of the social spaces and institutions affected by this new immigration and the types of intergroup dynamics it produced in all those spaces is beyond our scope here. We therefore concentrate on two areas: workplaces and public schools.

Workplaces and labor markets were indeed most affected by the sudden presence of Mexican newcomers, who altered the informal arrangements of the shop floor that long-term employees had worked out. Most accounts of this period reveal how, brandishing the immigrant ethos of hard work and the uncertainty of their legal status, newcomers would work quickly, breaking all kinds of production records. It is not difficult to imagine how this pleased managers and those who had recruited the new arrivals but also how it created tensions with long-term native workers and even long-established co-ethnics. A Mexican woman who had been among the group of recruited pioneers of the 1970s described the shop floor behavior of those who were arriving during the early 1990s:

> They [the newly arrived] were really bad, because they worked so hard.... It would take us two or three hours to creel a machine. When they got here, they would do it in a half-hour. It was really ugly. People worked liked that because they weren't legal. They were afraid of losing their jobs and worked overtime to pay for those jobs.

Functional to the goals of management to lower labor costs and raise productivity, this behavior combined with nativistic feelings to produce tensions in the carpet mills. These tensions exploded during INS raids of plants, when native workers would show agents in pursuit of fleeing undocumented immigrants where these were hiding. Despite these raids, immigrants continued to "colonize" workplaces, including the local poultry plant owned by ConAgra, which by 1997 was 80 percent Latino. Such "colonization" also meant changes in the labor market dynamics of carpet mill jobs. Because such jobs were abundant in Dalton, white workers were used to switch employers and posts often. As the inflow of Mexicans and other Latinos began to fill vacancies and to provide a plentiful source of mill hands, native workers could no longer sustain such labor market strategies. White workers resisted these changes in a variety of ways: moving to plants not yet populated by Mexicans and with expressions of indirect violence (that is, slashing the tires of vehicles owned by Latinos). According to plant managers interviewed in 1997, there was animosity between black and Mexican workers as well. In this context, the white and black local working-class complaint that "y'all are coming here and taking our jobs" was anything but a surprise.

It is worth noting that carpet industrialists had not been silent observers and beneficiaries of the ethnic transformation of worksites. Faced with labor shortages in the early 1990s, carpet manufacturers actually sent recruiters to south Texas, attracting Mexican American and Mexican workers to Dalton. Later on, mill owners advertised heavily in Spanish newspapers, radio and television shows, and on the town's billboards and walls, targeting Mexican and other Latino workers (Hernández-León and Zúñiga 2000).

Public schools were yet another social space where the ethnic make-up changed dramatically during this period. Where in the late 1980s, Hispanic students represented fewer than 4 percent of the total enrollment in Dalton Public Schools, by 1997 they were nearly 37 percent. Needless to say, neither the city nor the county's school systems were prepared to deal with such a growing proportion of students whose primary language was Spanish. Although both school districts participated in the Georgia Project from the beginning, the day-to-day inter- and intragroup dynamics in schools were charting their own complex path. Again, newcomers were not a homogeneous group. While one group of children and youths were migrating directly from Mexico, another was coming from Los Angeles and Chicago. Members of the latter group were bringing with them the behavioral patterns described in studies of (downward) segmented assimilation: oppositional attitudes, ethnic segregation, and interethnic confrontation (Ogbu 1987; Zhou 1997). Youth gangs soon appeared in Dalton High School and with them the familiar and sometimes exaggerated reactions of school official to anything that resembled gang colors, signs, and initiation rites. Facing cultural and linguistic hostility from authorities and teachers—who often would prohibit the use of Spanish in classrooms and school buses—many children and adolescents moving directly from Mexico have been quickly channeled into the ethnocultural resistance model. Overall, students, teachers and parents we interviewed recounted stories of segregation along ethnoracial lines, particularly in the upper grades.

At the same time, white parents were adopting a different yet familiar strategy of resistance: they were withdrawing their children from public schools and enrolling them in private academies in Dalton and Chattanooga. White student enrollment in Dalton public schools had dropped from a high of nearly 81 percent of the total in 1989 to about 49 percent in 1997. Although overall enrollment in the district had increased during this period, the absolute number of white pupils had declined by nearly 1,000. These parents were expressing their anxieties—and prejudices—about the effect of the immigrant inflow on their children's education as schools tried to accommodate and meet the needs of Spanish speakers. On the other hand, Mexican and other Latino parents were increasingly and forcefully vocal about the mistreatment and discrimination their children faced in schools and were questioning the good faith and seriousness of public education officials' efforts to address the needs of their offspring.

This brief look at these two social spaces—workplaces and schools—shows that the new visibility of Mexican immigrants had produced resistance, tension, and even conflict with local whites but also with African Americans. However, this would not be a fair description of the

period without recognition of a pattern of separate coexistence (Rodríguez 1999) between the various groups. Namely, a pattern of interethnic dynamics in which members of different groups would share or
alternatively use a given social space without engaging each other in
either conflictive or positive terms. Almost any space could be cited
as an example of separate coexistence: parks, shopping centers, and
churches.

Still, by the mid-1990s, vocal opposition to the immigrant inflow had
achieved new organized and informal expression. An anti-immigrant
group—Citizens Against Illegals—had been formed. This group and
the Ku Klux Klan organized a series of demonstrations in downtown
Dalton. In 1995, as part of Operation SouthPAW (Protecting American
Workers), the INS and the U.S. Border Patrol raided several major
carpet mills. The raids not only raised tensions to new levels but also
exhibited large local corporations, such as Aladdin mills, as the draw
and actual employment source for hundreds of undocumented immigrants in Dalton. More significantly, by September of that year, the city
and county governments and the INS set up the Immigration Task
Force office, jointly staffed by the local police and federal agents. The
local governments would pay for the costs associated with the office—
purportedly the first of its type in the country, as the *Chattanooga Free
Press* and its correspondent Tom Turner both reported ("100+ Aliens
Arrested in N. Ga., Ala.," June 21, 1995; "Immigration Force in Dalton
Notes 1st Year," September 30,1996, p. B1).

Yet the most significant of these developments was a wave of largely
anti-immigrant and anti-Latino letters to the editor published in the
city's newspaper—Dalton's *Daily Citizen News*—in late 1995.[1] In analyzing one of these letters, Edmund T. Hamann notes:

> Hispanics were labeled as a criminal subculture; Hispanics were
> characterized as guests and contrasted with natives; and Hispanics
> were labeled as uninvited which illuminates a distinction among
> long-time Daltonians between those who "invited" Hispanics (by
> employing them) and those who did not. With a leap of logic, the
> letter implied that the presence of Hispanics had imperiled the re-
> tention of English by English-speakers. (1999, 148)

Informal as it was, this was one of the most open and spontaneous
grassroots expressions of local opposition to Mexican immigration. As
the letters turned increasingly angry and xenophobic, the newspaper's
editors decided to temporarily suspend their publication. Needless to

say, this decision did not put an end to the feelings of opposition and discontent yet it closed one of the most public outlets for expression of disagreement with the changing ethnic landscape in northwest Georgia. Because *The Daily Citizen News* has traditionally played the role of voice of the local economic elite and the broader urban regime, the decision to stop publishing these letters was seen by many in the city as a move on the part of such elite to quell resistance to immigration. We contend that it also signified a turn in the stance of the industrial elite toward the dramatic transformations of the decade. From now on, it would not only not tolerate the most virulent forms of nativism and xenophobia but also not remain a relatively silent observer. We argue, in fact, that local industrialists and their spokespersons began to articulate a public discourse recognizing the importance of immigrants and their various contributions to the region.

THE PRESENT AND FUTURE OF INTERETHNIC RELATIONS: INTER- AND INTRAGROUP CONFLICT, ACCOMMODATION AND NOSTALGIA (1998 TO THE PRESENT)

We can cite several examples of the public attitude and discourse of industrialists welcoming immigrants; their informal sponsorship of the Georgia Project, the construction of soccer fields paid by carpet manufacturers, the establishment of a Hispanic Chamber of Commerce, the formal and informal recognition of Latino community leadership, and the conspicuous discourse that praised the "family" and "work ethic" values of Latinos. As other scholars have recognized, by extolling the virtues of immigrants, the industrial elite seemed to undermine all other workers that were not like them (Engstrom 2001; Hamman 1999). According to James D. Engstrom,

> What is dramatic in Dalton, however, is how quickly the discourse about hard work and loyalty switched from one ethnic group to another. Since the rise of the carpet industry in the 1950s, carpet manufacturers have sung the praises of native-born workers from Appalachia, but Dalton's corporate executives are now referring to the Mexicans as a "godsend" and the "lifeblood" of the industry. (2001, 50)

This new positioning of industrialists vis-à-vis the ethnic transformation of the local working class had multiple consequences. Although integration had nominally eliminated the notion that industrial jobs were the exclusivity of white workers, the small population of African Americans in the region had never challenged the numeric and cultural dominance of the white labor force. In a way, carpet mill jobs had remained one of the privileges of whiteness and the rapid and substantial arrival of Mexican immigrants undermined such privilege. The welcoming of Latino newcomers by a dominant segment of the urban regime— mill owners and their spokespersons—revived an old chasm between different class strata of white society. Now the issue was not unions but immigrants. On the one side of the divide were the industrial bourgeoisie, the political establishment, and sectors of the middle class who have found opportunities in this context of social change. On the other side, those opposing the immigrant presence were the white working class, low-income whites, and segments of the middle class.

It is obvious that the stance of carpet manufacturers did not eliminate prejudice and resentment against newcomers. At the same time, we have no evidence that such prejudice hardened either. We argue, instead, that the self-interest of the white industrial elite in Dalton did quell much of the backlash against immigrants and sheltered Mexicans and other Latinos from the most overt expressions of racism and nativism. A long-time Mexican American resident of Dalton who had many contacts with Anglos said in an interview in 1997 that native Daltonians disliked the now massive presence of Mexicans and disagreed with endeavors like the Georgia Project. According to him, the reason these people did not express their views openly was because "they are afraid of Bob Shaw and that's why they don't say anything." Bob Shaw is the head of Shaw Industries, the Dalton-based carpet manufacturer, the largest in the world.

Conversely, Mexican immigrants appeared to develop a sense of self-confidence and appreciation of their contributions to the local economy and community life. Welcomed by much of the economic and political elite of the city, newcomers provided us with responses that reflected this confidence. The same Mexican American stated in an interview conducted in the fall of 2001 that "in Dalton they [Anglos] got used to us [Mexicans]." Other informants made very similar remarks: "They [Anglos] are getting used to our [Latino or Mexican] culture;" "Can you imagine what would happen if all Mexicans in Dalton decided to stop working for one day?"

Working-class and disaffected middle-class whites have continued to express their resentment and prejudice, albeit in a private manner or in relatively closed political forums. These expressions include the rejection of bilingual education and bilingualism in general. A middle-class Anglo woman told us during an interview how at the end of the workday and in the intimacy of a small church group, another white woman had told her: "If I hear one more word of Spanish, I am going to throw up." However, disagreement about bilingualism did not pit whites against immigrants. The debate has in fact confronted the different segments of white society described earlier, giving way to an intragroup conflict. Although this debate is peppered with nostalgic references ("I want our schools to be the way they used to be") and concerns over economic and cultural threat ("Y'all coming here and taking our jobs"), the discussion is indeed about the future of Dalton and not about its past.

How have African Americans reacted and positioned themselves vis-à-vis Latino immigration? Despite their small numbers in the county, blacks are not a homogeneous group and have reacted accordingly, that is, providing different responses often along class lines. Although in the words of their leadership, black Daltonians have no power, politically active African Americans have seen Latino immigration as a way to overcome their marginal status. Black leaders have organized meetings with their Latino counterparts to find a common political agenda. These efforts stem from the recognition of the black leadership that in the wake of a massive inflow of Hispanic immigrants, African Americans were at risk of becoming "irrelevant." Indeed, in just one decade, blacks had become a distant second minority in Dalton and Whitfield (see table 10.1). According to our observations, these meetings have not always gone smoothly. In one of these events, for example, African American participants expressed their disagreement with the use of local resources to pay outsiders who tend to the needs of newcomers. Still, Mexican immigration had opened opportunities for black middle-class leaders who were brought to the table as issues of multiculturalism, minority rights, and political and social incorporation of immigrants have become part of the local debate. During the spring of 2002, local writer Daniel Cloud reported, the local chapter of the NAACP announced that they would begin a drive to register Latinos to vote ("NAACP Vigilant on Civil Rights," *Daily Citizen News,* March 31, 2002, p. 9).

Mexican immigration is recognizably more problematic for lower middle-class, working-class, and poor African Americans, who view immigrants as a source of competition and displacement at least at a symbolic level. Our observations suggest that, as in cities such as Los Angeles and Houston, the historic black neighborhoods of Dalton are no longer purely black. They are now comprised of a combination of immigrant Latino and African American households. Black lower-middle class interviewees reported being upset about the uses of housing and neighborhood space of newcomers (that is, overcrowding, raising chickens and growing food in backyards, stockpiling old cars). Black informants were also troubled by what they see as the "takeover" of semi-public spaces that sheer numbers have afforded Latinos. A frequently stated phrase among black Daltonians, according to our interviewees, succinctly summarized this issue: "Don't go to the mall or to the Wal-Mart on weekends because it's for the Latinos." Still, these respondents denied an actual change of their shopping and public space use due to the presence of immigrants.

Black interviewees consistently raised two other issues, which show that their perception of Latino immigration is not without ambiguities and contradictions. On the one hand, many of them expressed admiration for the entrepreneurial capacity and the social capital of newcomers. The evidence could not be more obvious; in a matter of years Mexican and other Latino immigrants had been able to establish numerous businesses, providing services to their own community. While not longing for the days of segregation, African American leaders argued that integration and mobility had in fact diluted the strong social capital that blacks could display decades before in northwest Georgia. On the other hand, these respondents also saw whites "catering to Latinos" and "providing things for Latinos to adjust," namely, facilitating incorporation and inclusion in a way that had never been available to African Americans (that is, business and housing loans, educational opportunities). At the same time, black Daltonians claimed that their struggles against segregation and discrimination had paved the way for Mexicans and other newcomers. In contrast with their white counterparts, none of our African American interviewees produced a nostalgic account of Dalton in the days before Latino immigration.

Although we have so far emphasized the immigration-induced tensions in intra- and intergroup relations, there is no question that accommodation and various other forms on nonconflict interaction are also an important part of the story. We argue, in fact, that the absence of overt intergroup conflict is a central dimension of the Dalton experience. Flexing its political and economic muscle, the city's industrial bourgeoisie set a crucial parameter of intergroup interaction, namely, that it would not support any kind of anti-Mexican or anti-immigrant movement, along with violent and overt nativism. Yet accommodation has been taking place in everyday life in many social arenas. Whites, blacks, and Latinos share leisure spaces, services, schools, and workplaces. Their mere demographic weight has turned Mexican and other Latino immigrants into an important group of consumers and local merchants strive to bring and welcome them into their stores. Also, observations we conducted in carpet mills showed Latino and black workers having lunch together and fraternizing during shift breaks. At the same time, native Daltonians are joining the Mexican soccer leagues and attending Mexican dances at the local fairgrounds. In these settings, we have observed white women skillfully dancing "quebradita" and other Mexican dances as a means to interact with Latino males. We corroborated these observations at the only Mexican cantina in town. This further suggests the existence of a field of interethnic sexual and personal relationships in Dalton—from prostitution and casual encounters to marriage and long-term partnerships.

Indeed, there is a growing number of mixed marriage households not only of whites and Mexicans but also of blacks and Latinos. More important, these marriages appear to happen at various class and income levels. We have identified mixed couples of low-income, working-class, and lower-middle class backgrounds. Yet another instance of accommodation comes from local schools, which have gradually incorporated the celebration of Mexican national festivities and holidays into their calendars. The school halls and classrooms now display Mexican symbols and postings in Spanish. In the religious field, the few local Catholics have seen the swelling of their ranks in a matter of years. These mostly white Catholics have come to accept the interaction with Latinos in mass and in various activities, including the construction of a new and much larger church. Finally, it is evident that the socialization experience of new generations of Daltonians is unfolding in a radically different social and cultural context when compared to their parents. White and black children are now regularly exposed to various aspects of Latin American cultures, including cuisine, music, and language. One cannot underestimate the interactions—material and symbolic—taking place in micro spaces, such as the many Mexican restaurants in Dalton and the other towns and cities in the region. The lobby of one of these restaurants is decorated with a mural that proudly depicts passages and icons of Mexico's history—from Tenochtitlan to Mexico City's modern stock exchange. Here, interactions and exchanges occur over the adaptation of food to local taste, music, and representations of Mexico in Georgia. The place is usually full at both lunch and dinner time.

CONCLUSION

The massive and sudden arrival of thousands of Mexican immigrants to Dalton has dramatically reshaped the ethnic and demographic landscape of this small city and its hinterland. As outsiders of the racialized social structure of the South, Mexicans "do not share the African American sense of structural barriers to achievement, racial alienation, or an ideology of exclusive entitlement" (Morawska 2001, 59) nor the sense of group superiority of whites. Although economically subordinate, Latino immigrants cannot be easily pinned down in this racialized structure and may for now avoid the highly charged debates on race and history, which exhibit the open wounds of this region (for example, the unfinished debate on the Confederate flag).

But the newly found Mexican presence has created its own set of antagonisms and forms of accommodation. What is most notable in the case of Dalton is that Latino immigration has fostered a split between different sectors of the white population. Led by carpet industrialists and members of the political elite, a loose coalition of stakeholders, including educators, business boosters, and middle-class professionals have "embraced" immigrants. This has occurred not without reservations and contradictions. Still, in supporting newcomers these actors carry out their own varied interests. The clearest and strongest of these interests is the need of the carpet industry of a reliable supply of labor. At the same time, the progressive elements of this coalition have articulated a vision of Dalton where there is room for bilingual schools, multicultural arenas, and mixed marriages, and for the political participation of immigrants. All these actors have rallied behind the Georgia Project, which may alternatively be interpreted as a form of neopaternalism (on the part of the industrial bourgeoisie) or as an earnest recognition that Dalton's immigration induced diversity is here to stay.

At the other end of the spectrum, dislocated low income and working-class whites, the lower-middle class and members of the middle class who feel symbolically threatened have not followed the cue of carpet industrialists. They question the legitimacy of the foreigners' presence, feel that they have had no input in the decisions and processes that have brought newcomers to town and are not willing to pay for the costs of immigrant incorporation. The absence of outspoken contestation should not be confused with silent acquiescence on their part. Many have taken their children out of public schools and some have altogether moved out of the county. Between 1990 and 2000, Whitfield County lost more than six thousand white inhabitants, a fact that cannot be explained solely on the basis of mortality and fertility rates (see table 10.1). It is clear that feeling displaced and threatened, some have voted with their feet by leaving.

Those who are staying are engaged, willingly and not, in the everyday negotiation and coexistence of different languages, religions, ethnicities, and lifestyles. Such negotiation is obviously not occurring in a leveled field but not even the most powerful stakeholders have an absolute control of the possible outcomes. There is indeed an emerging interracial landscape in this southern Appalachia locale with intergroup arrangements that are still in formation. The day-to-day interactions suggest the softening of lines that separate groups while tensions and class differences indicate the redrawing and invention of new boundaries.

NOTES

1. The events outlined in this paragraph are largely based in the account provided by Edmund T. Hamann (1999, 148–49).

REFERENCES

Anderson, Elijah, and Douglas S. Massey. 2001. "The Sociology of Race in the United States." In *Problem of the Century: Racial Stratification in the United States*, edited by Elijah Anderson and Douglas S. Massey. New York: Russell Sage Foundation.

Blumer, Herbert. 1958. "Race Prejudice as a Sense of Group Position." *Pacific Sociological Review* 1(1): 3–7.

Bobo, Lawrence, and Vincent L. Hughes. 1996. "Perceptions of Racial Group Competition: Extending Blumer's Theory of Group Position to a Multiracial Social Context." *American Sociological Review* 61(6): 951–72.

Carpet and Rug Institute. 2002. *Facts About the Carpet Industry: Industry Statistics*. Arlington, Va.: Carpet and Rug Institute, Inc. Available at: http://www.carpet-rug.com/drill_down_2.cfm?page=10&sub=3&requesttimeout=350 (accessed October 8, 2004).

Dalton and Whitfield Chamber of Commerce. 2002. *History of the Carpet Industry*. Dalton, Ga.: Dalton and Whitfield Chamber of Commerce. Available at: www.daltonchamber.org (accessed October 8, 2004).

Durand, Jorge. 1998. *Politica, modelo y patron migratorios*. San Luis Potosi, Mex.: El Colegio de San Luis.

Durand, Jorge, Douglas S. Massey, and Emilio Parrado. 1999. "The New Era of Mexican Migration to the United States." *Journal of American History* 86(2): 518–36.

Engstrom, James D. 1998. "Industry, Social Regulation, and Scale: The Carpet Manufacturing Complex of Dalton, Georgia." Ph.D. diss., Clark University.

————. 2001. "Industry and Immigration in Dalton, Georgia." In *Latino Workers in the Contemporary South*, edited by Arthur D. Murphy, Colleen Blanchard, and Jennifer A. Hill. Athens, Ga.: University of Georgia Press.

Flamming, Douglas. 1992. *Creating the Modern South: Millhands and Managers in Dalton, Georgia, 1884–1984*. Chapel Hill: The University of North Carolina Press.

Georgia Department of Education. Various years. *Georgia Public Education Report Card*. Available at: http://techservices.doe.k12.ga.us/reportcard/ (accessed October 1, 2004).

Hagan, Jacquie, and Néstor Rodríguez. 1992. "Recent Economic Restructuring and Evolving Intergroup Relations in Houston." In *Structuring Diversity*, edited by Louise Lamphere. Chicago: University of Chicago Press.

Hamann, Edmund T. 1999. "The Georgia Project: A Binational Attempt to Reinvent a School District in Response to Latino Newcomers." Ph. D. diss., University of Pennsylvania.

————. 2002. "*Un Paso Adelante?* The Politics of Bilingual Education, Latino Student Accommodation, and School District Management in Southern Appalachia." In *Education in the New Latino Diaspora: Policy and the Politics of Identity*, edited by Stanton Wortham, Enrique G. Murillo Jr., and Edmund T. Hamann. Westport, Conn.: Ablex.

Hernández-León, Rubén, and Víctor Zúñiga. 2000. "Making Carpet by the Mile": The Emergence of a Mexican Immigrant Community in an Industrial Region of the U.S. Historic South." *Social Science Quarterly* 81(1): 49–66.

————. 2003. "Mexican Immigrant Communities in the South and Social Capital: the Case of Dalton, Georgia." *Southern Rural Sociology* 19(1): 20–45.

Higham, John. 1999. "Instead of a Sequel, or, How I Lost My Subject." In *The Handbook of International Migration: The American Experience*, edited by Charles Hirschman, Philip Kasinitz, and Josh DeWind. New York: Russell Sage Foundation.

Johnson Jr., James H., Walter C. Farrell, and Chandra Guinn. 1997. "Immigration Reform and the Browning of America: Tensions, Conflicts, and Community Instability in Metropolitan Los Angeles." *International Migration Review* 31(4): 1055–1095.

Krissman, Fred. 2000. "Immigrant Labor Recruitment: U.S. Agribusiness and Undocumented Migration from Mexico." In *Immigration Research for a New Century*, edited by Nancy Foner, Rubén Rumbaut, and Steven Gold. New York: Russell Sage Foundation.

Loewen, James W. 1988. *The Mississippi Chinese*. Prospect Heights, Ill.: Waveland Press.

McDonald, Joseph A., and Donald A. Clelland. 1984. "Textile Workers and Union Sentiment." *Social Forces* 63(2): 502–21.

Morawska, Ewa. 2001. "Immigrant-Black Dissensions in American Cities: An Argument of Multiple Explanations." In *Problem of the Century: Racial Strati-*

fication in the United States, edited by Elijah Anderson and Douglas S. Massey. New York: Russell Sage Foundation.

Ogbu, John U. 1987. "Variability in Minority School Performance: A Problem in Search of an Explanation." *Anthropology and Education Quarterly* 18(4): 312–34.

Patton, Randall L. 1999. *Carpet Capital: The Rise of a New South Industry*. Athens, Ga.: The University of Georgia Press.

———. 2000. "Mass Production and the Rise of Shaw Industries." Available at: http://science. kennesaw.edu/org/academicforum/Patton.html (accessed November 15, 2001).

Rodríguez, Néstor. 1999. "U.S. Immigration and Changing Relations between African Americans and Latinos." In *The Handbook of International Migration: The American Experience*, edited by Charles Hirschman, Philip Kasinitz, and Josh DeWind. New York: Russell Sage Foundation.

University of Virginia Geospatial and Statistical Data Center. 1998. *United States Historical Census Data Browser*. Charlottesville: University of Virginia. Available at: http://fisher.lib.virginia.edu/census/ (accessed on March 20, 2002).

U.S. Department of Commerce. Bureau of the Census. N.d. *American FactFinder*. Available at: http://factfinder.census.gov/ (accessed on April 20, 2002).

———. 1973. *1970 Census of Population. Characteristics of the Population. Georgia*. Washington: U.S. Government Printing Office.

———. 1982. *1980 Census of Population. General Population Characteristics. Georgia*. Washington: U.S. Government Printing Office.

———. 1999. *U.S. Gazetteer: 1990 Census Lookup*. Washington: U.S. Census Bureau. Available at: http://www.census.gov/cgi-bin/gazetteer (accessed October 8, 2004).

Zhou, Min. 1997. "Segmented Assimilation: Issues, Controversies, and Recent Research on the New Second Generation." *International Migration Review* 31(4): 825–58.

Zúñiga, Víctor, and Rubén Hernández-León. 2001. "A New Destination of an Old Migration: Origins, Trajectories, and Labor Market Incorporation of Latinos in Dalton, Georgia." In *Latino Workers in the Contemporary South*, edited by Arthur D. Murphy, Colleen Blanchard, and Jennifer A. Hill. Athens, Ga.: University of Georgia Press.

Zúñiga, Víctor, Rubén Hernández-León, Janna Shadduck-Hernández, and M. Olivia Villarreal. 2002. "The New Paths of Mexican Immigrants in the United States: Challenges for Education and the Role of Mexican Universities." In *Education in the New Latino Diaspora: Policy and the Politics of Identity*, edited by Stanton Wortham, Enrique G. Murillo Jr., and Edmund T. Hamann. Westport, Conn.: Ablex.

INDEX

✕

Boldface numbers refer to figures and tables.

Chicano, meaning of and use of term, 238–39
childcare, lack of as barrier to English language acquisition, 37
Chinese Exclusion Acts, 6
Christmas tree industry, 60
churches and religious institutions: Dalton, Ga., 261, 262; Delmarva peninsula region, 170, 172, 174; Lexington, Ky. surveys, 190; Marshalltown, Iowa's Latino ministries, 146–47; Nebraska surveys, 34–35; Sampson County, N.C.'s Latino ministries, 72
Citizens Against Illegals, 264
citizenship theory, 157
Ciudad Nezahualcoyotl (Neza), 226–27
The Civilizing Process (Elias), 118
Civil Rights movement, 258
classic era, of immigration, 4–7
Cloud, D., 267
Cobos, J., 190
Cobos survey, 190, 195, 196, 197, 198, 202, 215n12
collective action, 108–12
collective violence, 111
college degree attainment, 27
Colorado: historical background, 7, 8–9; immigrant population (2000), **xv**; post-IRCA era (1990–2000), **10, 14, 15**; share of immigrants (1910–2000), **5, 10, 14**
community: definition of, 53; nature of, 124
Community Bridging Generations, 120
community social services. *See* social services
company housing, 64–65, 87, 91–94, 99n3
ConAgra, 262
construction industry, 161, **199**
contract workers, 61, 86–89, 168

Corchado, A., 117
Cornelius, W., 36
cosmopolitans, 235, 237
crab processing industry, 58, 66–69
crime: Houma, La., 89; Kennett Square, Pa., 115, 122; Lexington, Ky., 203; Marshalltown, Iowa, 142–43; Morgan City, La., 92
Crown Mill, 247
cultural values, loss of and identity formation, 43
culture of suspicion, 111
Current Population Survey (CPS), March supplement, 3

Dallas, share of immigrants (1990–2000), **15**
Dallas Morning News, 117
Dalton, Georgia: accommodation process, 268–69, 270; carpet manufacturing, 245–47, 261–62, 265–66; data sources, 257–58; immigration to, 249–51, 258–61; interethnic relations, 247, 253–55, 258, 260–69, 270; methodology, 253, 255–57; overview, xxv; population changes, 247, **248,** 249; racial-ethnic distribution in public schools, **250**; social class, 247–48, 251, 258–59, 266
Dalton *Daily Citizen News,* 264, 265
data sources: Dalton, Ga., 257–58; geographical analysis, 3; Kennett Square, Pa., 113; Lexington, Ky., 189–91; Louisiana, 80; Marshalltown, Iowa, 134; Nebraska, 24, 32; New York City, 227. *See also* census data
dating and relationships, 230
Davis, M., 203
day laborers, 45
Delaware, 155, **156**. *See also* Delmarva peninsula region

immigration law enforcement, in North Carolina, 50–52

Immigration Reform and Control Act (IRCA) (1986): amnesty and legalization provision, 11, 55, 225; Border Patrol expansion, 1–2, 12; consequences of, 1–2, 11–12; employment sanctions, 249; geographical analysis, 9–16, 18; impact on Kennett Square, Pa., 106–8; and undocumented workers, 11–12

income, 44, 237

incorporation: and contract employment, 88; economic factors, xix–xxi; future research topics, 98; Houma, La., 83, 86–91, 97; and legal status, xxi; Morgan City, La., 83, **86**, 91–97; in Nebraska, 27–28, 33–46; in New York City, 222–23; process of, 24–25, 84–86; and race, 220; and social networks, 85, 90. *See also* assimilation

Indiana: growth of immigrant population, xiv; historical background, 8; share of immigrants (1910–2000), **5, 10, 14**

informal economic activity, 53

In Search of Respect (Bourgois), 233

INS (Immigration and Naturalization Service). *See* Immigration and Naturalization Service (INS)

Integrated Public Use Microdata Samples (IPUMS), 3

integration, 25, 36–41, 188. *See also* incorporation

interethnic relations: between African Americans and Mexican immigrants, 66, 175–77, 202–5; Dalton, Ga., 247, 258, 260–69, 270; Delmarva peninsula region, 179–80; Lexington, Ky., 187–88, 201–6, 210–12; New York City, 227–29, 236;

Iowa: aging of population, 136; attitudes about immigration, 140–41; birthrate, 136; Excel plant opposition, 143–44; population, xiv, **30,** 133; share of immigrants (1910–2000), **5, 10, 14**. *See also* Marshalltown, Iowa

Iowa Commission on Latino Affairs, 148

Iowa Department of Economic Development, 143

Iowa Falls, Iowa, 143–44

Iowa-Nebraska Immigrant Rights Network, 47n5

IPUMS (Integrated Public Use Microdata Samples), 3

IRCA (Immigration Reform and Control Act). *See* Immigration Reform and Control Act (IRCA) (1986)

Irish immigrants, 220

Jim Crow laws, 258

Johanns, M., 38

Kansas: historical background, 7, 8–9; immigrant population (1990–2000), **30**; share of immigrants (1910–2000), **5, 10, 14**

Kaolin Mushroom Farms, 108

Kennett Consolidated School District (KCSD), 108

The Kennett Paper, 116, 117, 129n10

Kennett Square, Pennsylvania: Bridging the Community movement, 104, 119, 120–28; city profile, 104–5; community social services, 114; data sources, 113; history of immigration, 105–6; IRCA impact, 106–8; methodology, 113; overview, xxi–xxii; population changes, 107–8; protests against immigrants, 115–19; theoretical framework, 108–13